Nov 2010

Vimy

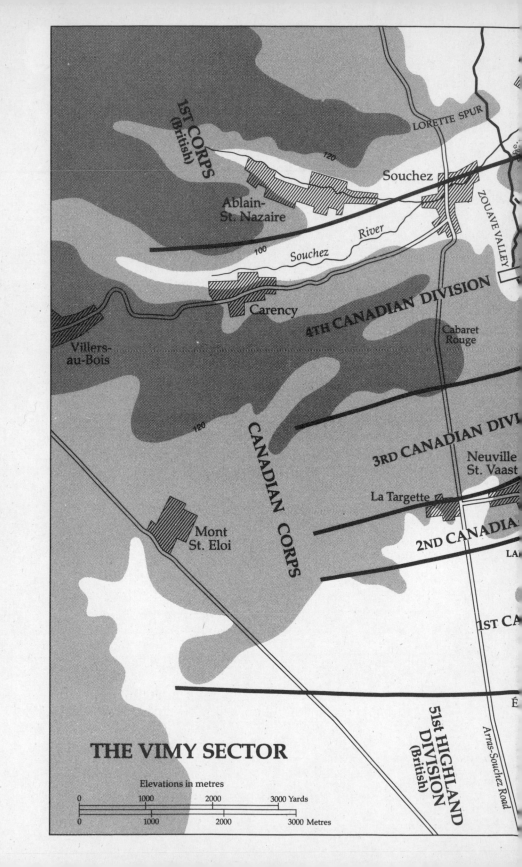

1ST CORPS
(British)

LORETTE SPUR

120

Souchez

ZOUAVE VALLEY

Ablain-
St. Nazaire

River

Souchez

100

4TH CANADIAN DIVISION

Carency

Cabaret
Rouge

Villers-
au-Bois

120

CANADIAN CORPS

3RD CANADIAN DIVI

Neuville
St. Vaast

La Targette

Mont
St. Eloi

2ND CANADIA

LA

1ST CA

51st HIGHLAND
DIVISION
(British)

Arras-Souchez Road

É

THE VIMY SECTOR

Elevations in metres

| 0 | 1000 | 2000 | 3000 Yards |
| 0 | 1000 | 2000 | 3000 Metres |

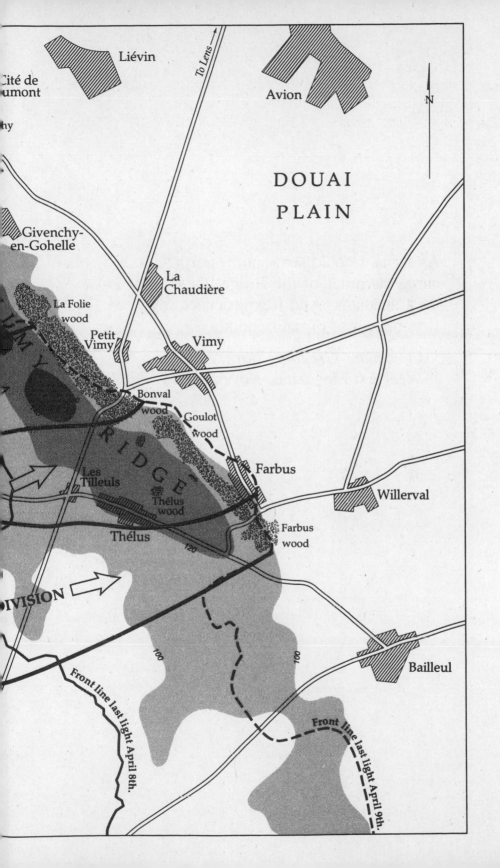

Liévin

Cité de
umont

hy

Givenchy-
en-Gohelle

Avion

To Lens

DOUAI
PLAIN

N

La Folie
wood

La Chaudière

IMY

Petit
Vimy

Vimy

Bonval
wood

Goulot
wood

RIDGE

Les
Tilleuls

Farbus

Willerval

Thélus
wood

Farbus
wood

Thélus

120

IVISION

100

100

Bailleul

Front line last light April 8th.

Front line last light April 9th.

As far as I could see, south, north
along the miles of the Ridge, there were
the Canadians. And I experienced my
first full sense of nationhood.

Lieutenant Gregory Clark, M.C.
Weekend Magazine, *November 13, 1967*

Vimy

by Pierre Berton

Anchor Canada

Anchor Canada and colophon are trademarks.

National Library of Canada Cataloguing in Publication Data

Berton, Pierre, 1920–
  Vimy

Includes index.
ISBN 0-385-65842-7

1. Vimy Ridge, Battle of, 1917. 2. World War, 1914–1918 –
Campaigns – France. 3. World War, 1914-1918 – Canada. I. Title.

D545.V5B47 2001   940.4'31   C2001-930603-2

Cover photo: Courtesy Provincial Archives of Newfoundland
  and Labrador (F 48-18)
Cover design: CS Richardson
Printed and bound in Canada

Published in Canada by
Anchor Canada, a division of
Random House of Canada Limited

Visit Random House of Canada Limited's website:
www.randomhouse.ca

FRI 10 9 8 7 6

Books by Pierre Berton

The Royal Family
The Mysterious North
Klondike
Just Add Water and Stir
Adventures of a Columnist
Fast Fast Fast Relief
The Big Sell
The Comfortable Pew
The Cool, Crazy, Committed
   World of the Sixties
The Smug Minority
The National Dream
The Last Spike
Drifting Home
Hollywood's Canada
My Country
The Dionne Years
The Wild Frontier
The Invasion of Canada
Flames Across the Border
Why We Act Like Canadians
The Promised Land
Vimy
Starting Out
The Arctic Grail
The Great Depression
Niagara: A History of the Falls
My Times: Living with History
1967, The Last Good Year

Picture Books
The New City (with Henri Rossier)
Remember Yesterday
The Great Railway
The Klondike Quest
Pierre Berton's Picture Book
   of Niagara Falls
Winter
The Great Lakes
Seacoasts
Pierre Berton's Canada

Anthologies
Great Canadians
Pierre and Janet Berton's
   Canadian Food Guide
Historic Headlines
Farewell to the Twentieth Century
Worth Repeating
Welcome to the Twenty-first
   Century

Fiction
Masquerade (pseudonym
   Lisa Kroniuk)

Books for Young Readers
The Golden Trail
The Secret World of Og
Adventures in Canadian History
   (22 volumes)

Contents

List of Maps

Maps by Geoffrey Matthews
Drawing of Vimy Ridge by Robert White

OVERTURE

Ten Thousand Thunders

5:30 came and a great light lit the place, a light made up of innumerable flickering tongues, which appeared from the void and extended as far to the south as the eye could see, a light which rippled and lit the clouds in that moment of silence before the crash and thunder of the battle smote the senses. Then the Ridge in front was wreathed in flame as the shells burst, confining the Germans to their dugouts while our men advanced to the assault.

Private Lewis Duncan to his aunt Sarah, April 17, 1917

Ten Thousand Thunders

It is probable that with the exception of the Krakatoa explosion of 1883, in all of history no human ears had ever been assaulted by the intensity of sound produced by the artillery barrage that launched the Battle of Vimy Ridge on April 9, 1917.

In the years that followed, the survivors would struggle to describe that shattering moment when 983 artillery pieces and 150 machine guns barked in unison to launch the first British victory in thirty-two months of frustrating warfare. All agreed that for anyone not present that dawn at Vimy it was not possible to comprehend the intensity of the experience. The shells and bullets hurtling above the trenches formed a canopy of red-hot steel just above the heads of the advancing troops – a canopy so dense that any Allied airplane flying too low exploded like a clay pigeon. At least four machines were destroyed that morning by their own guns.

The wall of sound, like ten thousand thunders, drowned out men's voices and smothered the skirl of the pipes – the Highland regiments' wistful homage to a more romantic era. It was as if a hundred express trains were roaring overhead. To Corporal Gus Sivertz, an optometrist from Victoria, the encompassing cocoon of sound was so palpable he felt that were he to raise a finger he would touch a solid ceiling. Individual noises, so familiar to the old soldiers at Vimy – the crump of naval guns, the bark and screech of the field artillery, the whine and clatter of the Vickers – were lost in the overpowering cacophony of the great barrage. Tons of red-hot metal hurtling through the skies caused an artificial wind to spring up, intensifying the growing sleet storm slanting into the faces of the enemy.

The earth reverberated for miles around, as in an earthquake, and the faint booming of the guns was heard by David Lloyd George, the British Prime Minister, at Downing Street in London. Some men could scarcely bear the sound. Lewis Buck, a lumberman from the Ottawa Valley, deep in a dugout with his fellow stretcher-bearers, thought he would go crazy from the reverberations above his head. But then, he reasoned, "this is what we came over for." Only the rats, he noticed, were unruffled by the noise.

The barrage began exactly at 5:30 A.M. Technically, it was dawn, but the first streaks of light in the east were obliterated by the driving storm. Shivering in the cold, tense with expectation, their guts briefly warmed by a stiff tot of army rum, the men in the assault waves could scarcely see the great whaleback of Vimy Ridge, only a few hundred yards away. It angled off into the gloom – its hump as high as a fifty-storey building – a miniature Gibraltar, honeycombed with German tunnels and dugouts, a labyrinth of steel and concrete fortifications, bristling with guns of every calibre.

The Germans had held and strengthened this fortress for more than two years and believed it to be impregnable. The French had hurled as many as twenty divisions against it and failed to take it. In three massive attacks between 1914 and 1916 they had squandered one hundred and fifty thousand *poilus*, dead or mangled. The British, who followed the French, had no better success. Now it was the Canadians' turn.

They lay out in No Man's Land, twenty thousand young men of the first wave, stretched out along the four-mile front, crouching in the liquid gruel of the shallow assault trenches or flat on their bellies, noses in the mud, holding their breath for the moment of the assault. With the optimism of soldiers in every battle in every century, they did not expect to die, for death, in their minds, was a catastrophe visited upon others. Surely if they did as they'd been trained to do, if they hugged that advancing wall of shells – the famous creeping barrage – they would survive the day.

Directly behind, ankle deep in water, greatcoats and puttees caked with mud, bayonets fixed, packstraps biting into their shoulders, a supporting wave of ten thousand more infantrymen blew on chilled fingers, puffed on hand-rolled fags, and fidgeted as they waited their turn to advance.

And behind them were seventy thousand more troops – gunners, stretcher-bearers, surgeons, cooks, transport drivers, mule-skinners, foresters, engineers, signalmen, runners, and brass hats – all hived in a bewildering maze of tunnels, dugouts, sunken roads, and trenches that wriggled for more than two miles in a crazy-quilt pattern behind the front lines.

The Canadian Corps (which included one British brigade) faced an incredible challenge. In one day – in fact in one morning – these civilian volunteers from a small country with no military tradition were expected to do what the British and French had failed to do in two years. The timetable called for most of them to be on the crest of the ridge by noon. And they were expected to achieve that victory with fifty thousand fewer men than the French had *lost* in their own frustrated assaults.

Few thought they could succeed. The Germans didn't believe that any force could dislodge them. A few days before the battle, one confident Bavarian put up a sign reading: "Anybody can take Vimy Ridge but all the Canadians in Canada can't hold it." A German officer taken in a raid before the battle told his captor: "You might get to the top of Vimy Ridge but I'll tell you this: you'll be able to take all the Canadians back in a rowboat that get there."

The new generalissimo, Robert-Georges Nivelle, agreed with the Germans. A few weeks before the battle he had declared flatly that the Canadian attempt would end in disaster. He allowed himself to be persuaded to go ahead with it by the British commander-in-chief, Douglas Haig, but even Haig seems to have had doubts. Certainly he saw Vimy as a limited objective at best, something to be won at enormous cost, with no chance of a breakthrough (he prepared for none). It's clear that he felt it would be hard enough just to hold the ridge in the face of the furious counterattacks for which the Germans were noted.

The Canadian Corps had been in the Vimy sector five

months, and they had known since late January that they would be given the task of seizing the ridge. Now they were as ready as they'd ever be. They were, at this point, the best-trained, best-equipped, and best-prepared troops on the Allied side. The Corps with its four Canadian divisions was remarkable in its homogeneity. In an army where divisions were shuttled about like chess men, the Canadians had stuck together, enjoying an *esprit* that was not possible for other British corps. They had been gassed at Ypres and blooded on the Somme, and the shoulder badge "Canada" had made them all brothers, no matter what their language or region.

From the moment he enlisted to the day of his discharge the Canadian soldier was under Canadian control. At Vimy, the men spoke a common idiom. There were certain things that were *theirs* and nobody else's, certain things they knew about that others did not know: Cyclone Taylor and Newsy Lalonde; Eaton's catalogue and Marquis wheat; CPR strawberries and Labatt's India Pale Ale; Tom Longboat, Kit of the *Mail*, Big Bear, and Louis Riel; Mackenzie and Mann; the Calgary *Eye Opener* and *Saturday Night*; Nellie McClung, Henri Bourassa, Pauline Johnson, and the Dumbbells. This was the glue that held them together and made them peacock proud. The British had done their best to frustrate this – to scatter the Canadian units through the British army; but the Canadians would have none of it.

"All we ask," a member of the Canadian Scottish wrote to his father, "is that we should not be drafted in with the Regular Battalions . . . we would be better by ourselves . . . we want to show by our own efforts that Canadians are as good as Territorials . . . a lot of our unique enthusiasm would be lost if we were doubled up with the Regulars. Take our own battalion; our physique is second to none; the standard of intelligence and individual initiative is, or certainly should be, higher than the ordinary British Regulars. That is why we want to be tried. . . ."

Now they were about to be tried. The Corps was up to strength: for the first time all four divisions would advance in line over a battlefield they had made their own. They knew every square inch of the ground. They had been trained meticulously to follow the attack plan to the minute. They had pinpointed the German gun positions, mapped the German trenches, and mined the German forward posts. Their moment had come. Peering out into No Man's Land a few seconds after the barrage began, they could see the German front line catch fire as a continuous line of bursting shells pounded the triple row of enemy trenches guarding the forward slopes of the ridge. This trench system stretched back for seven hundred yards. The first wave was expected to punch through it in just thirty-five minutes.

They could take some comfort in the spectacle opposite. An ocean of lightning seemed to have struck the German positions, obliterating everything and everyone who wasn't securely underground. A solid barrier of smoke and debris composed of burst sandbags, broken pieces of wood and equipment, and even human bodies was flung up from the opposing lines. "The pounding did not cease. In the space of an hour and forty minutes a quarter of a million shells would be thrown onto the German positions, a barrage rendered more deadly by a hail of seven million machine gun bullets."

At the same time, the earth trembled as mines, hidden in tunnels under the enemy positions, were touched off, creating miniature volcanoes – glowing infernos masked by pillars of black smoke. To add to the spectacle, huge drums of burning oil were hurled at the enemy strong points. When they exploded into flame they turned night into day, so that the whole ghastly battlefield was illuminated. It was as if a curtain had been suddenly raised to reveal a moonscape of shell holes and gigantic craters, crumbled trenches, broken wire, bits of wood and sacking, old skulls, all poking out of a porridge of gumbo through which the troops, burdened by forty-pound packs, would have to flounder.

Thirty seconds later, as the first wave of Canadians clambered out of the trenches there came a moment of spectacular beauty as hundreds of German rockets sizzled up from the dark bulk of the escarpment. These were SOS flares calling for an artillery bombardment of the Canadian front lines – four miles of dazzling fireworks, daubing the sky in gaudy streaks of green, yellow, orange, and red. For a few seconds the menacing scarp shimmered and danced in the reflective glow. Then those German guns that were still intact answered the call. But most had already been silenced by the Canadian barrage, and the remainder uselessly hammered assembly trenches that were already empty of men.

The Canadians lurched forward, loaded down with equipment, hugging the barrage. Most were frightened and many were terrified, but almost every man was more afraid of showing fear than he was of the enemy guns. Nobody hung back; that was not possible. They were like automatons, trained for months to respond instantly to any order.

Hundreds, in fact, bored by hours of waiting, stiff with cold, soaked through by gumbo, were eager to get under way – so eager that some got too far ahead of the main force and were killed by their own shells. Most were slightly tipsy on the strong army rum and some were roaring drunk. One diminutive platoon commander with the 4th Canadian Mounted Rifles was so intoxicated that he pointed his men the wrong way and ordered them to open fire on the shattered towers of the church at Mont St. Eloi, several miles behind the lines. His sergeant picked him up by the scruff of the neck and dropped him into a shell hole.

But even as the assault was launched men were falling. Royden Barbour, a young subaltern in the 25th Battalion from Nova Scotia, would have no memory of the attack. One moment he was going over the top, impressed by the perfection of it all – the pinpoint timing, the split-second barrage – elated to be a part of the action. The next, he was lying bleeding in a shell hole from wounds in his back and sides, with no idea of where or when he'd been hit.

At about the same time, Billy Buck was helping to pull his brother Lewis out of the trench, using their stretcher as a ladder. Lewis Buck wondered what he'd see first when he advanced. It came as a shock: there, hanging on the barbed wire, was a Canadian corpse blown to bits. The two stretcher-bearers had been told they'd be able to locate the wounded by a rifle stuck into the ground. Now, as far as the eye could see, the Bucks were confronted by a forest of rifles pointing at the sullen skies. Up ahead, the survivors followed the barrage.

One third of the Canadian guns had concentrated their fire on the main German trench system. The remainder formed part of the creeping barrage that moved just ahead of the advancing troops like a protective screen. Again, men would try to describe that deluge of exploding shrapnel. One likened it to a lawnmower cutting a field of grass, another to a rainstorm crossing a lake, a third to a moving Niagara of steel, a fourth to a curtain of water falling off a tin roof in a hailstorm, a fifth to a mass of shooting stars thicker than the Milky Way, a sixth to a line of red-hot fragments sizzling in the chill dawn. All agreed on one thing: the barrage was a moving shield that gave them confidence.

The barrage pounded the forward enemy lines – the mine craters and lightly held posts on the rim of No Man's Land – for three minutes, then crept forward at the rate of one hundred yards every three minutes, the troops walking closely behind it as they had been trained to do.

To former cavalryman Billy Bishop, now a pilot with the Royal Flying Corps, the scene below was astonishing. This wasn't war – no men charging forward, bayonets at the alert. Instead they seemed to be wandering casually across No Man's Land at a leisurely pace as if the whole thing were a great bore. From the air, the whole of No Man's Land appeared clean and white, fresh snow masking the usual filth and litter. Bishop half expected to see the men below him wake up and run, realizing their danger, but that didn't happen. He would see a shell burst, see the line of men halt momentarily, see three or four men near the burst topple over, see the stretcher-bearers run out to pick them up, while the line continued slowly forward. It was uncanny; Bishop couldn't get it out of his head that he was watching a game and not a conflict. Were those little figures below him real? He seemed to be in a different world looking down on a weird puppet show. But the artillery was real enough. From the Canadian gun lines at the rear he could see a long ribbon of incandescent light, and more than once he felt his plane jerk and heave as a shell whistled within a few feet.

On the ground the view was wildly different. A young private soldier from Sussex, New Brunswick, George Frederick Murray, had as good a vantage point as any, for he was waiting in reserve with the 5th Canadian Mounted Rifles almost at the very centre of the Canadian line and had time to absorb the spectacle unfolding before him. He looked up at the ridge and saw, through the wan light of breaking day, that the entire slope had become a shambles. Every foot of ground was churned and dug up; thousands of gaping shell holes were slowly filling with bloody water, arms, legs, pieces of dismembered bodies; and equipment of both sides was strewn about like garbage – abandoned rifles, steel helmets, bits of flesh, all bound together with a mucilage of mud over which long lines of haggard prisoners and the walking wounded stumbled and groped their way back to the Canadian lines.

And still the guns roared over the carnage.

BOOK ONE

Marching As to War

Q. Did you want to be in the war?
A. Yes.
Q. Were you crazy?
A. Yes, we were crazy, but we didn't know it.
Q. Did you have any idea what it was going to be like?
A. No, we didn't have any idea of what it was going
to be like.
Q. What did you think war was?
A. An adventure. We never thought about being
killed, you know. I thought I was going to be able to
come home and tell everybody about it. It never
entered my mind that I might not come back. We
wanted to get to it as fast as we could, because it
might be over before we got there.

Interview with Vimy veteran
Leslie Hudd, aged 86, August 25, 1983

CHAPTER ONE

Sam Hughes's Army

1

Almost every man who trudged up the slopes of Vimy Ridge on that gloomy Easter Monday in April 1917 had been a civilian when the war broke out, and this included four of the five Canadian-born generals who helped to plan the attack. In that last innocent summer of 1914, few expected that their lives and careers would be roughly altered by events that of course they could not foresee. Certainly, Arthur Currie, struggling to keep his foundering real estate business afloat in Victoria after the collapse of the Western land boom, had no inkling that he would, as a result of Vimy, lead the entire Canadian Corps in the final stages of a war few saw coming. The chief gunner at Vimy, E.W.B. "Dinky" Morrison, the man most responsible for the barrage that broke the Germans' back, was quietly editing the Ottawa *Citizen*, while David Watson, who would command the embattled 4th Division in the bloodiest encounter of the day, was running the Quebec *Chronicle*. Before the outbreak of the war, young Andy McNaughton, aged twenty-eight, was calmly pursuing a scientific career in the engineering department of McGill University. In less than three years he would so master the techniques of counter-battery warfare that 82 per cent of the German artillery at Vimy was rendered useless.

These were Saturday night soldiers, members of the militia, which had fifty thousand recruits on paper, most of them poorly trained and at least half either unfit for service or unwilling to serve. For Canada in 1914 had scarcely any military tradition, no military aspirations, and little knowledge of war. Out of a population of eight million, she had barely three thousand permanent force soldiers, and these were under British command. If Canadians were to fight and win battles they would have to start from scratch with no background of experience – and also no preconceived ideas, which was not necessarily a bad thing.

They knew very little about war – especially *this* war – yet under the stress of battle they found they could perform impossible feats for which they'd had no previous training.

At Vimy, Duncan Eberts Macintyre, a Saskatchewan storekeeper, became, in effect, the managing director of a brigade of three thousand men, the brigadier's right-hand man, every detail from rations to signals at his fingertips.

At Vimy, a bespectacled twenty-year-old medical student from the University of Toronto named Claude Williams – a man who had never fired a gun – not only operated a water-cooled, belt-driven Vickers but also taught others to do it and led them under fire.

William Markle Pecover was also twenty years old when the war broke out. He'd been teaching school in Manitoba for the previous two years. The only contact he'd had with his future enemies was the course in German he'd taken in high school. How could he know that those few half-remembered guttural phrases would one day be the means by which he would capture a dugoutful of prisoners?

Leonard Lynde Youell was working a fifty-five-hour week at the Toronto Electrical Company that summer. He'd got the job through the father of a friend. It paid fifteen cents an hour and he was glad to have it, for jobs were scarce and he needed money for his fees as a student at the university. Len Youell would not have believed that summer that in less than three years he too would be performing a strange, unwonted task: crouching in a forward observation post overlooking No Man's Land, with a telephone in one hand and a pair of binoculars in the other, correcting the ranges of the big guns at the rear by spotting the exact position of the shell bursts.

How could they know? Few Canadians gave much thought to events in Europe in those last peacetime months. People lazed on their front porches, or wound up the gramophone to listen to the great Al Jolson hit, "The Spaniard Who Blighted My Life," or Joe Hayman's smash best-selling recording of "Cohen on the Telephone." The English suffragettes were making more news than the German Kaiser, and the Keystone Kops were far better known than an obscure Austrian archduke.

Canada before 1914 was a peaceable kingdom and these were gentle times, where work was hard and pleasure innocent. Divorce was all but unknown; no decent woman was ever seen smoking a cigarette; saloons, where they existed at all, were male preserves. Sunday was sacrosanct; there was nothing else to do on the Sabbath but go to church. In 1912 Stephen Leacock caught the small-town mood of the country exactly in *Sunshine Sketches of a Little Town*, with its emphasis on local politics, backroom boozing, church socials and picnics.

For Canada was still a frontier country of farms and villages, of outdoor plumbing and rutted concession roads. The Model T, wheezing and coughing its way down the unpaved streets, was emerging as a symbol of a new and radically different era, and so were the ungainly mechanized tractors on the prairie farms. But the railway remained king. Two more transcontinental lines were being pushed westward to compete with the Canadian Pacific. Conceived at the height of the Western boom, they symbolized the ebullience of a nation that in spite of the boom's collapse still basked in the optimism of the frontier.

Wilfrid Laurier had said it: this was Canada's century! Nothing was impossible for a man who used his hands and his brains; hadn't that been proved time and again out West? Magazines like the new *Maclean's* (once the *Business Magazine*) glowed with true stories of men who'd pulled themselves up by their own bootstraps, penniless youths who had become millionaires.

To a very large extent the men who fought at Vimy had worked on farms or lived on the edge of the wilderness. Almost half the infantry came from west of Ontario, even though the Western provinces and territories made up less than a quarter of the Canadian population. An extraordinary number were English-born pioneers or their sons, men who had settled in the West during the immigration period and learned to adapt to unfamiliar conditions. ''You may be interested to know that most of the men in my platoon, as in the rest of the battalion, are farmers, ranchers, cowboys, trappers, etc. from the far west and northwest,'' Clifford Wells, a young archaeologist, wrote to his mother four days before the battle. ''Splendid stalwart men, most of them.'' One, Wells reported, was the champion rider of Alberta and Saskatchewan, king of the stampedes.

Such men were used to hard work, long hours, and rough conditions. At Vimy, far more time was spent in back-breaking toil – endless digging with pick and shovel, toting heavy loads over difficult ground – than in firing any weapons. The Canadians adapted easily to these familiar conditions, made the best of them, and used age-old Canadian devices, such as the Indian tumpline, to alleviate the work load.

These were men whose arms and shoulder muscles had been toughened by years of playing the two indigenous Canadian games, lacrosse and ice hockey. It was no great feat for them to march for hours with a rifle at the slope or high port, or to lunge with a bayonet. These were also men who were used to working with horses, who had laboured on the railways and in the mines, and who had tinkered with farm machinery. All these skills dovetailed neatly into the Vimy requirements, where thousands of feet of rails and plank road had to be laid, hundreds of yards of tunnels had to be blasted from the chalk, and fifty thousand horses had to be fed and cared for.

Trench life in France was appalling for everybody, but at least a good proportion of the men at Vimy had known what it was like to sleep out in the mud and rain, to eat a cold meal in the wilderness, and, in many cases, to knock over a deer with a rifle. It was the same with those in the sky above. All of Canada's leading flying aces came from backwoods communities, mainly from the West. In civilian life they were crack shots and good riders. After all, to manhandle a Sopwith Camel in the Great War wasn't that different from riding a spirited steed.

The Canadians who went off to war in 1914 from the fields

and the forests were not yet soldiers; in or out of uniform they could not have prevailed against a disciplined enemy. But they had guts and stamina and, perhaps more important, a habit of self-reliance that would help to carry them through those weary months when the mud and the vermin were almost unbearable, and those tense few hours when the guns roared and the trenches ran with blood.

2

The last day of peace was enlivened in Ottawa by a moment of pure farce, starring the Minister of Militia, Sam Hughes, the most belligerent public figure in a most unbelligerent nation. Hughes did not fight at Vimy, though he would have loved to; his battles were all political. In fact, he was finally kicked out of office by an exasperated prime minister in November 1916, just as the Canadian Corps was settling into the Vimy sector. Yet he deserves his place in the annals of the war in general and Vimy in particular because, without the force of that overpowering and maddening personality, it is quite possible that the Canadians would never have fought together as a united corps.

Hughes's astonishing career is marked by incidents so incredible as to give the serious researcher pause. Yet, at each encounter, one has the firm evidence of witnesses of impeccable veracity and sober mien. On this morning of August 3, 1914, there was one such present in the person of Charles Winter, the minister's private secretary.

Winter had arrived at 8:30, but Hughes was in his office before him, a massive figure with a square jaw and piercing blue eyes, now snarling and cursing and hammering on his desk. Spread before him was a copy of the Ottawa *Citizen* announcing that war had been declared against Germany and Austria by France, Russia, and Serbia. England had not yet declared, but a decision was expected when the Imperial cabinet met that afternoon. That was not good enough for Sam Hughes.

"They are going to skunk it!" Hughes cried, banging the paper with his fist. "They seem to be looking for an excuse to get out of helping France. Oh! What a shameful state of things! By God, I don't want to be a Britisher under such conditions . . ."

Winter intervened to point out that everybody expected the British cabinet to decide that afternoon, but Hughes was certain Britain would back down.

"They are curs enough to do it; I can read between the lines," he cried. "I believe they will temporize and hum and haw too long – and by God I don't want to be a Britisher under such conditions – it's too humiliating."

Hughes then asked if the Union Jack was flying over the building and Winter said he'd seen it up as usual.

"Then send up and have it taken down!" shouted Hughes. "I will not have it over our Canada's military headquarters when Britain shirks her plain duty – it is disgraceful."

Winter did as he was told. When the Militia Council met at nine that morning the offending banner lay neatly rolled on the Minister's desk. Only with great difficulty was he persuaded to return it to the flagstaff until the afternoon dispatches revealed whether or not the Empire was at war.

The episode was entirely typical of Hughes, a staunch Britisher but also a staunch Canadian nationalist, who was absolutely determined that Canada should not be a vassal of the mother country. In this he reflected a growing awareness on the part of his less bombastic countrymen. English-speaking Canadians were proud to be British, but they were also becoming intoxicated by the heady atmosphere of the boom years. For more than a decade the eyes of much of the world had been focused on the Canadian West. Scores of magazine articles, dozens of books had raved about this promised land. Canadians could be forgiven for being cocky about themselves and their country, and this cockiness would be reflected in the spirit of the troops who, after more than two years of battle, came into their own at Vimy.

On that Monday, August 3, the entire country awoke to the reality that war was inevitable. The European crisis had been on the front pages for no more than ten days, but now it was clear to the man on the farm, if not to Sam Hughes, that Britain would fight. It was a civic holiday in Ontario, and in Toronto, ten thousand people jammed the streets in front of the newspaper offices. Aflame now with war fever, they greeted each bulletin with a roar, flinging hats high into the air, waving Union Jacks, beating drums, and shouting out their enthusiasm. Similar scenes took place all across the nation. In Vancouver, it seemed as if the entire populace was on the streets to watch the Seaforth Highlanders on parade.

The following day, as if to match the fervour of the populace, the temperature soared, reaching 101°F on the prairies. By evening, the news was out: Britain was at war. Almost everyone (except Sam Hughes) assumed that Canada was at war as well, not as a full partner, not as an ally, but as a subsidiary force. The Canadian war effort was to be organized by the British. Canada would be fighting for the Empire, for British ideals. As the *Mail and Empire* of Toronto explained: "For all practical purposes the wishes of the British war office govern the raising of Canadian contingents. . . ."

Most English-speaking Canadians thought of themselves as British first, Canadian second. In spite of the waves of European and American immigrants who had helped people the West, the majority of Canadians outside Quebec were either British born or of British stock. Any schoolchild opening a Canadian reader was caught by the phrase "One Flag, One Fleet, One Throne," which appeared with the Union Jack as the frontispiece.

English Canada's heroes were English mariners and soldiers – Drake and Nelson, Wellington and Cromwell. English Canada's great holidays – Victoria Day and the Glorious Twelfth – were British. Most school texts were published in England and peddled by Canadian jobbers. Kipling, the voice of Imperial Britain, was probably the most quoted poet in Canada, followed by Robert Service, whose mimicry of the master's style caused him to be known as "the Canadian Kipling." The *rightness* of all things British was unquestioned. The Canadian way was the British way, except in Quebec, which had its own heroes, holidays, and poets and its own differing attitude to nationalism and European war.

But in those days of "exaltation and enthusiasm," to use the Prime Minister's phrase, everyone seemed caught up in the excitement. "We stand shoulder to shoulder with the British Dominions in this quarrel," Sir Robert Borden told the House, and even Henri Bourassa, the Quebec ultra-nationalist, murmured approval. Later Bourassa had a change of heart: England's war was not French Canada's war. But there were some in Quebec who attacked that stand as treason.

By and large the continental immigrants did not join the rush to enlist. The Slavs and the Scandinavians stayed on their new farms. The Germans found it difficult to fight their countrymen. The Doukhobors, Mennonites, and Hutterites would not fight for religious reasons. And many of the Americans who had swarmed into Saskatchewan and Alberta a few years before went back across the border.

It was the British and especially the British-born who flocked to the colours in the early days of the war and who made up the bulk of the Canadian Corps at Vimy. To many there was no question of choice: the Old Country was in danger. "What outfit are you going to join?" was the way a friend put it to F.C. Bagshaw, an English immigrant in Winnipeg. It did not occur to either of them that there was any other decision or that Bagshaw, at thirty-five the oldest man in the 5th Battalion, might beg off because of his age.

Like Fred Holm, another immigrant, whose family came from Bristol in 1910 because there was no work in England, they joined because, in Holm's words, "it's in the blood . . . it was the right thing to do." That attitude was general and was echoed in the words of the youngest son of Nellie McClung, the well-known novelist, who told his mother: "I want to go–I want to help the British Empire–while there is a British Empire!"

But not all of those who fought at Vimy joined for reasons of patriotism, though most used that excuse. In many ways, the stampede to the recruiting offices in 1914 resembled another stampede, seventeen years before. When the

Klondike fever struck, thousands rushed off to the frozen North, not because they really believed they were going to get rich (as they pretended), but because they were active young men, bored with life, seeking adventure in a distant clime – and also because everybody else was going, and so it was "the thing to do."

The thing to do! It is a phrase that reoccurs in the reminiscenses of Vimy veterans. Everybody, it seemed, was going. Nobody wanted to be left behind. If your entire college class or church club was signing up, would you want to be the only holdout? As Gordon Shrum was later to admit, he went because everybody he knew was going, and he feared that if he didn't follow the crowd he'd be ostracized. A gunner with the 29th Battery at Vimy, Shrum went on to a distinguished career in science, education, and public service in British Columbia.

That was it: if you didn't go you were an outcast or something close to it. The fever was epidemic, especially in the West. In Vancouver the men's club of a local Presbyterian church signed up en masse. In Moose Jaw, one hundred members of the Legion of Frontiersmen simply took possession of an east-bound train, with or without paying the fare, and were carried to Ottawa, where they joined the newly formed Princess Pats. In Winnipeg an entire baseball team enlisted; in Kamloops all the carpenters building a local hospital walked off the job and joined up; in Saskatoon, twenty-six members of the city band signed on.

Whole communities were ravaged by mass enlistments. The saddest, perhaps, was the little town of Walhachin, B.C., which became a ghost village in the post-war years because every able-bodied man had joined the army and few had returned. An empty cricket pitch suggested the Imperial make-up of the community.

These early volunteers did not fear death; they feared that the great adventure would end before they could take part in it. The worst conditions failed to damp their ardour. In Winnipeg, the old Horse Show building used as a barracks was so cold that several young recruits, unable to get decent clothing, died of pneumonia. In spite of that the troops continued to sing the sardonic verses of "When the War Is Nearly over We'll Be There."

As late as 1916, when some young women who had no real notion of what the war was about were handing out white feathers to shame the reluctant, the fever was still raging, in spite of–or perhaps because of–the news from the front. The universities were combing their classrooms to raise special battalions of students and graduates who would fight shoulder to shoulder and thus retain some of the camaraderie of campus life. When Dr. William Boyd, a veteran of the field ambulance in France, returned to recite John McCrae's poem "In Flanders Fields," twenty members of the graduating class of Manitoba College rushed to the recruiting office to become ambulance drivers themselves.

Others joined for reasons that might be described as selfish, though in the mud of Flanders that didn't matter a hoot. A great many simply wanted a free ride across the water, a chance to visit their homeland, a quick holiday before the war petered out, as it most certainly would in a few months. Harold Barker, an eighteen-year-old from Gloucestershire, was one of these. He'd come to Canada in 1911, spotted an orchard near Winchester, Ontario, got off the train, and taken a job picking apples. Since that moment he'd thought only of returning home. He didn't join the army to fight for his country; he knew nothing *about* his country! He joined the army because he was homesick. He got more than he'd bargained for. On the morning of the Vimy battle, Corporal Harold Barker, a scout with the Royal Canadian Regiment, was hit by one of his own shells and dragged off the field bleeding from wounds in the mouth, chest, legs, and back.

Ben Case joined the army because he hadn't studied for his exams. He couldn't face the prospect of failing and he didn't have a job prospect, so at 9 A.M. when the examinations started at the University of Toronto, he was standing at the Dufferin Gate of the Canadian National Exhibition grounds, waiting to enlist. On the morning of the Vimy battle, Ben Case, by now a telephone lineman, was crouching in a pit, half deafened by the barrage, aware only that his comrade, "Tubby" Turnbull, had been killed by a splinter of shrapnel.

Jack Quinnell joined up because it would mean one less mouth to feed back home. He was sixteen years old when he enlisted, a gangling redhead with innocent blue eyes, one of seven children in a family where money was tight and food scarce. Who, in his position, would not have signed up? The private soldier's pay of a dollar ten a day sounded like a small fortune, and in addition there was free food, free clothing, free travel, and the prospect of adventure. Like the others, Jack Quinnell hadn't the slightest idea what he was in for. But on the afternoon of April 9, 1917, when his regiment was blown to pieces in a vain attempt to seize the highest point of the ridge, and Jack Quinnell lay half buried by an explosion, he knew that he had earned his pay.

To these men, raised on Tennyson and Kipling, war was all dash and colour, evoking words like "gallantry," "courage," and "daring." War was men in brilliant costumes galloping about on splendid horses. War was an arm temporarily in a sling, a bandage draped rakishly across a forehead, a sabre scar ennobling a cheek.

Canadians of 1914 had never been exposed to war – only to the romantic paintings reproduced in school texts or the dramatic engravings in the illustrated magazines. War to them was Wolfe expiring gracefully on Abraham's Plain or Brock dashing up the Queenston slopes, sword flashing in the sunlight. War was the Métis driven from the gun-pits of Batoche, or the Bengal Lancers jousting with the hill tribes of the Punjab, or the Welsh holding out against the fuzzy-wuzzies at Rorke's Drift. War was Gunga Din and the Soldiers of the Queen, all in scarlet and gold. In 1914, the only memories Canadians had of war were the reminiscenses of the rough-riders who returned from South Africa with tales of derring-do, chasing the Boers across the veld.

There was no organized pacifist movement in Canada; in fact war was not necessarily thought of as a bad thing. Arthur Lower, who was to become the country's leading social historian, remembered discussing the subject in June, 1914, with a friend. They decided that "a nice little war would be just what the country needed to cap its development and give it a sense of corporate unity." Lower lived to regret that prescient remark, which came true in the grisliest manner.

War, then, was an adventure, and it is safe to say that most, if not all, of the young men who fought at Vimy saw it that way. To William Pecover, the Manitoba schoolteacher, it was just that: something he couldn't afford to miss – going overseas on a ship! When two of his school pals joined up in Brandon he didn't waste a minute in joining them. Leslie Hudd, a former Barnardo boy and a member of the Sherbrooke Militia, who was only seventeen, put his name in for the cyclist company even though he'd never ridden a bicycle because it sounded suitably dashing and because he knew that the cyclists were being sent to France quickly. His attitude changed drastically after he was gassed at Ypres.

Like the young men who swarmed to the recruiting offices, terrified of missing out on the "fun" (as more than one termed it), the army brass was convinced that the conflict would end quickly. In the early months of the war, the army was rigorously selective. One man was turned down because he weighed only a hundred pounds, another because he had a job and the orders were to sign up the unemployed first, a third because his chest expansion wasn't ample enough. (This was the determined Fred Holm, who worked out for weeks at the Toronto YMCA to build himself up.)

Will Bird, a future novelist from the Maritimes, was turned down because he already had a brother in the service and it was thought unfair to his widowed mother to hazard both sons. But by 1916, when the war was gobbling up the flower of Canada's youth, considerations like these were tossed aside, and all these men found themselves fighting at the Battle of Vimy Ridge. This change of attitude was brought home graphically to Dodge Rankine, a young McGill student who, to his disgust, was turned down in 1914 because he'd once had typhoid. Two years later, when Rankine encountered the same doctor at the recruiting office, things were radically different.

"What do you want, Dodge?" the doctor asked.

"I want to join the artillery."

"Open your shirt," said the doctor, briefly applying a stethoscope to his chest. That was the end of the medical. "The boat leaves at four o'clock," the doctor explained.

By the end of the month, Rankine was in France. The following spring he was helping to operate one of the big siege guns in the great barrage at Vimy.

By the time he joined the army, Rankine was twenty-one, but thousands of others had not yet reached voting age. The impression left by the contemporary photographs and paintings and also by the later Hollywood war movies is deceptive. We think of the soldiers of the Great War as grown men, mature in years and experience. In fact, this war was fought to a considerable extent by teenagers. The moustaches, the sunken eyes, the hollow cheeks mask the truth – that many of these youths, trained to kill and be killed, would in normal times still have been in high school. They badgered their parents for permission to go until the parents gave in.

A young Regina teenager named Bob Owen was one of these. Twice he ran away from home to join the army. Twice his widowed mother brought him back. Finally, after pleading and cajoling on his part, she reluctantly agreed to let him enlist. The local postmaster confronted him as he boarded the train to the East, the cars full of teenagers like himself, all eager for the adventure of their lives. But young Owen – he was just seventeen – had a release signed by his mother in his pocket. He looked out of the window as the train started to pull away and witnessed a spectacle that became affecting only in retrospect. There on the platform were other mothers, all crying. As the train moved slowly out of the station the women began to run along the platform beside it, clutching their sons' hands, refusing to let go until the train had to be stopped to disengage them. Finally, the train puffed away, the mothers still weeping and waving goodbye to their children, in many cases forever.

3

On August 24, the first militia units began to straggle into the new camp in the township of Valcartier, Quebec. Here, on a sandy plain covered in scrub bush sixteen miles northwest of Quebec City, some thirty-three thousand members of the Canadian militia were to be trained for overseas service.

The Scots were the first to arrive, men from the various Highland units who would form the new 16th Battalion, Canadian Scottish. They were unusual in that most were old soldiers. Three out of four had seen service in one of ninety-five different units, ranging from the Australian militia to the Chinese army. It was as well that they had had some military experience because the training at Valcartier was almost non-existent.

Physically, the camp itself was a remarkable accomplishment. In less than a month this wretched piece of bush land, bisected by the Jacques Cartier River, had been transformed into a bustling military camp, complete with roads, water mains, railway sidings, stores, showers and movies for the troops, three miles of rifle range, and twenty-eight thousand feet of drain pipe.

There was only one problem: nobody seemed to know from day to day what was going on. There was little time for training, and the organization of the troops was chaotic; after all, the men had poured in from some two hundred militia units. Every officer was kept in doubt as to whether or not he would go overseas. One battalion had three lieutenant-colonels on strength; another had four prospective seconds-in-command and only one horse for all. A third battalion arrived fifteen hundred strong and was broken up for reinforcements. Still another turned up with eleven officers and only fourteen rank and file. One adjutant who suddenly found himself without a staff had to type out orders himself and in doing so got the carbon paper reversed. His orders could be deciphered only by holding them before a mirror.

Some of the volunteers' early enthusiasm was badly shaken at Valcartier and not just because of the inadequate tents, the lack of greatcoats, or the incredible mix-up of stores and equipment. It was Sam Hughes himself who helped shatter morale among all ranks but especially among the officers.

As one of them noted, most of their time seemed to be taken up listening to Hughes, sitting on his horse, haranguing the troops and berating their officers. That was, of course, an exaggeration. Yet that image – the posturing figure in the red-tabbed uniform, the chill blue eyes, the hard, square jaw, the pompous phrases – was one that would remain with them and, in later years, symbolize Valcartier.

For Valcartier was Hughes's creation, a memorial to his single-minded ability to get things done and to the personal idiocies and imbecilities that forced the nation's leaders to question his sanity. From the Governor General, Prince Arthur, Duke of Connaught, on down the consensus was that Hughes was mentally unbalanced – "off his base," to use Prince Arthur's phrase. Borden's deputy, Sir George Foster, believed it. "There is only one feeling about Sam. That he is crazy," he wrote in his diary on September 22. Claude MacDonell, a prominent Tory M.P., believed it. "The man is insane," he told Borden in November. Joseph Flavelle, a leading financier who encountered Hughes in 1916, believed it. Hughes, he concluded, was "mentally unbalanced with the low cunning and cleverness often associated with the insane." And Borden himself believed it. In his memoirs he described Hughes's conduct and speeches as "so eccentric as to justify the conclusion that his mind was unbalanced."

By mid-September, 1914, the Prime Minister was receiving "astonishing reports as to Hughes's language and conduct" at Valcartier. Borden's informants were impeccable; they included the Governor General himself. The King's son felt it necessary to tell the Prime Minister that Hughes's language to his own officers in front of the troops was "violent and insulting" and that they were "generally enraged."

It boggles the mind that this posturing and bigoted Orangeman, who ran the army as his own personal fiefdom, should have remained in office for more than two years after the war began, insulting everybody from the King's representative to the entire French-Canadian community (and thereby exacerbating a widening split in the country that would lead, after Vimy, to a major national crisis).

Why didn't Borden fire him? The blunt answer is that Hughes scared him silly. The mild and courteous prime minister couldn't summon up the courage to have it out with a Tory stalwart who bullied, blustered, lied, and bluffed his way out of the tightest corner. Hughes fought back at the slightest reproof with long, vituperative letters of self-vindication refusing ever to apologize for his sins, announcing that he was "loved by millions" and comparing his critics to yelping puppy dogs vainly chasing an express train.

He insulted everybody from the secretary of the Toronto Humane Society to the Anglican Bishop of Montreal. When the Bishop complained about the lack of Anglican padres in the forces, Hughes unleashed a string of profanity at him. When the animal lover inquired about the mistreatment of horses at Valcartier, Hughes called him a damn liar and physically ejected him from his office.

This was the man, in charge of the nation's military defences since 1911, who announced blandly at the war's outset that he could personally raise forty divisions to fight the Germans, who wore his uniform to cabinet meetings and exclaimed that if the war wasn't over by spring he would take the field himself, a prospect that terrified and appalled his colleagues.

It is a democratic tradition that the military should always be under civilian control and that generals should have no politics. The problem was that in Hughes's case there was no such division. He had made himself a lieutenant-colonel in the militia and after a few months had promoted himself to major-general. As such he ran the army and thought nothing of promoting his political friends as honorary colonels.

He could not abide being wrong, for his ego was monumental. Encountering an officer on leave he mistakenly addressed him as captain and when told the man was only a lieutenant promoted him on the spot. "Sir, I know what I'm talking about," said Hughes. He was out of line, of course: politicians can't promote officers, but then Hughes was always out of line. He paid no more attention to military etiquette than he did to cabinet solidarity. He broke the rule that officers should never be dressed down in front of their troops. "Pipe up, you little bugger, or get out of the service!" he shouted at one who spoke too quietly. He created new battalions, scrapped old ones, moved others about like puppets, decided who would go overseas with the first contingent, who would stay behind.

He hated the British Army and especially the permanent force, whom he referred to publicly as a bunch of barroom loafers. He had been a staunch militia man since the days of the Fenian raids. He'd run afoul of the British brass hats in the South African War and felt aggrieved because he hadn't been awarded the Victoria Cross – indeed, he seems to have believed that he should have had *two* V.C.s. He refused to take any advice from the regulars and, in his laudable but misplaced nationalism, was convinced that the untrained Canadians were better than their seasoned British counterparts. He publicly told one man who wore four decorations on his chest that it would be a crime to allow him to lead men to the front.

Hughes could not stand being under the thumb of the British. He would later help to lever the British commander of the 1st Division, and later of the Canadian Corps, out of his job. Lieutenant-General Sir Edwin Alderson was a hero of the South African War but no match for Hughes, who shot off a "poisonous telegram" (in the words of the CPR's Thomas Shaughnessy) attacking the new divisional leader and suggesting that it would be better if he himself took command. The insult was aggravated by the fact that the telegram, which went to his London agent, Colonel John Wallace Carson, was not sent in code.

In Hughes's eyes the British Dominions should be equal partners with the United Kingdom, in no way subservient one to the other. It would be almost two decades before this autonomy was enshrined in the Statute of Westminster. In that sense, Hughes was a man ahead of his time – but only in that sense. Yet when Hughes is assessed these sentiments have to be taken into account and weighed against the mountain of gaucheries, barbarities, vulgarities, and blunders that have made him the laughing-stock of history. Hughes was an impossible man; yet without his single-minded and often belligerent posturing it is doubtful whether the Canadian Corps would have come into being as a united national force to fight and win the Battle of Vimy Ridge.

He must also bear most of the burden for the fact that the first contingent left Canada without any real training. Hughes's own military philosophy was antediluvian and his refusal to listen to the regular British staff officers in Canada was tragic. He had no use for the Royal Flying Corps – didn't believe that airplanes had any military value – and his personal tactics seemed to hark back to Waterloo. A group of the Governor General's Bodyguards was being taught drill at Valcartier one day when Hughes, resplendent in red tabs and on horseback, arrived with an escort of cavalry, lances poised ("He's not entitled to that," one old soldier whispered). Hughes wheeled his horse, turned to the troops, and cried: "Form square!" The men looked at him blankly. The manoeuvre had long since been struck from the training manual, yet nothing would do but that the corporal in charge must shuffle his men around and get them kneeling with bayonets fixed.

"Now," rapped Hughes, looking straight at Private Frank Yates. "What do you do after that?"

Yates looked at him blankly.

The corporal kicked Yates in the rear and whispered: "Unload."

"Unload, sir," said Yates, and Hughes seemed satisfied.

Later that night Yates and the others discussed the incident. "Good God," said one. "What sort of army are we in?"

Trained or not, the first contingent was ready to leave for England early in October of 1914. Hughes was convinced against all evidence that the Canadians were fighting fit. Sitting astride his horse, addressing the men on the eve of their departure overseas, he launched into a speech, later damned by Borden as "flamboyant and grandiloquent," that was clearly based on Napoleon's famous address to the armies of Italy. "Soldiers!" cried Hughes. "The world regards you as a marvel. . . . Within six weeks you were at your homes, peaceful Canadian citizens. . . . Today [you] are as fine a body – Officers and Men – as ever faced a foe. . . .''

This was laying it on pretty thick. There was no evidence that the world had any regard for these eager but innocent young Canadians in their ill-fitting uniforms and badly made army boots. But there was much more, for Hughes went on and on, reeling off a long list of his accomplishments at Valcartier, announcing that there would be ''no faltering or temporizing'' (whatever that meant) and praising the ''indomitable spirit'' with which they would ''triumph over the common enemy of humanity.''

At one point, to the bafflement and astonishment of the troops, Hughes broke into a long stream of sentimental poetry before telling them the one thing they didn't want to hear: that some would never return. No matter: ''The soldier going down in the cause of freedom never dies. Immortality is his. What recks he whether his resting place may be bedecked with the golden lilies of France or amid the vine clad hills of the Rhine? The principles for which you strive are eternal.''

Even in that era of purple oratory this was too much. Hughes had expected the plaudits of the nation. Instead, all he got was merriment. The Prime Minister put it concisely enough in his diary that same evening. ''Everybody laughing at Sam's address,'' he wrote.

But now, to his dismay, Borden found that Hughes was determined to accompany the first contingent to Britain. The Governor General was as much opposed to that as the Prime Minister. The prospect of the gauche and posturing minister loose among the stiff-necked and proper English sent shivers down their spines. Hughes would be seen as representing the Canadian government when, in fact, he rarely bothered to check with anybody to avoid committing a gaffe.

Yet Hughes had every reason to want to shake up the British. He was convinced, rightly, that Lord Kitchener wanted to separate the Canadian battalions and dovetail them into the regular British forces. If that happened the Canadian identity would be lost, swallowed up in an ocean of Tommy Atkinses.

In the end he got his way, but not before he had, in his

fashion, arranged for the embarkation of the troops. He refused to allow anybody but himself to organize this task and, in a speech a few weeks later, claimed that if it hadn't been for him, the entire convoy of thirty ships might have been sunk by German submarines. Modesty was never one of Hughes's failings.

In fact, the embarkation had been badly muddled. In the words of Colonel J.F.C. Fuller, who handled the Southampton end, one of the transports, S.S. *Manhattan*, "closely resembled a Noah's Ark." Scores of officers and men, having missed the ships they were supposed to sail in, simply climbed aboard the *Manhattan*, whose holds were already jammed with baggage that had arrived late. To Fuller's absolute bafflement, some units actually disappeared and others were created while at sea. One infantry battalion, for example, finding time heavy on its hands, looted the *Manhattan*'s hold, discovered several cases of spurs, and arrived in England as an untraceable cavalry regiment.

Thus did the vanguard of the Canadian Corps arrive on British shores. If somebody had told Fuller that these same men would form the nucleus of the small force that gave Great Britain its first victory of the war, one might have pardoned him for smiling.

Hughes was already in London. He did not travel with the contingent but, having seen the troops off, boarded a fast liner and reached England ahead of the soldiers. There, resplendent in his tailored whipcord and red tabs, he headed for the War Office to beard Lord Kitchener in his den.

Only a man of Hughes's temperament and ego could have stood up to the terrifying victor of Khartoum, whose steel blue eyes and monstrous moustache dominated the recruiting posters in London. Kitchener had already overruled Hughes's three suggestions for a Canadian commander, appointing instead his own choice, General Alderson. Now he proposed to take complete control of the Canadians.

Kitchener talked to the Canadian like a stern uncle reproving an errant youth.

"Hughes," he said, "I see you have brought a number of men from Canada; they are of course without training and this would apply to their officers. I have decided to divide them up among the British regiments; they will be of very little use to us as they are.''

''Sir,'' said Hughes, ''do I understand you to say that you are going to break up these Canadian regiments that came over? Why, it will kill recruiting in Canada.''

''You have your orders,'' said Kitchener, shortly. ''Carry them out.''

''I'll be damned if I will,'' said Sam Hughes and, turning on his heel, marched out.

According to Hughes, Kitchener had the agreement of the Canadian High Commissioner, Sir George Perley, that the troops would be regarded as purely British and that Canada should have nothing to say in their management. Indeed, when Hughes met Perley a day or so later, the High Commissioner asked him, ''You do not pretend, surely, to have anything to do with the Canadian soldiers in Britain?''

To this Hughes replied that the entire British government and the War Office must understand that the officers and men, being in the pay of Canada, should be controlled in Canada, in Britain, and at the front by the Canadian government, except for the command. As he wrote to Borden some years after the affair: ''I determined that Canada was not to be treated as a Crown Colony and that, as we paid the bill and furnished the goods, which in nearly every instance were better than the British, I would act.''

This was Sam Hughes's finest hour. There would be no more. Over the next two years he would stumble from blunder to blunder, from scandal to scandal, from gaucherie to gaucherie before he was finally forced out of office. And yet for all his braggadocio, for all his political cronyism, for all his incredible egotism, his slanderous insults, his barefaced prevarications, this strangest and most eccentric of all Canadian politicians had one last achievement to his credit. The united Canadian Corps stood as a symbol of a nation emerging from the colonial shadows. The victory at Vimy would confirm the growing realization that Canada had, at last, come of age.

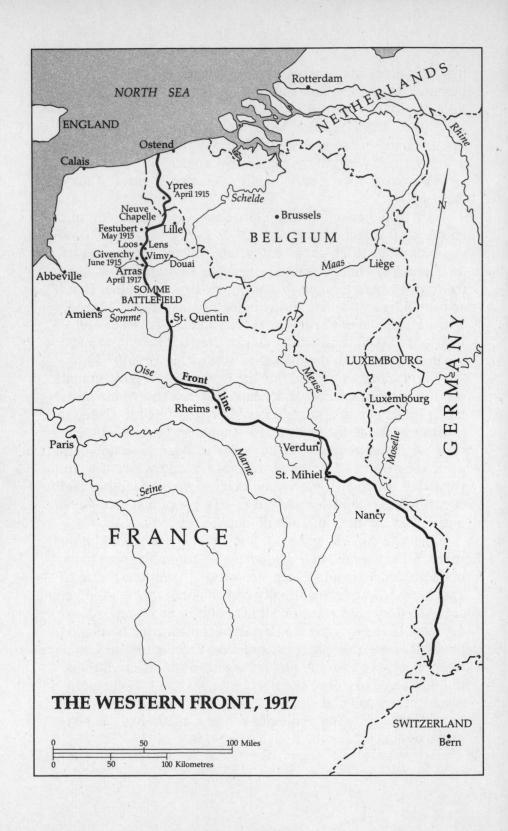

NORTH SEA

ENGLAND

Rotterdam

NETHERLANDS

Ostend

Calais

Ypres
April 1915

Schelde

Brussels

Neuve
Chapelle

Festubert
May 1915   Lille

BELGIUM

Loos · Lens

Givenchy   Vimy
June 1915

Douai

Maas   Liège

Abbeville

Arras
April 1917

SOMME
BATTLEFIELD

Amiens   Somme   · St. Quentin

Rhine

N

LUXEMBOURG

Oise   Front

line

Meuse

Luxembourg

Rheims

Moselle

GERMANY

Paris

Verdun

St. Mihiel

Marne

Seine

Nancy

F R A N C E

THE WESTERN FRONT, 1917

SWITZERLAND

Bern

| 0 | | 50 | | 100 Miles |
| 0 | 50 | | 100 Kilometres | |

CHAPTER TWO

A Ribbon of Deadly Stealth

1

On Thursday, October 14, 1914, England got its first proof that the Empire was responding to the call to arms. The Canadian contingent had arrived unexpectedly at Plymouth to provoke a welcome that resounded across the kingdom. When the news spread over the seaport the British went crazy. For two days as the Canadians disembarked, people swarmed to the dockyard waving hats, flags, and any other patriotic emblem available, showering the soldiers with cigarettes, chocolates, apples, and bottles of whisky and gin, and singing an unfamiliar song called "Tipperary." On the quayside, the riveters aboard a dreadnought under construction had chalked huge letters on the plating: "Bravo Canadians!"

As the men tramped through the streets to the waiting trains that would take them to the training fields on Salisbury Plain, cheering crowds marched alongside. At every station, throngs were on the platform shouting themselves hoarse. It was widely reported that the hated Kaiser was in a rage over the new arrivals. When told that Canada had sent her sons in thirty ocean liners to the help of the mother country he was said to have shouted, "Sons! Slaves! They will go back in thirty rowboats!" No one revealed how this remarkable piece of military intelligence had got through so quickly to the Kaiser's enemies.

The Times made much of the fact that the Canadians were different from the English, though "British in the best sense." They were, the paper reported, sterner and sturdier than the typical English recruit, "the type of strong clean limbed Briton at whom one instinctively takes a second look in the street."

In the months that followed other differences were noted with less enthusiasm, especially by the British staff officers. In the eyes of many Englishmen, the Canadians were a wild, undisciplined lot and therefore ineffective by British Army standards. There was nothing sheep-like about them. At the Valcartier camp, when the same movie was shown once too often, they had gone crazy, torn down the YMCA tent and set it afire. Now, in the Old Country, they refused to conform to the rigid class lines that divided privates, NCOs, and officers into watertight social compartments – as in the railway coaches and in the pubs, with their three segregated bars.

Military etiquette based on social class was foreign to the young men from the farms and the forests – including those who had fled the strictures of British society to enjoy the open-handed style of the frontier. It was difficult to call a man "sir" when he'd held a job similar to yours in civilian life. Saluting – which seemed very like a peasant's knuckle to the forehead – did not come easily. The British tommies saluted every officer they saw, even across a broad roadway; the Canadians saluted only when they felt like it.

When Sergeant Cassels, a newly promoted NCO in the 16th Battalion, was told he couldn't walk down the streets with a private soldier, he tore off his stripes. "I'm not a sergeant any more," he declared. Others were just as appalled by class divisions. Captain Hal Wallis, a Westmount man from 7th Brigade headquarters, came back from officers' school shaking his head over his encounter with an outcast from that group. Why, asked Wallis, would the other officers have nothing to do with him? "I am not a gentleman," came the reply. "I worked for the post office."

The absence of distinctive class was, however, an asset for the Canadians. It meant that ability won out over élitism. Neither birth nor marriage nor social position counted in the selection of Canadian officers. By 1916 political clout didn't help, either.

In Britain, class was everything. The command and fabric of the regular British army has been described by one critic as having "stiffened into a sort of Byzantine formalism." The other ranks, who belonged to the lower class, were expected to obey orders without question and without any real knowledge of the military situation, which was considered too deep and complicated for them to grasp. Such was the gap between officers and men that any private soldier who did try to ask a question of his seniors was considered by his own fellows a traitor to his class – "cosying up to the toffs." Even in 1917, when the British army had been bled white, promotion from the ranks was not usual.

Canadian private soldiers thought nothing of entering a saloon or a private bar in a British pub. In one fashionable West End restaurant, the shocked patrons were treated to the spectacle of a company sergeant-major parading between the tables accompanied by a private playing the pipes.

The hierarchy took a dim view of such shenanigans. Captain Andrew Macphail, a medical officer with the first contingent and a distinguished McGill academic, whose letters home were studded with wry comments, was told by a British staff officer that the Canadians were being kept out of action because they were unruly and mutinous. The Canadians, for their part, were often intolerant of the English to the point where the courtly fifty-year-old doctor found that, as a Canadian, he must be extremely guarded aboard buses and trains lest he leave himself open to insult. Macphail had two brothers also serving in the forces, both as officers. These members of a well-to-do, literary family (for Macphail was an essayist and an editor as well as a professor of the history of medicine) were bemused by the roughness of the troops under them and also their own colleagues. Jim Macphail found he had to restrict passes by as much as 20 per cent because so many Canadians were drunk in public places. As he wrote to his brother John, "many of the officers are quite uncouth, often showing hilarious amusement at English customs, money, food and drink."

The troops had to be lectured constantly on the subject of discipline. It took considerable patience to teach men used to the wide open spaces of prairie, mountain, and seacoast that they couldn't leave camp on a whim without a pass, that they mustn't overstay their leave, and that each soldier had a duty to keep his conduct sheet clean. At Plymouth, scores had tumbled off the ships and headed for the nearest pub, so many

49

that in the days that followed, special trains – "Drunkards Specials" – had to be requisitioned to take the absentees on to Salisbury after the Military Police rounded them up. It wasn't easy to get such men to conform. At one point the 1st Division was warned that if discipline didn't improve, the entire unit would be broken up.

The Canadians improved, but they were never subservient. When the 2nd Division arrived similar problems came up. On the *Sardinia*, the entire company revolted and wrecked three canteens after it was discovered that one of the bakers aboard had spat tobacco juice into his flour bin. Pay night in the lines of the Nova Scotia Rifles was described as such a shambles that no officer attempted to control his troops; the Cape Bretoners were allowed to run wild until hangover time the following day.

No wonder, then, that some British staff officers looked down on the Canadians as little more than a rabble. After all, they were colonials, weren't they – what could one expect? Moreover, they were inexperienced. Kitchener didn't believe that any Canadian officer was fit to command a unit larger than an infantry brigade, and no one can fault him for that, although he conceded they might later command divisions if they proved themselves as brigade commanders in action. That is exactly what happened after the Second Battle of Ypres.

Douglas Haig himself was baffled by the independence of the Canadians – and not just by the unruliness of the ordinary soldiers. It was the publicly expressed insistence on an independent command that perplexed the British commander, who later confided to his diary that "some people in Canada regard themselves rather as 'Allies' than fellow citizens of the Empire." That, of course, was the exact point being made to Kitchener by the unspeakable Hughes. But to Haig, a Dominion was still a colony. Indeed, in those early months, the line of responsibility was more than a little muddy. As first commander of the Canadians, the British general, Alderson, found himself in the bewildering position of being responsible to Kitchener, who had appointed him, and also to the Canadian government in the person of Hughes, who didn't want him. Legally, the men he commanded were members of the Canadian militia – volunteers on active service defending their country abroad. Thus there was a basis for the Canadian control that was gradually assumed as the war lengthened. Canadian divisions were not to be shuffled like cards into the British corps. Well before the troops moved into the Vimy sector it had become clear that the Canadians actually were allies and not Haig's "fellow citizens" – and that they had no intention of being treated as lesser mortals.

2

Salisbury Plain was a horror, but the Canadians didn't complain. "It's all a blooming picnic to me now," wrote one private in the Canadian Scottish to his family. "I only wish you were with us to share the fun."

The fun took place on a wasted plain, empty of fences, houses, or people. The season was the wettest in years – in a seventy-five-day period there were only five dry days. The chalky soil had long since been trodden into a quagmire. The huts and tents were overcrowded, illness was widespread; everyone, it seemed, suffered from 'flu, and there were 1,249 cases of venereal disease. Snow and heavy mists curtailed training. The food was terrible, roads were often rendered impassable by blizzards, and the troops spent more time rebuilding the camp than they did in training. The Canadian Scottish, for example, spent 130 days in England but trained for only 40.

In addition, in spite of Sam Hughes's boast that Canadian goods were "in nearly every instance better than the British," much of the Canadian equipment was defective. Horse transport vehicles had to be replaced because of the weakness of the materials or the lack of interchangeable parts. Harness was generally unsuitable. Motor lorries broke down. Only five battalions had the superior British Webb equipment; the rest were equipped with the inferior leather Oliver equipment – Sam Hughes's choice – which meant that the soldiers had no packs and no means of carrying an entrenching tool. Hughes had even allowed his secretary to take out a patent for a so-called trench spade with a hole in the blade so that soldiers could protect themselves while peering at the enemy. The government ordered a quarter of a million; none was used.

Worst of all were the Canadian-made boots. In the words of the London *Truth*, they "soaked up water like blotting paper" and were soon replaced with British footwear. It was the same with the cloth made for Canadian uniforms; it was so inferior that all Canadians in Britain had to be refitted. Two members of parliament were forced to resign over the "boots scandal." Profiteering, greed, patronage, and political cronyism, together with Hughes's misplaced nationalism, were conspiring to sabotage the Canadian forces. It was not an auspicious beginning.

In the face of this, the troops remained irrepressibly cheerful and eager to exchange the mud of the training fields for the gumbo of Flanders. They simply had no idea of what they were in for. Nobody told them. The reports from the front, written by jingoistic correspondents or filtered through army censors, gave few hints of the horrors that lay ahead. Only when they landed in France did they get an inkling of what was coming, and only then did the schoolboy enthusiasm start to flag.

When Leonard Youell, a Canadian liaison officer, reached a French port with his battalion, he was struck by the spectacle of a solitary figure standing on the dock. He was, thought Youell, perhaps the most dilapidated human that he had ever seen, a contrast to the fresh-faced Canadians with their polished boots and glistening cap badges. An exuberant newcomer shouted the rallying call, "Are we downhearted?" and the entire battalion replied with a rousing "No!" But a silence fell after the man on the dock looked up and retorted, "Well, you bloody soon will be."

If these Canadians had no real idea of what lay ahead, those at home had even less. Later generations raised on revisionist tales of the Great War – on the poetry of Sassoon and Owen or the novels of Romains and Remarque – find it hard to believe that the folk back home saw the war not as a hell on earth but almost as a kind of adolescent romp. It was not until the next decade that the novelists and poets as well as the returned soldiers managed to convey something of the ghastliness of those fifty-two months. By and large, the First War was not the holocaust for civilians that the Second became, but for the men in the trenches of that earlier conflict war was far more dreadful than it was for those in the foxholes of its successor.

The 1st Division arrived in France in the early spring of 1915, after their stint of training on Salisbury Plain. Only then did they begin to comprehend what they were in for. By the time of the gas attacks in the Second Battle of Ypres – in late April and early May – they had a pretty good idea. This was not the kind of school-book war that was part of the fuzzy background of their youth. It was, in fact, a throwback to medieval times when men with catapults hurled rocks and flaming missiles at walled and moated fortresses, whose defenders responded with showers of arrows and vats of boiling pitch. This was siege warfare brought up to date, the catapults replaced by howitzers, the crossbows with Vickers guns. But the principles were the same.

It was not possible to dash around the flanks because in this war there were no longer any flanks; such was the legacy of the machine gun. The Western Front was anchored by the North Sea on the left of the Allied line and the twin barriers of the Alps and the Black Forest on the right. For all that distance – more than three hundred miles of crow-flight, much longer by serpentine ditch – the trench systems of the two adversaries stretched in a double line never more than a few hundred yards apart.

This was static warfare, the warfare of attrition, where the gain of a few yards of ravaged real estate was hailed as a victory. But the real purpose was to kill so many of the enemy that he could no longer function. It was confidently believed that the mounting pile of corpses would force him to sue for peace. And so on both sides men crouched like hogs in the mud, waiting for one of those appalling ventures into blood-letting that every commander since Hannibal has tried to avoid but that could not be avoided in the Great War – a frontal assault against a heavily prepared fortress position. And Vimy Ridge – south of Ypres, north of the Somme – was the greatest German fortress of all.

And yet, in the thousands of letters home, yellowing in family archives, there are remarkably few hints of the war's reality. The letters are generally brief and often impersonal.

"Censoring letters . . . is absolutely the most monotonous and tiring job we have to perform," the young machine-gun officer Claude Williams wrote to his mother two days before the Vimy battle. "Letter after letter, everyone saying the same thing – first of all acknowledging a parcel, then they say they are well, afterwards the weather, finishing up with their opinion of when the war's going to finish." On the evening after the Vimy battle, following a day of bitter struggle, M.E. Parsons, a runner with the 2nd Division, opened a letter from his mother. "We do hope you are not near that dreadful fighting," she wrote. Parsons picked up one of the Field Postcards or "Whizbangs," which the troops were encouraged to use, ticked off the two lines on the printed form – "I am quite well" and "I hope to be home soon" – and mailed it home.

The Whizbangs were a convenient way of telling family at home nothing, except the fact that you were alive or wounded. Like Parsons, the sender simply ticked off the appropriate sentences. Letters had to be posted unsealed, the envelopes closed only after an examination by a company officer. Those who attempted to report the worst horrors usually found that these passages had been removed. But few bothered. One of the remarkable things about the Great War was that hundreds of thousands of soldiers on the Western Front practised a form of self-censorship, following an unwritten law that no one should discourage the people at home. Blue envelopes were available for those who preferred to have their letters censored at base rather than by their own company commanders. William Pecover, the young Manitoba teacher, got twenty-eight days' field punishment when he tried, unsuccessfully, to circumvent the censor by using a rough code in such a letter.

And so the brutal truth never got through, and Canadians were lulled by a false picture of a struggle in which their clean-limbed, courageous boys, heroes all, fought against a black-hearted and beastly enemy.

Why this conspiracy of silence? There was more than one reason: Sergeant James Montgomerie of the Black Watch, for instance, laundered his letters because he didn't want the people at home to be sorry that he'd joined up with such enthusiasm. How was it possible to rush off to war, eyes glistening, bands playing, patriotic slogans on your lips, with everybody cheering you on, only to discover you'd been had? Nobody wants to be seen as a fool.

Besides, real soldiers didn't whine. The gallant understatement, the light quip in the face of adversity, this was part of the traditional image of the fighting man. The youngsters who flocked to the colours had been raised on tales of the British stiff upper lip under pressure – the Light Brigade stoically charging the Russian guns, the schoolboy rallying the ranks with the cry of "Play up! Play up! and play the game!"

More important, however, was the general feeling that it was bad for civilian morale and hence the war effort to emphasize the casualties and conditions, and callous to terrify one's mother unnecessarily with tales of bloated bodies rising out of the slime or cronies trying to stuff their entrails back into their abdomens.

With one or two notable exceptions the generals and staff officers who committed thousands to the slaughter rarely saw the results of what they'd done, and the men in the forward areas, in the words of Andrew McNaughton, "didn't know enough to resent it." In 1917 they hadn't yet realized it wasn't the kind of thing to be expected of men at war.

But perhaps the overriding reason why the men at the front had no desire to speak the truth about conditions in the trenches was that these conditions truly *were* unspeakable. Even in 1985, old men in their nineties, veterans of Vimy, asked to describe the mud and the lice, the filth and the rats, could only shake their heads and say, "You had to be there. It's not possible to describe it to somebody who wasn't."

You could, if you wished, recreate something approaching the trench life in Flanders during those years. You could dig in your backyard a ditch about eight feet deep, fill it during a rainstorm with two feet of thick clay mud, and then crouch in it, day and night, for a week, living on tinned bully beef, a few slices of mouldy bread or hardtack, and plum jam. Yet even if you filled the ditch with live rats and infested it with so many lice that your shirt crawled, it would still be a pale counterfeit of the real thing. The ceaseless rumble of guns, the crack of bullets overhead, the crump of trench mortars, the stench of mangled bodies, and the command on certain nights to emerge from your filthy hole and crawl in terror across No Man's Land – these cannot be simulated.

Nor can the uncertainty. Any healthy young man can survive a few days in a ditch, but *four years*? A week in a ditch, a week out, bored to death, committed to back-breaking toil, with only a little leave, no chance of seeing home and family and no idea when it would all end – this was the lot of those who survived. Small wonder that they did not attempt to describe the indescribable.

Half a century later, one Canadian who was there did undertake to describe trench life and came as close to it as any, perhaps because he was a journalist and a raconteur – one of the best Canada has produced. Gregory Clark's picture of the trenches, delivered as part of a CBC interview forty-eight years after Vimy, deserves to be quoted at length:

> . . . [the] historians . . . have forgotten to remind us of one thing, that from the sea up near Ostend, some hundreds of miles, waving and weaving across Belgium and down through France over hill and valley, and plain and river, down across and back up into the mountains, three hundred and some miles . . . was this ribbon of stealth. Some places it would be only a

mile wide, other places, because of the flat terrain, it was wider. This ribbon or belt of absolute stealth, day and night, week after month after year for four years – never changing; this band of deathly stealth in which no man moved or spoke loudly.

When you entered it from behind whatever hills or other cover enabled you to be yourself (chatting and marching and slouching along with your unit) suddenly you entered this strange, mysterious, unearthly land of stealth. And in that stealth, millions of men . . . lived years of their lives. . . .

There were sounds: there was the distant sound of the guns firing. There was the weird, unearthly howling of shells . . . the crack and explosion of shells. There would be strange, meaningless rifle shots, little random unassociated rattles of half-dozen bursts of machine guns in the night. . . . These sounds in this stealth only accentuated it and gave it a more unearthly and slightly lunatic sense. You were living in this strange, weird and wonderful thing not a little while. Battles came and broke it and smashed it into a thousand million pieces but then the battles subsided and the stealth returned.

Now they speak of trenches in this strange ribbon of deadly stealth across Europe. Trenches is too romantic a name. . . . These were ditches. . . . As time went by we had no garbage disposal, no sewage disposal – they became filthy. You threw everything you didn't want out over the parapet. . . . And if you ever stood at a place where, with powerful binoculars, you could look at the trenches you saw this strange line of garbage heap wandering up hill and down dale as far as the eye could see. And in that setting men lived . . . year after year [in] . . . a sort of garbage dump ditch . . . the latrines were little trenches off the main trench. These, when they became too offensive, were filled in and a new one dug; but these main trenches were held sometimes months on end. They became very sour. The smell . . . in those dugouts was a sour, strange odour overlaid in winter by the smell of coke gas. . . .

This land of stealth went through towns, villages but mostly through farm fields, abandoned and of course running wild with turnips and some other farm crops. A weird tangle – you [would] think it would come alive with game, but no. There was nothing in it except rats by the countless million. I don't think it was possible to exaggerate the number of rats in that stealthy land – and [they] added that last mad feature. Wherever you went, in daylight and at night, the whole place was squeaking and squealing with these huge, monstrous rats living on this garbage. . . .

The tension never for one moment relaxed. The stealth never relaxed day or night, winter, spring, summer, autumn. The tension never ended. You never knew at what moment one of those perfectly meaningless sounds . . . would get you. . . . It wouldn't have taken a great deal in this dreadful, prehistoric circumstance for men to have lost heart and they never did. We had a thing called shell shock in our war. . . . A great many of us were hostile to the phrase. . . . It wasn't anything of the kind. It was just fatigue – not so much in battle as in these long intervals of living under these conditions. . . .

3

Although the men at the front never really told their families the truth about the war, it is possible to detect a subtle lessening of enthusiasm in the letters they dispatched to Canada after a spell in the trenches. The correspondence of Claude Williams, the medical-student-turned-machine-gunner, provides one example. Williams, a gung-ho enthusiast if there ever was one, didn't use the Whizbang forms; his letters are long and effusive. The early ones, from Shorncliffe, Kent, where he trained in 1916, fairly bubble with excitement. "Oh, it is grand to be a Machine Gunner!" he wrote home in July. "We are just aching to go," he exclaimed in August. "You should just see the scramble to discover who has been signed on the next draft. I have known four or five pounds being offered for a man's place . . . but it is never accepted."

Williams had wanted to join the infantry, specifically the PPCLI, but was turned down because he wore glasses. His father, an army padre and a friend of Sam Hughes's, got him into the officers' training course at Niagara camp in May of 1915. There he was chosen to be part of a machine-gun unit

58

privately raised and paid for by Colonel John Labatt, of the Ontario brewing family. Now, more than a year later, he feared nothing so much as the possibility that he'd be made an instructor and miss the fun. If so, he told his family, "I will deliberately make the poorest marks possible. . . . " If necessary, he would stow away to get to France; other officers had already done that.

His correspondence continues in this vein. News of the Somme massacre only made him more eager to join the fight: "I have been so sick of waiting whilst every other fellow gets ahead of me. . . . " Finally, in October, 1916, as the first Canadians began to move toward Vimy, the call came. To Williams it was "almost too good to be true . . . the next happiest time since I heard I was to take out a commission. . . ."

Once he was in France, however, Williams's letters lost some of their glow. In training there he saw a man blown to shreds while handling a Mills bomb, the officer next to him decapitated, a third badly maimed. One morning two soldiers were shot by a firing squad. "I am enjoying this fine," he hastened to add, but then: "Please excuse this letter's lack of neatness. I am covered in mud . . . writing by candlelight."

His next letter, from the trenches before Vimy, was positively peevish. He berated his family for making light of his condition. "I don't see anything amusing about writing by candlelight, that is all we have here, you can't even get a coal oil lamp of any kind, nothing but candles. . . . It is pitch black without them."

At this point Williams was plastered with a thick layer of mud from his head to his boots. It had poured rain all night. The trench was a quagmire. Parts of the walls had caved in, burying half the ammunition. The roof and stairway of his dugout were threatening to collapse, and the men had been roused to stand by with picks and shovels. Water tumbled down the steps like a miniature Niagara, and Williams and his batman found themselves struggling frantically to dig themselves out before the whole thing gave way. The mud was so deep that one of the platoon runners had been stuck waist deep and forced to leave his boots in the glue before he could be extricated. This, of course, was standard stuff, but Williams made it clear that it wasn't a matter for family jocularity.

Yet Williams soon got over his pique and, like almost every other man in the trenches, continued to reassure his family in his letters home. "It is the greatest fun, slop, slopping for miles without a dry spot anywhere," he wrote to his mother in November after a dreadful day spent with a working party in the rain. To his father, in January, he apologized because "on reading over this letter the tenor sounds far from cheerful." Low spirits, Williams emphasized, "have no place in the trenches," adding "I don't think you should show it to mother."

By that time, the entire corps was dug in below the slopes of Vimy Ridge, and every Canadian in Europe was, like Williams, learning to endure the unendurable. They had looked out into the night and seen, glowing like embers in No Man's Land, the red eyes of the foraging rats – the same rats that ran across their faces as they slept and whose bites scarred their legs to the kneecaps. They had turned their shirts inside out, night after night, running a cigarette lighter along the seams to kill the lice that crawled by the hundreds through their clothing. They had seen mud so bad that the horses died of exhaustion trying to pull loads through the gumbo. They had seen men in shock cry and shiver if a shell dropped a hundred yards away, and they had seen others shoot themselves in the foot or chew a thread of cordite from a rifle cartridge to turn themselves into hospital cases – anything to escape, if only for a few days. Hideous death had become a familiarity; men learned to use human shinbones as coat hangers and corpses as benches to keep their backsides out of the mud.

For two years, from Neuve Chapelle to the Somme, Canadians had been fighting and dying in Flanders. They made their reputation in April 1915 at the Second Battle of Ypres. The French Zouaves, surprised and terrified by the first gas attack of the war, fled the salient, leaving a four-mile gap in the line. But the Canadian 1st Division – those who had joined up in those first enthusiastic days – held fast, filled the gap and, choking and gasping in the yellow cloud of poison, pressed urine-soaked handkerchiefs to their noses and prevented a German breakthrough. The cost was terrible: more than six thousand casualties out of a divisional fighting strength of ten thousand . . . But by standing fast the Canadians prevented a rout that could have changed the course of the war.

The Ypres catastrophe bred in the Canadians a suspicion of British and French rigidity. The system didn't allow for any real feedback of ideas up or down the chain of command. The brass hats didn't believe the lower classes in the lower ranks were bright enough to think for themselves. Junior officers were given little leeway in responding to orders. You did what you were told, and you didn't question the word from on high. That did not sit well with men like Arthur Currie, a brigade commander at Ypres, whose tactical handling of his own troops brought him a promotion shortly afterward.

The Canadians were infuriated by the staff work at Ypres. Their British superiors had repeatedly ignored warnings of an impending gas attack. By the end of March, 1915, German prisoners were telling their interrogators specific details about gas cylinders stored in the enemy trenches. One captured German told of batteries of such cylinders placed every forty metres along the front. A few reconnaissance patrols were sent out to confirm these reports, but nobody took the findings seriously. When one French general warned of possible use of gas his superior ignored him as a credulous fool. The feeling at the top was that the Germans would never be so ungentlemanly as to use gas against their enemies.

Other reverses followed – at Givenchy, where the maps turned out to be grossly inaccurate; at Festubert, where the preparation was hasty and inadequate; and at the St. Eloi craters, where the advice of Canadian leaders was overridden by that of the British commander. But it was at the Somme in the summer of 1916 that the Canadians learned, at dreadful cost, how not to conduct a war.

The Battle of the Somme began on July 1, 1916. Its purpose was twofold: to achieve a breakthrough in the line and to relieve pressure on the French, who were defending Verdun to the south. By the time it petered out the following winter, gaining nothing but the possession of a few acres of ground, all four Canadian divisions had been blooded. The first three divisions fought from September 3 to mid-October when they went north to the Vimy front. The newly created 4th Division stayed on the Somme from October 10 to the end of November when they joined their comrades at Vimy.

What is loosely described as the Battle of the Somme was actually a series of battles, a mosaic of ghastly setbacks and minor victories in which the obstinate British commander, Sir Douglas Haig, who seemed to learn very little from adversity, threw away tens of thousands of lives by repeating tactics that had proved ineffectual on the first day of the struggle.

Indeed, the early tactics at the Somme were reminiscent of those nineteenth-century wars when men armed with muskets marched solidly forward in line, shoulder to shoulder, spraying lead at their enemies. The rifle and the machine gun had long since replaced the musket, but the British troops still attacked the German positions in closely packed waves. The men, lined up like ten pins, each wave from fifty to one hundred yards behind the next, depended on an artillery barrage to soften the German positions, but in every case the barrage was too little and too late.

The idea was that the Germans would be pinned down in their dugouts by the barrage, sitting ducks when the British reached them. But the advancing troops were too far behind the barrage. When it lifted and moved on, the Germans simply leaped out of the trenches and, with their machine guns, mowed down the rows of British, many of whom were still far from their objective, held up by the heavy wire entanglements that masked the German positions.

In the first day of the Somme battle – the day that was supposed to blast a gap in the German line that would start the troops forward on a dash to Berlin – almost sixty thousand men were killed or wounded. The blood-letting continued all that summer. The Newfoundland Regiment, in one single tragic day, lost 710 of its 801 officers and men. Incredibly, the same tactics continued, and the lessons of the Somme only began to sink in when the Canadians attacked Courcelette in mid-September.

Here, for the first time, a new expression entered the military lexicon: *creeping barrage*. Now the wall of shells crept forward just ahead of the advancing troops in hundred-yard lifts at three-minute intervals. Thus the Canadians were able to reach the enemy before he had a chance to rise out of the protecting trenches. And they moved forward not in a blind and steady advance but in a series of bounds, each to a specific, predetermined objective, and each one covered by artillery fire. It was this innovation, refined to the split second and drilled into every man on the Vimy front, that helped the Canadian Corps seize the ridge from the Germans.

At Courcelette, the Canadians showed an initiative that was rare among the Allied troops in the Great War. Having captured their objective, a sugar factory and a farm on the outskirts, they kept on straight through the village, taking a thousand prisoners and holding their ground against the inevitable counterattacks, a bold stroke praised by the High Command as "without parallel in the present campaign." It was this action that confirmed them as shock troops. As David Lloyd George, the British Prime Minister, was to put it in his memoirs, "Whenever the Germans found the Canadian Corps coming into the line, they prepared for the worst."

The Somme was the training ground for Vimy – but at the cost of twenty-four thousand Canadian casualties. The worst experience came in October with the Canadian assault on the Regina Trench, a strongly fortified line that was the Germans' second position in the battle for possession of the Thiepval Ridge. The trench held out. The British artillery failed to cut the German protective wire, and so the German machine gunners could not be dislodged. Although there were plenty of shells available by this time, the British gunners were still husbanding their supplies, out of habit. Thus the trench remained intact.

It would be up to the 4th Division to try to take the trench, for the other three, sadly depleted by the events of that bloody summer, had already been taken out of the line. They were a subdued company, moving north through the rolling farmland of Picardy toward the Vimy sector. Duncan Macintyre, the one-time prairie storekeeper, now a staff captain with the 2nd Division, rode back along the line of march to meet his brigade, the 6th, on its way out. These were all Westerners from Vancouver, Calgary, Winnipeg, and the Territories. To Macintyre, astride his horse on a little rise, they seemed a surprisingly small group, winding along the valley road out of La Vivogne so slowly that they scarcely seemed to be moving.

He cantered forward and spotted a man he knew well, Major Alex Ross, leading his old battalion, the 28th, composed entirely of Northwesters.

"Where's the rest of the battalion, sir?" Macintyre asked him.

"This is all of the battalion, Mac," replied Ross in a choked voice, and Macintyre could see the tears glistening in his eyes.

There were more losses to come as the 4th Division prepared once again to attack the Regina Trench. On October 25, "the day of death" as it came to be called, the 44th, a Winnipeg unit, lost two hundred officers and men. Once again, the artillery barrage was insufficient to quiet the enemy fire. As the Canadians advanced across No Man's Land, they could see the German machine gunners emerging untouched on the parapets. At last, on November 10, the barrage was perfected and the trench taken. The 4th Division vacated the charnel house of the Somme and moved north to join its fellow divisions holding the line at Vimy.

They had all suffered a costly lesson. When Greg Clark joined the 4th Canadian Mounted Rifles in the Vimy sector that month, he figured that there were 4,200 members of that regiment whom he had never seen and would never know. They had been there in France before him and now they were gone. At the Somme, the battalion had gone into action 1,200 strong. In six weeks it had suffered a thousand casualties.

Some of the platoons, with a normal strength of thirty-eight, were down to ten men. Thus the Corps that fought at Vimy was a mixture of hardened veterans and raw newcomers.

There were other changes. Sam Hughes had finally been given his walking papers that month, fired after nine days of soul-searching by a vacillating prime minister who could not, in the end, stomach a grossly insulting letter. The Ross rifle, which Hughes had espoused with all the fanaticism of a dervish, had also been discarded in favour of the more rugged Lee Enfield. The snipers loved the all-Canadian Ross, which was a marksman's delight, but the ordinary soldiers hated it because it jammed in the mud. Ignoring orders, they threw it away and picked up the British weapon from the nearest corpse. Alderson, the British commander who had had the temerity to attack the Ross, was also gone, a victim of Sam Hughes's pique. His replacement, Lieutenant-General Sir Julian Byng, was a tougher nut for Hughes to crack.

Three months before, on August 17, the two had dined for the first time in France and discussed the matter of promotions and appointments within the Corps. In his usual bombastic manner, Hughes told Byng that he had never made a single mistake in his selections during the whole time he had held office and proposed to continue to make all appointments.

The Corps commander replied that he would always make recommendations to the Minister as a matter of courtesy. Nevertheless, the moment that Hughes attempted to override his suggestion, then he, Byng, would resign – a politically disastrous eventuality. That was that. Hughes had met his match in the deceptively casual general with the iron will.

Byng had had plenty of time to study the failures at the Somme during those autumn days when his troops were attacking Courcelette and later the Regina Trench. At Vimy he proposed to put these lessons into practice. More than anything else, the Somme had demonstrated the need for more careful training and meticulous preparation. New tactics were required; the creeping barrage would have to be perfected. Better intelligence was needed. The enemy guns would have to be pinpointed and destroyed before the men on the ground could move; that meant artillery men with more elastic minds and a scientific approach to the art of gunnery. And better fuses would be essential if the shells were to destroy the enemy wire.

A more flexible, less blinkered approach to static warfare was needed. There must be closer liaison with the air force, and better communication between the high command and the troops in the mud. Nothing could be taken for granted. It wasn't good enough to assume that the German wire was cut or the trenches pulverized; somebody had to find that out. The lower ranks had to be given a better idea of what was planned and then trained to act on their own, instead of blindly following orders worked out by staff officers miles behind the lines.

All this would take time, for the morale and the strength of the four Canadian divisions were badly shattered. The old soldiers who sat in the trenches before Vimy were weary of battle while the newcomers, arriving by the thousands, were nervous, green, and unblooded. To weld the Canadian Corps into a cohesive fighting force would require initiative, understanding, and innovative leadership of the highest order. The Battle of Vimy Ridge was still five months away.

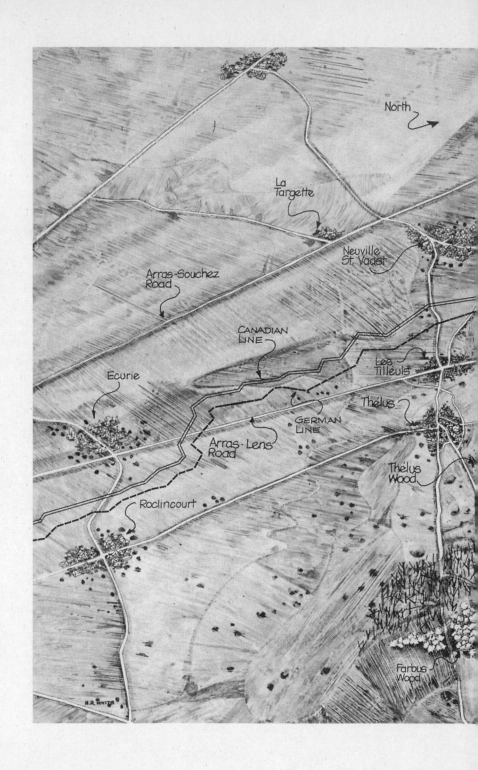

North

La Targette

Neuville St. Vaast

Arras-Souchez Road

CANADIAN LINE

Les Tilleuls

Écurie

Thélus

GERMAN LINE

Arras-Lens Road

Thélus Wood

Roclincourt

Farbus Wood

H.R. WHITE

Souchez · The Pimple · Souchez River · Zouave Valley · Givenchy-en-Gohelle · Hill 145 · La Folie Wood · La Folie Farm · Petit Vimy · La Chaudière · Bonval Wood · Vimy · Goulot Wood · Farbus · Willerval

The
Ridge

BOOK TWO

The Build-Up

What I want is the discipline of a well-trained pack of
hounds. You find your own holes through the hedges.
I'm not going to tell you where they are. But never
lose sight of your objective. Reach it in your own way.

Lieutenant-General Sir Julian Byng to his officers,
Vimy sector, 1917

CHAPTER THREE

Marking Time

1

By mid-November 1916, the Somme offensive had petered out and the British Army in northern France, shivering in the coldest winter in half a century, was marking time. The shattered battalions of the Canadian 4th Division, which had fought so hard to capture the Regina Trench, had moved north to join their compatriots. By December, the exhausted Corps was united again, strung out thinly for ten miles along the Artois sector between Arras to the south and Loos to the north.

Change was in the wind. The French commander, Joffre, had been cast aside in favour of the more aggressive Nivelle. The vigorous Welshman, David Lloyd George, had replaced the lethargic Herbert Asquith as Prime Minister of Great Britain. In spite of Haig's doubts, these new and powerful personalities were determined to transform the war of attrition into a decisive war of movement. But before the great breakthrough could be achieved, one obstacle had to be eliminated. The Vimy bastion must be captured and held.

Tactically, the ridge was one of the most important features on the Western Front, the anchor point for the new defence system that the Germans were carefully and secretly preparing to thwart the expected Allied hammer-blow.

There it lay, facing the Canadian lines – a low, seven-mile escarpment of sullen grey, rising softly from the plain below, a monotonous spine of mud, churned into a froth by shellfire, devoid of grass or foliage, lacking in colour or detail, every inch of its slippery surface pitted or pulverized by two years of constant pounding. At first glance it didn't seem very imposing, but to those who knew its history and who looked ahead to that moment when they must plough forward and upward toward that ragged crest aflame with gunfire, it took on an aura both dark and sinister.

The high crest of the ridge – the part that counted tactically – lay between two river valleys, the Souchez to the north and the Scarpe four miles to the south. This would be the Canadian objective, but that wasn't yet clear in December and wouldn't be until early February, when the entire corps was squeezed into this four-mile sector. The ground between was shaped like a great pie section because the Canadian lines didn't parallel the ridge but veered away from it at an angle. At the southern boundary, the Canadians were four thousand yards from the crest, at the north, a mere seven hundred. Between lay No Man's Land, a spectral world of shell holes and old bones. Down its midriff a ragged line of gigantic craters marked the sites of earlier mine explosions in the failed struggles to capture the ridge. Some were so vast that Canadian sentries and snipers held one lip while the Germans squatted on the opposite rim.

Beyond the crater line – in places no more than a few dozen yards away – three parallel rows of German trenches zigzagged along the lower slopes of the ridge, protected by forty-foot rolls of heavy steel wire with razor-sharp barbs and machine-gun nests in steel and concrete pillboxes.

Behind these forward defences rose the dark bulk of the escarpment, which more than one new arrival likened to that of a gigantic whale. Its highest point, Hill 145, rose 470 feet above the plain to form the mammal's hump. A mile to the north, on the edge of the Canadian sector, was a small knoll, poking up like a pimple on the whale's snout and called, naturally enough, the Pimple.

A mile south of Hill 145 was another hill near whose slopes was sprawled a farm that was no longer a farm – La Folie. Two miles south of that, straddling the crest near the right of the corps boundary, was a village that was no longer a village – Thélus. Directly in front of these ruins, high on the forward slope, stood the fragments of Les Tilleuls (the Linden Trees), a hamlet that was no longer a hamlet, clustered in a grove that was no longer a grove. These dead communities added to the starkness of the scene and hinted at the intensity of the struggles that had gone before. Veined by trenches, honeycombed with tunnels, bristling with gun emplacements, crawling with snipers, this formidable rampart had been in German hands since October 1914. The Germans intended it to stay that way.

From their vantage points on the crest, they had an uninterrupted view for miles in every direction. Behind them, among the forests that still cloaked the steeper eastern slopes and hid their big guns, lay small, red-roofed villages not yet entirely shattered by shellfire: Givenchy-en-Gohelle, in the shadow of the Pimple, Vimy and Petit Vimy directly to the east, and, to the south, the village of Farbus, sheltered by Farbus Wood. Far to the rear lay the spires and slag heaps of Lens, the heart of France's coal mining region, now denied to the Allies. Here was life, movement, and colour: carts and lorries clattering along the Lens-Arras road, freight trains snorting past on a rail line that once was French, peasants toiling in the fields, troops moving about in broad daylight, smoke pouring from the big stacks at Lens – and all this spectacle shielded from the soldiers of the King, observable only by a handful of brave men in captive balloons and by the young knights of the Royal Flying Corps.

To the west, the Germans looked down on a dead world, stretching back for more than six miles, in striking contrast to the scene behind. Back of the line of craters they could see the blurred contours of the Canadian forward trenches and behind these two more lines – the support and reserve trenches. Farther back, parallel with the trench lines, were three deeply sunk roads, and beyond these the Arras-Souchez highway.

Bisecting this lifeless, underground domain were the great communication trenches, which sheltered the troops moving up to the front at night; one was four miles long. For nothing moved above ground by day, and even the nights were hazardous, especially when the German flares banished the covering gloom. The swampy Zouave Valley on the northern edge of the Canadian sector was a hunting ground for German snipers and gunners. The Canadians called it Death Valley; every man who crossed it did so in full view of the enemy. There were trenches there, too, but these were generally so full of liquid mud that many preferred to chance a quick nocturnal dash above ground. That was a court-martial offence, but many accepted it: anything – an enemy bullet, an army trial – was better than strangling in a river of running slime.

The Canadians had one advantage. The German defences on the forward slopes of the ridge were also exposed, and the time would come when the Canadian guns would blast them into rubble. But for the moment the Germans had the upper hand. For six and a half miles, every piece of Canadian equipment, every gun, every ammunition dump, every lorry pool, every ration depot – everything that could be blown apart or could give the Germans some inkling of what was to come – had to be concealed in pits or camouflaged or hidden behind folds of ground or copses of foliage.

The safest places of all were the big subways that went as far back as Neuville St. Vaast and as far forward as the front lines. The Germans knew they were there but had no clear idea of what was going on below ground. The presence of those subways – a dozen of them – some nosing forward inch by inch, foot by foot, dozens of feet below the surface, was the hole card in the game of poker being played out that winter in the shadow of the ridge.

In this ravaged world, the French villages were little more than heaps of rubble. Arras, three miles to the south, which would give its name to the great spring offensive of which the Vimy attack was a part, was a shell. Restaurants, stores, cafés were battered to bits; the cathedral was a wreck, the railway station a ruin. Ecurie, on the southern border of the Canadian sector, once a haven for French farmers, was no more than a name on a signpost, a flattened expanse of brick dust, bisected by roads that could be used only at night. Neuville St. Vaast, once the White City of Flanders, was a desert of rubbled chalk, its inhabitants long since fled. Someone had erected a bitter sign: THIS WAS NEUVILLE ST. VAAST. Only in the cellars, tunnels, and caves below the surface, which concealed railway terminals, gun positions, and troop facilities, did life go on. The town cemetery was devastated, every monument knocked down, the vaults smashed, the coffins shattered. Beneath the broken trees, skeletons of Frenchmen long gone lay contorted among the clumps of rank grass.

Souchez and its neighbour, Carency, had been blown away to their foundations by the dreadful struggle of 1915. One foggy morning Bob Brown, a Scottish immigrant from Regina, explored the ruins of Souchez with two others. The town was out of bounds, and Brown was curious to know why. He soon found out: Souchez was a human abattoir. Skeletons lay everywhere. At one point he found a spot where a Frenchman had been standing, rifle in hand, at the moment a building was hit. The man's skeleton, still clutching the rifle, lay under a heavy beam. A trench dug across the main street and filled with skeletons had yet to be covered over. But the most affecting symbol was the schoolhouse, its roof gone, its walls blown in, but the teacher's desk still standing with the roll book marking the day the school had been forced to close. Brown tore out the page, pocketed it, and left Souchez to its ghouls and ghosts.

The ridge and its environs stank of death, and the trenches were sour with it. One of the first things that hit the newly arrived Canadians was the evidence of old and monumental struggles. At the ridge's northern end, above the Souchez River, a promontory named for the Abbey of Notre Dame de Lorette butted out at right angles. Here the French had managed at fearful cost to wrest the plateau from the Germans, and the evidence of that struggle for what they then called La Butte de la Mort (the Hill of Death) was everywhere. When Will Bird, with his sensitive writer's perception, first saw the carnage on the Lorette Spur, it made his flesh crawl: he had never before seen so many grinning skulls. Here was a maze of old trenches and ditches littered with the garbage of war – broken rifles, frayed equipment, rusting bayonets, hundreds of bombs, tangles of barbed wire, puddles of filth, and everywhere rotting uniforms, some French blue, others German grey, tattered sacks now, holding their own consignments of bones.

Farther south lay the Labyrinth, another city of the dead, a bewildering network of caves, tunnels, trenches, and dugouts, circulating and radiating in all directions. Here again French and Germans burrowing beneath the ground had blown each other up and fought hand to hand with knives and clubs. French equipment, human bones, wire, and scores of home-made bombs – jam tins filled with scrap-iron, nails, and stones – lay everywhere. In the Aux Ruitz cave, it was said, there were so many dead that one tunnel had to be walled up.

Through this tangle of decaying artifacts the souvenir hunters picked their way, insensible to the heart-breaking evidence of human waste. As Private Donald Fraser, a six-foot Scot from Calgary, confided to his journal, ''rifling the dead used to be considered in pre-war times a ghoulish business but over here the dead are of no account, they are scattered all over the battle area.'' An inveterate collector, Fraser spent many of his spare hours cutting the buttons off the tunics of corpses.

There were subtler hints, however, of those earlier battles, certain nocturnal sounds – mere whispers between the crump of the guns – that could send a shiver up the spine of those who had been hardened by a long acquaintance with the dead. In the French cemetery at Villers-au-Bois, thousands of temporary crosses marked the resting places of those bodies that had been awarded a formal burial. On each of these crosses, the French had placed a small tri-coloured metal triangle as makeshift identification. In the night, when a chill breeze sighed through this city of the dead, the men in the trenches could hear the eerie clink-clink-clink of these thousands of tin triangles, a reminder of the vast and ghostly army that had preceded them.

2

For the Germans, most private soldiers felt no emotion other than a mild curiosity. The only Germans they really saw were either corpses or prisoners; the others kept their heads down or appeared as shadowy figures in the night raids that were a feature of the winter stalemate. The prisoners looked weak and weedy, but then prisoners generally do. Andrew Macphail thought them "cancerously yellow," and Claude Williams thought they were "a very bowed, sickly looking aggregation." But much of that was wishful thinking.

The men opposite were Prussians and Bavarians. The latter were considered the better fighters, probably because the Prussian division included men of other nationalities, many of them dissident and willing to surrender. Their main complaint was the poor quality and scarcity of their clothing. The Allied blockade had done its work. Some men had no underwear. Shirts were no longer wool but thin cotton; some were woven of wood fibre. Prisoners told stories of starvation in the enemy lines, one Pole complaining that he'd had nothing but bread, jam, and tea for weeks, which was unusual. The Canadians, who were really not much better off, rose to the occasion. One of the Nova Scotians decided to taunt the Germans by holding up a loaf of bread on a bayonet to show how well his side was living. Almost instantly a German bayonet appeared on the far side of No Man's Land. On it were stuck *two* loaves of bread. Between the opposing sides there existed a rough camaraderie born of common misery. When the Canadians first reached Vimy Ridge, a sign was hoisted above the German trenches: WELCOME CANADIANS. Another read: CUT OUT YOUR DAMNED ARTILLERY. WE, TOO, WERE AT THE SOMME.

To the people back home – the young women handing out white feathers, the editorialists declaiming from their office chairs, the politicians making bold speeches on behalf of war loan campaigns – and, indeed, to the senior officers at the front, the enemy was known as the Hun or the Boche, terms devised to suggest a primitive bestiality. But to the men in the front lines, the German was universally and familiarly known as Fritz (or to the airmen as Jerry). The attitude was jocular, as expressed in such songs as "Keep Your Head Down, Fritzie Boy."

Letters and wartime reminiscences suggest that the Canadians often resented their own brass more than they disliked the grey-clad German. You shot at him because he was shooting at you, but it wasn't a personal matter. He too was wallowing in the mud, only a few yards away.

Will Bird, who reached France at the end of December, spotted his first uncaptured German on the second night of his sentry duty. Shivering at his outpost in No Man's Land, the young Nova Scotian could hear the Germans walking about in their trenches, coughing in the cold, and turning the creaking handle of a windlass hauling up chalk from a half-finished dugout. Suddenly a Canadian flare burst in the sky above, bathing the German positions in an eerie light. There, standing waist high in the opposing trench, less than a hundred yards away, was a young boy – no more than a teenager. Both men froze, as they'd been taught to do when a star shell exploded, but Bird knew the boy had seen him. They stared at each other for a moment, two young men made enemies by forces over which they had no control. Then, suddenly, the German waved at Bird. Some impulse caused Bird to wave back too. The German vanished, and the brief instant of eye contact between two men ended; but Bird never forgot that moment.

Bombardier Jim Johnson had a similar experience on December 24, 1916. He was called to the parapet by his officer and, peering over the sandbags, was astonished to see an entire body of Germans, two hundred yards away, receiving their Christmas rations in full view of the Canadians.

"What would you do in this case?" asked the officer.

"I think this is Christmas Eve," said Johnson tentatively.

"Oh, yes it is," the officer said. "But in case someone gets trigger happy, you fire a shot close enough to them as a warning."

Johnson let go with a single round, placed about twenty feet to the left. The Germans scrambled for cover, but one man hesitated, turned, and raised his hand toward Johnson in a salute. Johnson was glad he hadn't followed the rule book.

The senior command was death on this sort of demonstration, no matter how tenuous, for everybody was supposed to hate the Hun. Earlier cases of Christmas fraternization had caused great uneasiness among the generals on both sides: what if the soldiers simply stopped fighting each other? So concerned were some staff officers at Vimy that on Christmas Day, 1916, some units cancelled the rum ration. But the Princess Pats got an extra ration that day and proceeded to arrange a truce with their opposite numbers. Private Norman Keys, a Montrealer who spoke German, acted as spokesman in the exchange that followed in No Man's Land. Like his comrades, Keys was wearing his new rubber boots and fresh clothing issued that morning, and smoking a Christmas cigar – all of which impressed the Germans. Orders from above quickly put an end to the fraternizing and shelling resumed.

The Royal 22nd or "Van Doos" were less charitable than the Princess Pats. Yuletide or no Yuletide, they raided the German lines and stole all their Christmas presents. At Vimy there was little peace and only a modicum of goodwill toward the men on the far side of No Man's Land.

3

The Western Front was never quiet. Even in those early months, when the Canadians were supposed to be recuperating from the butchery of the Somme, the guns on both sides continued to fire. The trenches may have been eight feet deep, but the men in them never felt safe from the rain of Whizbangs, Minnies, Jack Johnsons, Rum Jars, and Coal Boxes, whose ingenious nicknames masked their deadly purpose. They could only hope that if a shell landed in their section, it would explode on the far side of one of the traverses, which were spaced out at intervals all along the zigzag line.

The Minnenwerfers or "Moaning Minnies" were slow but deadly. Their range was short, their concussion dreadful. They were lobbed in a high arc over No Man's Land – two hundred pounds of high explosive – leaving at night a faint trail of sparks that caused the uninitiated to believe they were dud flares. The old hands, who saw them coming and knew what they were, could not escape a creepy tingle in their spines as they ran away from the expected point of impact, flung themselves flat in the mud, and waited for the earth-shaking explosion, which could blow a crater ten feet or more wide and send debris, sandbags, and human fragments flying in all directions. Even if the shell didn't score a direct hit, the concussion could kill. Jim Johnson, the Winnipeg bombardier, had a close call that winter when the Germans got the range of his mortar. Johnson heard the shell coming and had managed to scramble a hundred yards from the target when it landed, demolishing the mortar and exploding all the ammunition. The concussion ripped his tunic down the seam from collar to waist and also burst the seams in his pants. As he struggled to his feet, nearly naked, an officer rushed up from the communication trench. ''What the hell happened to your clothes?'' he asked severely.

The German mortar shells also arced high over No Man's Land to drop vertically into the crowded trenches. In the argot of the soldiers, the smaller ones were ''piss tins'' and the bigger ''rum jars.'' They varied in length from two to three and a half feet—as big as a nail keg—and were filled with scrap-iron. They operated on a time fuse that allowed no more than an instant's warning.

The German 5.9- and 8-inch shells were named for Jack Johnson, the famous black boxer, and sometimes called ''coal boxes'' because of the black smoke that erupted from the explosion (the Allied shells, which used lyddite as an explosive, sent up yellow smoke). But the greatest source of irritation was the smaller whizbang. The nickname, which to this day evokes the Great War, describes the sound: a whiz when it left the gun, a bang when it hit the parapet. But, as Claude Williams discovered, this small, 3-inch shell of low trajectory travelled so swiftly there was scarcely any time between the whiz and the bang to take cover.

Williams reached the Vimy sector in the late fall, bursting with enthusiasm, a stocky, bespectacled young officer in impeccable whipcord and tightly rolled puttees, his boots and

Sam Browne glistening with polish. For more than a year he had chafed with impatience, waiting to get in on the fun; now he had finally achieved his ambition. It seemed too good to be true. Nor did his early enthusiasm entirely wane. He exulted in trench life, actually looked forward to quitting the monotony of the billets in the rest area. He loved the sight of the Canadian incendiary shells firing the German dumps and lighting up the night. Yes, there was mud and bitter cold, but in his letters home he made light of it. It was "just part of the life and it isn't a bad life at all, nobody is grumbling about it." There were some minor irritations – on some occasions he had to go all day without washing his hands and twenty-four hours without a bath. His batman, however, had once gone without a bath for three months during the Somme action; or so he claimed. Williams was less fastidious in other matters. He combed through the human garbage that littered the Lorette Spur until he'd collected enough French and German bones to construct a skeleton, which he kept under the bed in his dugout.

The men in the machine-gun company were less enthusiastic about the war and not at all enthusiastic about Lieutenant Williams. Like so many new and ardent young officers he was a stickler for discipline, especially the discipline of dress. In spite of the mud and the watchful enemy he wanted his men shaved and scrubbed clean, their buttons polished, their clothing neat. But these veterans of the Somme had different priorities. Private Fraser, the inveterate souvenir hunter, who served under Williams, was one who "resented this from a newcomer who had yet to obtain battle experience and be able to differentiate between important and unimportant things."

Then, on January 3, 1917, Claude Williams received his baptism of fire. Until that moment the German shells had passed harmlessly over his head. Two days before Christmas he had even been able to pause in a letter to his mother and note: "Here come some 'Whistling Willies' " – and then continue his report about the weather without a tremor. But on January 3 the Willies got to him.

He was sloshing through a mud-filled trench when he heard the whiz and then the bang of a German shell. Down he went into the mud, half stunned by the concussion, then was up again trying to reach the nearest dugout before a second explosion, only to find that one of his rubber waders was half off. It was impossible to do anything but crawl.

Williams felt like a man having a nightmare when some *thing* is chasing you and you can't move. A second *whiz* . . . another *bang*, and Williams, dropping his head onto his arms, felt himself half smothered in mud. Now he scrambled forward to the dugout as a third shell exploded at the exact point he'd just left, blowing up the trench and blocking the dugout's entrance. Another landed on the top of the dugout, which creaked and groaned with the force of the explosion, snuffing the candle and leaving him in darkness.

Williams forced his way out and back into the trench as another shell dropped up ahead, half filling the passageway with muck. Now he realized he was moving directly into the drop area, where the shells were thickest. He couldn't turn back, could only pray that nothing would come too close. Suddenly there was another dreadful whiz, and Claude Williams knew it was going to drop right on him – there was no escape. He fell into the bottom of the trench and rolled himself into a ball, waiting for the worst.

The concussion all but deafened him. A yard ahead a vast hole appeared, and an instant later clods of earth began descending on him, some chunks so big they knocked the breath from his body. More and more dirt fell, and Williams now feared he would be buried alive. Finally it stopped; he pinched himself and discovered that he was still in one piece with many bruises but no broken bones.

Farther along the trench, Williams's men could hear the explosions. Along came Williams's sergeant, a Somme veteran named McGirr, laughing at his officer's plight. "I don't think he will bother you again about being good soldiers in the trenches," Sergeant McGirr told his men. A few moments later a bedraggled Williams appeared and collapsed, totally unnerved. It was, in the opinion of Private Fraser, "an effective cure. . . . No more word about being fancy-line soldiers." Three days after his narrow escape Claude Williams wrote to his mother: "Nothing much of importance happened last week – still plodding along in the same old way."

For most of that record winter, the Canadians were cold, wet, hungry, tired, and (though they did not admit it) frightened. The cold was unbelievable. The temperature did not rise above zero Fahrenheit for one month. The ground froze two feet deep, making it impossible to bury the horses and mules that died of cold and exposure. This was not the dry cold that the men of the prairies and the Northwest were accustomed to. Fog and rain mingled with snow and sleet; the water in the shell holes froze overnight; the mud turned hard as granite so that men were actually wounded by flying chunks of earth. They clumped along the duckboards, swathed in greatcoats and jerkins, hooded by balaclavas under their steel helmets, their rifles wrapped in sacking; and they took their boots to bed to keep them from freezing stiff. It was so cold the bread froze after it came from the ovens and had to be cut apart with a hacksaw. Colds were so common that before a man could be sent to the rear he had to be suffering from pneumonia.

At other times the weather turned balmy, and the mud, the dreadful clinging mud, reappeared. Nothing sapped the soldiers' morale more than this ever-present gumbo, so gluelike that the strongest boots had their seams wrenched apart by men's efforts to struggle out of the morass. Leslie Hudd, the foundry worker from Sherbrooke who had joined the cyclists because the job sounded dashing and romantic, was one of a group who weighed a typical mud-soaked greatcoat. It tipped the scales at forty-seven pounds. Others cut off the skirts of their greatcoats with jack-knives to make them more manageable and were promptly fined a dollar apiece for destroying government property.

The mud flowed like gruel around men's puttees, filled their boots, squeezed into their socks, and had to be scraped out from between the toes with a knife. Trench mats – "bath-mats" in the soldiers' argot – made of slatted wood, like ladders, were supposed to keep the men's feet above the mud. But these were soon swallowed up. In some places three layers of mats were dug up, the earliest having been laid by the French in 1915.

If a man slipped and fell in a muddy trench he could easily vanish and smother in the mire, invisible to those who came behind, slogging over his body. One eighteen-year-old, Gordon Lawson, was flung forward when a broken trench mat flew up and hit him in the stomach. Lawson felt one foot on his buttocks and another bite into his shoulders as the file began to move over him. Kicking wildly, he managed to alert the third man in line, who extricated him just in time.

There was no real remedy, as Corporal Eric Forbes of the 6th Field Company, Engineers, realized when the commanding general of his division, Henry Burstall, arrived at his trench. Burstall was wearing hip waders because the mud and water had reached mid-thigh. As the general stepped out onto an unanchored trench mat, Forbes shouted a warning. It came too late. The mat came up, struck the general in the face, and knocked him into the gruel up to his waist.

"Corporal," cried the general. "I want these trenches pumped out. Get the pumps!"

Forbes well knew that no pumps were capable of doing the job; but Burstall was adamant. "I'll get the pumps for you," he said. "I'll send pumps up."

But, as Forbes remarked that night to his fellow engineers, you might as well try to pump the Atlantic Ocean dry. The pumps never arrived.

Andrew Macphail once spent five hours trying to negotiate a trench with mud reaching to his knees and shrapnel screaming overhead. It took all his energy to extricate each foot before lurching forward, ever aware that if he toppled he'd smother under the tramp of those behind. It was, as he confided wanly to his diary, "all so unlike the pomp of war." This was not the Scots Greys galloping down the slopes of Waterloo or even Middleton's scarlet-clad volunteers leaping out of the rifle-pits at Batoche. Each time Macphail went to the front he confessed to a new sense of desolation. Even when the sun came out in an occasional blink it brought out "the hideous detail: a German with a leg bone protruding, a cow's head, rifles and bayonets rusted and bent, the raw, gaping trenches and the men performing menial tasks, scraping their boots, shovelling mud, rubbing their extremities with whale oil to prevent trench feet."

The whale oil came up in jugs, ice cold. Each man was required to rub it on every twenty-four hours, for it was a crime to suffer from trench foot. But some men were too weary to use it and others purposely courted the affliction in order to escape the trenches. Will Bird saw one man who could no longer walk taken out on a stretcher, his feet huge blobs of misshapen flesh, ready for amputation. The ailment became so bad that winter that if a man was evacuated for trench foot, his entire unit was punished by a loss of leave for two or three months. In Arthur Currie's 1st Division, officers were ordered to witness their men applying the whale oil; if a soldier had to be evacuated, his superior could be court-martialled.

It wasn't enough that the men in the forward lines were wet, cold, and weary; they were also hungry. As the Canadian railway contractors and logging firms had learned in the early days of the century, men can abide harsh conditions if the food is plentiful and good, but in the forward trenches before Vimy, the fare was monotonous, skimpy, and cold. A single potato was considered a luxury. As many as seven men were required to share a loaf of bread. For Will Bird, these were the hungriest years of his life. He was so famished that if he spotted a fragment of hardtack trampled into the mud, he would seize it, rub it clean, and wolf it down.

In the front line the food was eaten cold – mainly bully beef, biscuits, cheese, or plum-and-apple jam – from mess tins washed out in shell holes. Scores suffered from skin diseases because of the lack of vegetables. The divisional ration dumps were usually eight or ten miles behind the lines at the railhead. From there, each morning, horse transport brought supplies forward to battalion stores, where they were sorted into gunnysacks for platoons and sections and moved farther up by limber, light railway, or pack mule. Ration parties from the support trenches took them into the front line, but a stray shell or a sniper's bullet often meant that the men at the front went hungry, maddened sometimes by the odour of the sausages the Germans were cooking only a few yards away.

After a tour of duty at the front everyone was exhausted, and that included junior staff officers – men like Captain Duncan Macintyre, late of Moose Jaw. One night in February, Macintyre dragged his weary body back to Mont St. Eloi, reaching brigade headquarters in a battered chateau at 2 A.M., took off his muddy boots and equipment, rolled into his sleeping bag on the hard floor, and slept like a dead man. When he awoke late the next morning in bright sunlight, he discovered that an enemy shell had destroyed the right wing of the chateau, causing seventeen casualties. While Macintyre snored, as if under ether, others were working to haul out the wounded and bury the dead.

It was hard to stay awake, even if sleep itself meant death. Leslie Hudd, the cyclist, worked all day until he was exhausted and then discovered that he would have to stay up all night on gas patrol in a lonely part of the front line. He tried to stay awake, leaning against the back of the trench to support himself, but his eyes closed, and the next thing he knew his company commander was standing in front of him.

"Are you awake?" the officer asked. Hudd nodded.

"No you weren't," the officer told him. "You were asleep. You know what that means?"

"I could be shot," said Hudd, miserably.

"Hudd," said the captain, "I don't know how I'm going to get you out of this."

By this time the wretched cyclist was shaking like a leaf.

"I'll leave it to you, sir," he said. "I'm guilty. You caught me at it. I just dropped off not five minutes ago."

Hudd's young superior was faced with an agonizing decision. He was, in effect, judge, jury, prosecutor, and executioner. If he reported Hudd, the sentry's blood would be on his hands and his first victim would be not a German but a fellow Canadian. So he told Hudd quietly that if he promised not to say anything, he wouldn't report the dereliction. Leslie Hudd breathed a sigh of relief.

For many others, sleep was almost impossible, even in the support trenches where the dugouts were. In Claude Williams's dugout there was barely room enough to turn around, and Williams, as a machine-gun officer, had more space than most. To reach his underground room Williams had to go down a flight of stairs on all fours. The room was three feet high; two bunks took up three quarters of the space, a table an eighth, a small stove a sixteenth; that left a tiny area to move about in. If one man wanted to use the table, the other had to get into bed. Williams accomplished this difficult feat by crawling *under* the table, slipping his feet into his sleeping bag, and wriggling in the rest of the way by a series of convulsive twists and squirms. A rat the size of a cat had gnawed a hole in the bottom and kept trying to get into the bag with Williams, who spent most of a sleepless night kicking it out.

4

The only bright spots at the front were the arrival of mail and parcels from home and the daily rum ration. Even the strictest temperance advocates came to realize the morale-building effect of a stiff tot on a cold night or before a trench raid. The Reverend Charles Gordon, better known as Ralph Connor, the novelist, shelved his temperance principles during the war and declared that "rum is an absolute necessity to the soldier in the field. I would rather dispossess them of their rifles. . . ."

In the rest areas, the troops enjoyed the unbelievable luxury of a bath or shower, even though the shower might be only half a bucket of water. Many, like Claude Williams's batman, went for weeks without even a change of underwear. In the shell holes and trenches of Vimy there was water, water everywhere, but clean water for bathing was hoarded as carefully as cigarettes.

Some fortunate men were billeted during these rest periods in the homes of the French who, in spite of their own short rations, were unfailingly hospitable. Corporal Harold Barker, the Gloucestershire farmer, added to his workload by helping a French farmer with his chores in exchange for bread. He never forgot the taste of the loaves, fresh and crusty, as they came from the outdoor oven. Some of the hosts even cleaned the boots of the men who stayed with them. Claude Williams told his mother that the French housewives refused to take money from the men whom they deluged with coffee – as much as fifteen cups a day. "You could never believe that people could take such utter strangers into their homes and treat them as one of the family," he wrote.

Sometimes the hospitality went further than that. Victor Wheeler, a virtuous young signalman from Calgary, was billeted with other members of the 50th Battalion in a farmer's barn. One morning, he was sitting in the kitchen drinking fresh cow's milk when the youngest daughter smiled at him, and opened her hand to reveal a contraceptive.

"Voulez vous aller à ma chambre à coucher avec moi, Monsieur?" she invited. To Wheeler's astonishment, the mother nodded cheerfully and invited him to accept. Wheeler, who kept a pocket Bible in his tunic and neither smoked nor drank, stiffly refused the offer. He never knew whether it was made for monetary reasons, personal pleasure, or as an act of patriotism, but he did notice that the girl's unmarried sister was already bringing up two children whose father was said to be unknown.

There were other diversions, ranging from the travelling theatrical groups, such as the famous Dumbbells, to the local bordellos. George Henry Hambley, a future United Church minister from Swan Lake, Manitoba, was shocked by the presence of bawdy houses among the ruins of Neuville St. Vaast. "They have right in town here licensed houses of debauchery," he wrote in his diary, "and it is the most common thing. . . . Even these old married women are after our lads – and how can the poor lads help it I don't know, when the temptation is so great and the access so horribly easy. . . .

Yet it is too bad . . . that our lads who have been comparatively perfectly clean and innocent have to be drawn into the vortex. . . ."

With such delights awaiting them only a few miles to the rear, it's no wonder that men prayed for a "blighty" – a small wound that would not incapacitate them for life but would get them out of the line for a month or even a week. Such men were looked on with envy by their comrades; the pain of a bullet in the fleshy part of the arm or leg was nothing to the ecstasy brought on by visions of crisp hospital sheets and decent grub. Victor Wheeler observed one such moment of elation while standing next to his friend Dicky Moore, watching an aerial dogfight involving the famous von Richthofen. As the flimsy craft wheeled and circled above them, a stray bullet pierced Moore's left foot. Moore cried out, not with pain, but with delight.

"Oh," he shouted, "it's a beauty, Vic! What a present from the Red Devil! It's a Blighty, I'll bet a dollar."

And off he went to the luxury of a hospital ward, far from the rats, the lice, the cold food, and the ever-present mud.

CHAPTER FOUR

The Byng Boys

1

On January 19, 1917, Henry Horne, the dapper commander of the British 1st Army, informed Julian Byng that in the coming spring offensive the Canadian Corps would be responsible for capturing all of the four-mile crest of Vimy Ridge except for the Pimple. The British 1st Corps, also in Horne's army, elements of which would be placed under Byng's command to strengthen the assault, would protect the Canadians' left flank. On the right, the British 3rd Army astride the River Scarpe would attack simultaneously on an eight-mile front. The exact date had not yet been set, but the timetable called for the job to be completed before April 1. Byng and his staff had about two months to plan the operation and train the men.

It wouldn't be easy. Raw reinforcements were still pouring in to fill the gaps in the ranks of the battered battalions. The veterans of Ypres and the Somme had learned something about war and discipline, but the new men could not be described as trained. These small-town Canadians would have to be drilled day after day, week after week to walk at a steady pace, timed to the second, directly behind their own barrage. This would require more than courage: it would require discipline; and the Canadians, as Byng well knew, were notorious for being undisciplined.

But the discipline would not be mindless. Unlike most British senior officers, Byng insisted on treating his troops as adults. The old assault machine in which every soldier was an automaton, blindly slogging forward without any clear idea of the battle plan, was about to be scrapped. At Vimy, Byng was determined that everyone would know exactly what was planned.

This represented a radical change in orthodox military

thinking and it came from one who, at first glance, appeared an unlikely choice to lead the rambunctious Canadians into battle. On paper he seemed the very personification of the stiff-necked aristocrat. His father was an earl, his mother a peer's daughter and a Cavendish at that – the bluest of the bluebloods. His grandfather had been a field marshal. He himself was a product of the playing fields of Eton, an intimate of royalty whom the King addressed by his nickname, Bungo. He came from the cavalry, a service so myopic that some of its officers – Haig was one – believed the bullet was not made that could stop a horse. His military background was pukka sahib: he had served in the outposts of Empire – India, the Sudan – where the British lived by the old rules, making no concessions to climate or environment, buttoning their collars tightly in the heat of the noonday sun, spurring their ponies across Imperial polo fields, enjoying ritual stengahs on the porches of their bungalows.

Yet perhaps more than any other Byng belied the image of the spit-and-polish Great War career officer. He was casual in his dress, spartan in his habits, affable with all ranks, and, above all, unorthodox. He had none of the stand-offishness associated with his class; his senior Canadian commander, Arthur Currie, was far more aloof than Byng.

But Byng shared with Currie and the other Canadians a flexibility of mind, a refusal to conform to outworn rules, that won the day at Vimy. Andrew Macphail, who loathed most politicians and staff brass, was uncharacteristically enthusiastic about Byng. "This is a soldier!" he scribbled, "large, strong, lithe, with worn boots and frayed puttees."

Byng had no desire to command the Canadians, of whom he knew next to nothing. The task was forced upon him, and since he was already a corps commander in the British army, it could not be considered a promotion.

"Why am I sent to the Canadians?" he wanted to know when the transfer order came in May 1916. "I don't know a Canadian. Why this stunt? I am sorry to leave the old Corps as we are fighting like hell and killing Boches. However, there it is. I am ordered to these people and will do my best but I don't know that there is any congratulation about it."

Still, he had nothing to lose. Since he hadn't been promoted, he didn't have to keep in with the politicians to hold his job, as Sam Hughes had found out the previous August.

As it turned out, the appointment was one of the happiest of the war. Byng was the right man at the right time in the right place to take over the Canadian Corps from Alderson. It was a unique command. In the British Army, a corps wasn't much more than a skeleton headquarters in which divisions came and went, dealt like cards according to the needs or whims of the general staff. The four Canadian divisions, however, were always kept up to strength. In fact, the 5th Division, still in training that January in England, was about to be broken up to reinforce the units in France, so that every battalion in the field would have one hundred more men on strength than its establishment called for. At full strength, a British division numbered about fifteen thousand men. At Vimy the Canadian figure exceeded twenty-one thousand. Julian Byng's Canadian Corps, then, was more like a small army.

His personal style fitted that of his new command. In the larger units of the Allied armies during the Great War, the commander was a vague and distant figure who never ventured into the front lines and was rarely seen by the private soldiers. But Byng's links to his troops were forged early in the game. He seemed to be everywhere, usually on foot, his boots spattered with mud, questioning, chatting, observing the ordinary soldier at work and at rest. Soon the Canadians began to call themselves the Byng Boys, after a popular musical revue at London's Alhambra Theatre.

Byng preferred to live like the rank and file as closely as was practical. Because the troops got so little leave, he took very little himself; in the four war years his wife saw him only five times. The food at Corps headquarters was execrable. Not for Julian Byng the long, candlelit dinners with which most of the senior staff indulged themselves. He shovelled down whatever was offered and rose from the table to go back to work. After King George had the misfortune to lunch with him in France he insisted to Queen Mary that he'd been poisoned. "Bungo didn't live – he pigged . . ." was the way the King put it.

Duncan Macintyre once spent a day guiding Byng around the Ypres salient. Byng wanted to see everything, so they both crawled out to observation posts and snipers' nests and through tunnels. At noon, Byng squatted on a firestep in the front line, pulled a sandwich from his pocket, chewed on it, then lit a pipe and enjoyed a short chat with the men at the point where fighting was heaviest.

The physical descriptions of Byng by those who knew him are fascinating because no two are quite the same. Some call him big, some tall; some say he wasn't tall but lithe, others that he was bulky. All say he was strong, with a strong jaw, strong hands, and a strong walk. The picture that emerges is one of a powerful and commanding presence, fit and muscular. He was fifty-four and looked younger, a handsome man with knowing blue eyes framed by a lean face, brown as shoe leather, and a large military moustache. In his photographs he looks a little terrifying, and he could be terrifying. But he also had the common touch.

He did not stand on ceremony, did not even take his hand out of his tunic to return a salute, merely raising it courteously inside the pocket. At a corps inspection, where a general and his staff customarily trotted down the road on sleek chargers, the new commander came into the horse lines through a hedge, jumping the ditches, as Andrew Macphail put it, "as unaffectedly as a farmer would come into a neighbour's place to look at his crops."

Byng's inspections, unlike so many others, were starkly thorough, never perfunctory. He never kept the troops waiting but arrived promptly to the second. Once, it was said, he turned up seven minutes early and hid behind a hedge with his staff until the exact moment. Shiny buttons did not impress him; well-scrubbed mess tins did. He was an expert on the equipment of the ordinary soldier, from rifles to small packs. Nor did he indulge in the pleasantries that so often accompanied these rituals. As one officer in the 44th (Winnipeg) Battalion put it, "afterwards officers go around wringing their hands while hard-boiled sergeants burst into tears." Major-General David Watson's diary entry for December 15, 1916, at Vimy, speaks for itself. The 4th Division's commander wrote a little ruefully that Byng had inspected the 54th Battalion from the Kootenay district of British Columbia and found it "in a most unsatisfactory state, dirty, and unorganized, and told Colonel Kemball so very plainly."

But he cared about his men. In India, years before, his first action had been to alter the high collars of the men's jackets so they could wear them open in the sweltering heat. To Byng, a soldier was never a cipher, never a statistic on the casualty lists. There was a strong religious streak in Byng. Macintyre once heard him say that he never ordered so much as a patrol to go over the top without getting down on his knees and praying for their safe return.

It was said of Byng that he could converse on subjects as far apart as Confucius and Canadian ducks. He had forgotten more than most of his junior officers had learned, for he had been a professional soldier and a keen student of military tactics for thirty-three years.

He had commanded the South African Light Horse during the Boer War, and in that free-wheeling atmosphere he made his reputation as a daring and often unorthodox commander. It was there that his character was moulded. Byng, the tireless young colonel, followed a different drummer from his colleagues'. In London on leave, while others were playing polo or dancing at fashionable clubs, Byng was down at the Smithfield Market learning about meat, trying to outwit the contractors who were supplying an inferior product to his troops.

When war broke out in 1914, he was a major-general in the Egyptian command. He distinguished himself at Ypres, was knighted, promoted to lieutenant-general, and sent to Gallipoli, where he drew up a successful plan to evacuate the embattled troops with a minimum loss of life. For that he received the blue ribbon of the Bath and, after a spell in Egypt, command of the Canadian Corps.

Now he was determined that every man under him would know his task when Zero Hour dawned. "Explain it to him again and again," he told his officers. "Encourage him to ask you questions. Remember also, that no matter what sort of a fix you get into, you mustn't just sit down and hope that things will work themselves out. You must *do* something in a crisis. The man who does nothing is *always* wrong."

This kind of attitude fitted the Canadian character and helped to win the battle that followed. It was surely Byng's greatest moment, as he himself acknowledged when he was elevated to the peerage. Four years after the battle he would be Viscount Byng of Vimy, Governor General of Canada. It is one of the ironies of history that future generations would remember him more for the constitutional battle with Mackenzie King that he lost than for the bloody battle he won on the muddy slopes of a battered ridge in France.

2

Six hundred thousand Allied soldiers had been killed or mutilated on the Somme, including twenty-four thousand young Canadians. Julian Byng was determined that there should be no repetition of that blood-bath, which had seen men with little training and less understanding of battle hurled in dense waves against the German machine guns. The Somme's lessons must be studied and applied to the exercises that would take place behind the Canadian lines beyond reach of the enemy guns.

The man chosen to report on the Somme experience was Arthur Currie, the senior divisional commander and Byng's most trusted general – the man who took command of the Corps when Byng was absent and who would shortly replace Byng as its commander.

In December Byng had given Currie two tasks: first, to analyse the Somme battle and report on the lessons learned; second, to advise how those lessons might be applied to the infantry tactics and training at Vimy. The methodical Currie took three weeks to prepare his first report on eleven foolscap pages. He had plunged into the second when he received a signal honour: he was the only Canadian chosen by the British to accompany a group of officers invited by the French to visit the Verdun battlefield in the first week of January. At Verdun the carnage had been even worse than on the Somme; there were lessons to be learned there, too.

The French invited questions and Currie was ruthless in his curiosity. As one British officer put it, "he pumped everyone dry." He was not prepared to accept the word of the French brass hats; he checked every statement against the experience of junior officers and often discovered that the seniors were wrong in their assessment. The result was another careful analysis of what could be learned from the Verdun experience. After Currie finished his second Somme report, he began, on January 20, to give lectures on tactics to the senior officers of the Corps. It was his findings that dictated the way in which the troops were trained for the Vimy battle.

Here was a remarkable figure, plucked from obscurity by the onrush of history. A failed real estate operator in Victoria, close to bankruptcy, without professional military experience, Currie had risen to major-general in less than three years and would soon climb up another notch in the military hierarchy. With only a high school education and a third-class teacher's certificate, he would be propelled after the war into the principalship of Canada's most famous university, McGill.

It is inconceivable that a man with Currie's background could have risen past field rank in the British Army, where education and breeding counted for more than tactical skills. But Currie was not the only unschooled Canadian to wear a major-general's red tabs. His colleague David Watson, commander of the 4th Division, had never got past Grade 8. Unlike Currie, Watson had enjoyed a spectacular business career. An orphan in Quebec City, he had gone to work as a youth on the commercial side of the Quebec *Chronicle* and ended up owning it. His rise in the ranks from militia private to lieutenant-colonel, and then to wartime major-general, was equally startling. Now he was a junior to Currie, a lean and supple man with an old, lined face, cadaverous and saturnine. The marks of Ypres, where he had personally carried out a wounded man under heavy fire, were on him. At forty-eight, he was the oldest of the divisional commanders and looked even older. It was said that Ypres had aged him ten years.

In his own meteoric rise, Currie had leaped over two other officers, both his seniors in age and experience. Louis James Lipsett, commander of the 3rd Division, had actually taught Currie tactics in Victoria when the latter was a militia colonel. A firm-jawed Irishman, Lipsett was a professional soldier, lent to the Canadians during the war as commander of Winnipeg's Little Black Devils. There the Imperial officer became a convert to the Canadian style.

Lipsett was much loved, for he was tireless in the care he took of his men. His troops were well aware of his dictum that no officer should think of his own comfort until the ordinary soldiers were fed, warmed, and sheltered. His blunt declaration, as a battalion commander at Ypres, that he would "stick to the last in the trenches" was legendary, as was his fearlessness under fire. Any officer who showed the slightest fear, he warned, would be sacked. He himself liked to prowl the front lines in order to be close to his men.

Will Bird ran into him one night in a crater post fifteen yards in front of the main trench. The strange officer seemed genuinely interested in Bird's background, asking about his home in Nova Scotia and his years out West working for various eccentric ranchers. When he revealed who he was, Bird was stunned and tongue-tied, whereupon Lipsett pulled a snapshot from his pocket to identify himself, making Bird promise he wouldn't tell his mates. Perhaps because of these nocturnal ramblings, Lipsett didn't survive the war; a sniper's bullet got him in 1918. But Will Bird never forgot that meeting and kept the photograph for the rest of his life.

Henry Burstall, commander of the 2nd Division, was that rarest of all Canadian birds, a regular army officer. A Quebecker, Burstall had had more experience than any of the others. He had been to the Klondike as part of the Yukon Field Force, had fought in the Boer War, had served with the South African constabulary, and had been selected as aide-de-camp to the Duke of Connaught during the latter's vice-regal tenure. A big, bluff six-footer with a hearty laugh that hid an inner shyness, he had been selected to command the 2nd Division over Garnet Hughes, son of the Minister of Militia, whom Borden was trying to placate just before firing him. But Byng would not tolerate political interference, especially in the case of Brigadier-General Hughes, an indifferent leader at best.

On paper, all three of these men seemed better fitted than Currie for command. Currie didn't *look* like a general. There are fashions in the military image just as there are in women's hats. Currie did not adhere to the Great War stereotype of a ramrod-fit, gimlet-eyed, lean-faced, moustached leader. Haig looked the part and so did Currie's divisional colleagues, with their firm, chiselled features and clipped military moustaches. Currie was one of the few senior officers who was clean shaven. His face was flabby, he sported a double chin, his eyes were a watery blue, and he was shaped like a gigantic pear. He was, in fact, so bulky that he had difficulty making his way through the narrower trenches. There was nothing dapper about Currie: his uniform always looked a little sloppy. His men called him, not without affection, "Guts and Gaiters."

Looks were deceptive. Currie was one of the most admired commanders on the Western Front. Borden considered him the equal of any corps commander in the war. Byng, going through a list of possible Canadian chiefs of staff, put his thumb against Currie's name and said, "Of him, there are no 'ifs'." Philip Gibbs, the war correspondent, said that Currie reminded him of Cromwell. And Lloyd George, praising his "great ability and strength of purpose," would settle on another Currie trait: his "lack of fetishism." Currie, the civilian soldier, had no old fetishes to expunge. He approached each problem with an open mind, and it was this that appealed to the British Prime Minister, whose loathing of Sir Douglas Haig bordered on the pathological.

"The ablest brains did not climb to the top of the stairs," Lloyd George wrote ruefully of the British officer class. "Seniority and Society were the dominant factors in army promotion. Deportment counted a good deal. Brains came a bad fourth. . . . The only exceptions were to be found in the Dominion forces." If Lloyd George had been able to buck the system he would eventually have made Currie commander of all British forces with the Australian general, John Monash, his chief of staff. Even the tough little Welshman could not achieve that goal, but had the war continued past 1918, it would have come to pass.

3

Currie was not a military genius. The Great War produced none, at least on the Allied side. But he was a good tactician with a high sense of the practical and a strong capacity for administration. His grasp of detail was awesome, and his memory for names and faces seemed infallible. It was said of Currie that if you met him once, he'd remember your name four years later. He certainly knew his NCOs by name. One of his battalion commanders once came to him requesting that a sergeant-major, Jim Watchman, be given leave to get married. Said Currie: "You mean the man the fellows call Mustang Pete?"

His sense of tactics under pressure came to the fore at Ypres. When his flank was threatened, he threw away the rule book, abandoning the standard linear defence and opting for the kind of all-round defence that would become common in the Second War.

He was cool to the point of austerity, his features rarely betraying any emotion. Nothing seemed to ruffle him. He never raised his voice in anger. The only hint of displeasure was a sharp glint in his pale eyes. Andrew McNaughton, the counter-battery officer, who liked him – for Currie was a gunner who spoke the language of the artillery – found him "pretty sticky to deal with," meaning that Currie could not be shaken by colleagues, underlings, or the high command.

F.C. Bagshaw, then an orderly-room sergeant with the 5th Battalion, a Saskatchewan regiment, had a first-hand view of Currie's legendary coolness under fire at Ypres. On April 24, 1915, the third day of the attack, he looked up from the mud of the trench to see a portly officer casually strolling along a ridge, oblivious to the sniper fire around him. Finally the officer jumped down and made his way along the trench line. It was Currie. "Who was that shooting at me?" he asked, in the same casual way a friend might say, "Who was that waving at me?"

"That was the enemy, sir," someone replied. Currie appeared quite unperturbed.

He showed the same courage in standing up to the High Command in 1915 when he thought the orders were wrong. As a junior brigade commander he bitterly protested what he believed were premature orders to go on the attack at Festubert and also, a month later, at Givenchy. For this he was rapped on the knuckles, but he wasn't cowed. Told by the divisional staff that the order had come from the corps commander, he responded that "it is quite time that some corps commanders were told to go to blazes."

The attacks failed at great cost, proving Currie's point. What had bothered him was sloppy preparation: not enough time set aside for reconnaissance. In the opinion of Brigadier-General Jack Seeley, the Canadian cavalry commander, Currie had "an almost fanatical hatred of unnecessary casualties." How ironic, then, that ten years later Currie, of all people, would have to defend himself against a newspaper's libellous charge that he had needlessly sacrificed Canadian lives in the final days of the war.*

It is a measure of the admiration in which Currie was held that his disagreements with the higher-ups did not stand

* The offending article, which appeared in the Port Hope *Evening Guide* (owned by the Hughes family) in June 1927, was written by the most unsavoury of Liberal hacks, W.T.R. Preston. Currie won his suit for libel after a long and sensational trial, but the damaging effects on his health and reputation were lasting.

in the way of his promotion. He had tangled with Sam Hughes before the war, refusing to take part in a church parade for an organization he felt had political overtones. Hughes confronted Currie in Victoria but backed down. "Well, Currie," he said, "I came out here to get your scalp but you're all right." At that time Hughes and his son, Garnet, were both Currie supporters.

In Victoria Currie had been a prominent Liberal, but by 1917 he was fed up with politics. He had no friends at court, no political allies, and sought no favours. "I do not believe in mutual admiration soldiers," he once said. He was an advocate of promotion on merit, not political pull.*

He was concerned about his men and made it clear to his junior officers that the care of their troops must take precedence over their own personal comfort. That concern extended to an almost obsessive insistence that everyone from private soldier on up should know exactly what he was to do in battle. He had an ability, during inspections, to seize upon the most moronic member of a company and pepper him with questions, believing that if the slowest came up with the right answers, the rest must know their business. As a result, the cannier platoons would pick out such men in advance and give them a cram course before Currie arrived.

In the training plan that followed Currie's winter assessments of the Somme and Verdun, he and Byng made sure that every man would be told the details of the plan of attack – everything except the date. Each soldier would know not only his own task in the assault but also the tasks of others; thus, if necessary, a private could take over from a corporal, a corporal from a sergeant, a sergeant from an officer. Indeed, there would be times when the casualties were such that

* It was this attitude that led indirectly to the famous libel action. When Currie was promoted to corps commander after Vimy, Sam Hughes lobbied to have his son replace him as commander of the 1st Division. Currie, who had a low opinion of the younger Hughes's military abilities, bluntly refused. "I will get you before I am finished with you!" Garnet Hughes threatened. And he did. The offending article was clearly inspired by father and son.

sergeants ran companies and sergeant-majors ran battalions.

This was unprecedented in the British Army. "Maps to section leaders," was Currie's dictum, and that was unprecedented, too. The idea that every section of six or nine men would be given a detailed map of their portion of the front, that every lance-corporal would see his line of advance marked out on paper, was something new. It had the morale-building effect of making each man feel that he was trusted, that his leaders considered him intelligent enough to be let in on what had been secret information in previous battles. For the assault on Vimy Ridge, the Canadian Corps distributed forty thousand such maps to men newly trained to act when necessary on their own initiative rather than to follow orders blindly.

4

Arthur Currie's record confirms the old adage that in certain men the furnace of battle causes hidden qualities to bubble to the surface. For there was little in Currie's background to suggest his later military prominence. He was a big but sickly Ontario farm boy, suffering from stomach complaints, which, when they returned in early adulthood and later in the war, hinted at psychosomatic roots. He had moved to Victoria at the age of seventeen and taught school on Vancouver Island until he was twenty-two. Then his life reached a crisis point. He'd been in the non-permanent militia for two years and had achieved the rank of corporal. At that point he was offered a commission, which he desperately wanted to accept. But he could scarcely afford it on his teacher's salary of sixty-two dollars a month. It was then that his stomach trouble returned.

Victoria had by far the most highly stratified society of any city in Western Canada, and there is little doubt that Currie coveted the status that a militia commission would bring in a community dominated by Imperial officers, not to mention the upper caste of the British Navy stationed at the Esquimalt base. Currie's social aspirations may be gauged by his change

104

of name. His immigrant grandfather's "Corrigan" had already been transformed to "Curry." Now the grandson adopted an even more acceptable spelling. And he rejected the more plebeian Methodist Church of his mother for the more fashionable Church of England.

A militia commission cost money. An officer had to pay for his own expensive kit and was expected to give his pay to the mess. And Currie also wanted to get married: his English-born fiancée had a double-barrelled name, which made her more than socially acceptable in Victoria. There was nothing for it but to quit the classroom and go into the insurance business and later into real estate. In those yeasty days of Western expansion these were much more attractive vocations.

He joined the Masons and became president of the Young Liberals but spent most of his free time in the local armouries. He was an ardent and energetic citizen soldier, out on the rifle range every Saturday, up at 6 A.M. to shoot during the summer months. By the time the great land boom swept Western Canada, Arthur Currie was colonel of his regiment and senior partner in a real estate firm.

Those were heady days. With a population of thirty thousand, Victoria boasted 111 real estate agents like Currie, most of whom plunged wildly in the belief the boom would never end. Currie was a victim of his own unbridled optimism. The bubble burst, and by 1913, almost broke and due for militia retirement, the future general was about to fade into obscurity.

At this point he was suddenly pressed to take over command of a new militia unit, and a Highland unit at that – the 50th Battalion, known as the Gay Gordons, after the mother regiment in Britain. He could scarcely afford the splendid but expensive (and for a man of Currie's physique slightly ludicrous) Highland kit, let alone the mess bills and his expected contributions to the regiment. But he could not resist. And when he was offered an overseas brigade the following autumn of 1914, he could not resist that either.

What was not known to the officers who served under him, and to only a handful who served over him, was a truly dreadful secret. Currie kept it locked within himself for all those years at Ypres, Festubert, Givenchy, the Somme, and Vimy: a secret that must have caused his stomach to turn and his dreams to become nightmares. For nearly three years, as he later admitted, it was the last thing he thought of at night and the first thing when he awoke each morning.

To be blunt, Currie was an embezzler. He had diverted eleven thousand dollars of the regiment's funds, intended to pay for uniforms, to cover his own personal debts. There were extenuating circumstances involving the Gordon Highlanders' honorary colonel, William Coy, a newly rich New Brunswick entrepreneur who bought himself social status in Victoria by promising to underwrite the regiment to the tune of thirty-five thousand dollars. Coy not only welched on the deal but also bought up Currie's note at a fat discount. Bankruptcy would have meant the end of Currie's career as an officer and the collapse of his social position, and so he appropriated the government's cheque intended for the regimental contractors.

In France, Currie was bombarded with letters demanding explanations or payment. To these he did not reply – *could* not reply. In Victoria, his friends tried to raise money to cover the missing sum; but Victoria was floundering in depression, and the debt remained outstanding. Borden was brought into the matter – he had received, in 1915, an anonymous letter calling Currie a thief – and so was Sir George Perley in London. Currie's delinquency was a court-martial offence; but how could you court-martial Canada's best soldier? That would shatter both army and civilian morale. And so for three years the government, the army, and the contractors themselves conspired in a cover-up that would end only in the fall of 1917, when David Watson of the 4th Division and Brigadier Victor Odlum, both wealthy men, lent Currie the necessary funds.

Of Currie's inner turmoil the officers and men rehearsing day after day the careful plans for the attack on the ridge knew nothing. The big, fleshy face remained impassive, the pale eyes clear and unblinking. No lines of worry creased that smooth brow, no hunch of the shoulders betrayed the shadow of the Damoclean sword that, during those final days before Zero Hour, hung suspended over the senior divisional commander of the Canadian Corps.

5

Byng and his staff knew very well that all the training in the world would not save the Canadian Corps if the German wire remained intact. The British High Command had been sobered by the tragedy of the Somme, where twenty thousand British soldiers, on the first day of the offensive, had been blown to bits. The guns had not been able to cut the enemy wire, which formed an impregnable barrier, eighty feet thick in places. The rolls of heavy, tempered steel were as high as a house, with five-inch barbs, stronger and thicker than anything seen on a rancher's fence. To get caught on that wire was to suffer a fearful fate.

In the Second World War, the Canadian troops, marching on manoeuvres, used to sing a silly song:

> *Has anyone seen the sergeant?*
> *I know where he is*
> *I know where he is*
> *I know where he is.*
> *Has anyone seen the sergeant?*
> *I know where he is,*
> *Hanging on the old barbed wire.*

The implications of that piece of gallows humour, revived from an older conflict, were lost on most of the young men studying the more adventurous tactics of fire and movement. It dawned on only a few that the sergeant, hanging on the old barbed wire, was enmeshed like a fly in a web, unable to advance or retreat, impaled on the barbs, blood pouring from a dozen gashes, a sitting target for the German machine gunners.

The nocturnal moaning of such men, dying slowly in No Man's Land without hope of succour, haunted many a veteran of the Somme, as it must have haunted Byng. That is why he and his brilliant chief gunner, Brigadier-General Edward "Dinky" Morrison, the former newspaperman, pressed hard through every available channel for supplies of the new No. 106 fuse, which allowed shells to explode on contact with the wire rather than above it.

What was good enough for Henry Shrapnel in the eighteenth century wasn't good enough for the siege warfare of the twentieth, but it took the Allied commanders two years to realize that. Shrapnel was designed to kill men, and it was horribly effective: when the shell burst it released hundreds of steel balls, which whirred through the air, scything down everyone in their path. But it could scarcely make a dent in the wire. Thousands of soldiers, deceived into believing that a pathway had been cleared in front of the enemy trenches, found themselves trapped in a tangle of barbs. Immobilized, they could only wait for the machine guns to tear them to pieces.

The solution to this catastrophe was the development of the new fuse and the abandonment of shrapnel as a wire cutting device. The fuse caused each high-explosive shell to burst on contact, driving deep into the heart of the wire, tearing it to shreds and ripping great gaps through which the attacking troops could pour. When the new fuses began to reach the Vimy sector in mid-January, Byng and Morrison could breathe more easily.

Like the cavalry, the artillery was one of the most conservative arms of the service. The senior British gunners, with one or two admirable exceptions, were still fighting the Boer War. At the start of the war they treated the machine gun as a toy. The Germans had fifty to a division, the British only two. Kitchener, under pressure from Lloyd George, then Minister of Munitions, thought four would be a luxury. The scrappy little Welshman went behind his back and ordered a speed-up in production. By November 1916, with Kitchener dead, the British war office was asking for sixteen machine guns per battalion. By the end of the war, the number had risen to eighty. But in that first year the Allies had stubbornly refused to understand the new style of battle that the invention of the machine gun had brought to France.

Hundreds of thousands of men were slaughtered because the generals were still thinking in terms of bayonet and pikestaff. In one tragic incident, 6,000 French soldiers, massed in a sector only 2,400 feet wide, were ordered to advance with fixed bayonets, forbidden even to pull the triggers of their rifles. Half died in the attempt, but that did not stop their leaders from ordering a *second* identical suicide bayonet attack into the spray of German machine-gun bullets!

Byng had no intention of repeating this folly. The new commander was good at picking men; Winston Churchill had once served under him in South Africa. Three of his staff officers would later rise to become Chiefs of the Imperial General Staff. Most of the staff was British; Canadians were only beginning to gain the experience to achieve staff rank. But now, with the help of his colleagues, Byng reached down and plucked out the youngest brigade commander in France to take charge of counter-battery work.

On January 27, Andrew George Latta McNaughton, aged twenty-nine, was named Counter-Battery Staff Officer and given carte blanche to focus his scientifically trained mind on the twin problems of pinpoint intelligence and pinpoint accuracy. The post was a new one. McNaughton would have to develop the techniques of counter-battery work from scratch. But before the war was over he would be acknowledged by both the Allies and the Germans as the best artillery officer in the British Empire. And when, a generation later, Canada raised a new army for a new war, McNaughton would be its first commander.

Like so many of the unconventional leaders in that conventional first war, McNaughton was a Westerner, the son of Scottish pioneers. He grew up in Moosomin, then a tiny hamlet in the old North West Territories. There he learned to ride, shoot, hunt, and fish, activities that nurture self-reliance. At brigade headquarters he slept on the floor, spurning a mattress, perfectly content to open a tin of bully beef for his supper.

A crack shot, he also brought to the artillery an intimate knowledge of horses – invaluable in those pre-mechanized days – and a questioning mind. As a boy he had been fascinated by explosives: he was always blowing up things, building small cannons out of lengths of pipe stuffed with black powder. But it was at McGill that his mind was trained under such physicists as Ernest Rutherford, the future Nobel prize winner. Electrical engineering was in its infancy. A new device known as an oscillograph had just been developed, and McNaughton was later to put that to good use at Vimy. He would, in fact, bring a scientist's mind to every aspect of counter-battery work, from gun barrel wear and the effect of wind on shell velocity to the technique of spotting the precise position of an enemy weapon by observing its muzzle flashes.

He had already made a considerable reputation. Currie had spotted him as a comer and so had Morrison, the chief gunner. He was known as a hard worker: when he first arrived at his battery he had put reveille back one hour. And he was well liked: his men called him Andy. Now Byng sent him south, too, to see what the French had learned at Verdun and the British at the Somme.

Off went Andy McNaughton in a spanking Napier motor car all to himself, feeling that he was now Somebody – a sinewy black Scot, somewhat dishevelled and shaggy, with deep-set, burning eyes. In later years when he commanded the Canadian Army of the Second World War, he was photographed by Karsh with a vast greatcoat draped across his shoulders, those dark eyes glowering into the distance, as if with some suppressed fire. It made him seem larger than life and more than a little terrifying; in reality he was a slight, mild man who rarely raised his voice and was more scientist than soldier. But he was firm and he was stubborn. His staff saw him sack a senior officer once – or rather didn't see it. The man walked into McNaughton's office to emerge, after a short period of silence, white and shaking – ordered to take the first boat home. But it had all been done without the C.O. raising his voice.

McNaughton learned little from the French. Their high

command told him one thing about counter-battery work, the middle command another, the men in the trenches something else again. Clearly the brass was woefully out of touch with the front line. At British 5th Corps, however, he encountered an unconventional gunner, Lieutenant-Colonel A.G. Haig, who happened to be a cousin of the British Commander-in-Chief. Haig, who had fought in the mountains of Burma where unorthodox methods were essential and the High Command a long way off, told McNaughton something of his experiences and experiments with flash spotting and sound ranging. In the weeks that followed, McNaughton was to develop and fine-tune these techniques, right to the moment of the Vimy attack.

CHAPTER FIVE

The Raiders

1

On February 2, Julian Byng gathered his senior officers together at Camblain l'Abbé, a French chateau just beyond the far limit of the German guns. There he crisply outlined the dimensions of the task that faced the corps.

From this moment on the rear areas began to buzz with activity. In addition to the the normal duties of army personnel – clerks and cooks, gunners and surgeons – a bewildering variety of other skills were needed. The preparations for the battle would require the combined talents of loggers, locomotive engineers, tunnellers, carpenters, track crews, tailors, telegraphers, train dispatchers, road builders, and, sadly, grave diggers, for the cemeteries must be ready to receive their tribute.

But first, the divisions had to be reorganized. The corps front of ten miles was reduced to four. Currie's veteran 1st Division came down from the north to take its place on the right of the line, as military tradition dictated. Henry Burstall's 2nd Division, next in seniority, would move into the line to the left of Currie. The next two would follow, again in order of seniority and experience, right to left. They would hold their sectors without further shuffling until Zero Day, memorizing the ground on their immediate fronts. Every man was expected to be as familiar with the battlefield as he was with the streets of his home town. Every shell hole, every pitted decline, every battered tree and stump, every fold and hump, every trench, tunnel, and sap, every gun emplacement and sniper's roost must be pinpointed on maps and registered in men's minds so that, if necessary, they could walk blindfolded across No Man's Land and still know where they stood.

Some of this could be achieved through aerial observation, through the interrogation of prisoners, and through the wizardry of McNaughton's team of scientists, who would shortly begin to locate the German guns through the new techniques of flash spotting and sound ranging. But there was no substitute for first-hand knowledge. To know the ground the troops had to crawl over it. That was one of the main purposes of the trench raids, which began as early as December and reached a crescendo in February and March.

The trench raids were a Canadian invention. Until the Canadians came along nobody–not the British, not the French, not even the Germans – had considered the possibilities of raiding one another's lines between major offensives.

The first trench raid was staged in the Ypres salient on the last day of February 1915 by the Princess Pats, six months before the Canadian Corps was formed. One hundred men took part in a smash-and-grab attack that destroyed thirty yards of German trenches. Five Canadians were killed in the fight, eleven more wounded.

But the credit for developing the trench raid into a sophisticated concomitant of battle is generally reserved for Victor Odlum, who in November 1915 commanded the 7th (British Columbia) Battalion. His was one of two units that carried out a successful double attack that month across the Douve River. It was the first in the Corps's experience and it became a model for the scores of raids that followed.

The front was quiet at the time. Odlum's troops were bored and cold. It is said that somebody suggested a raid on the German trenches simply to relieve the monotony. Odlum seized upon the idea and made it his own. The raid was meticulously planned – the 170 volunteers rehearsed for ten days – and the results were overwhelmingly successful. The Canadians took the Germans by surprise and suffered only two casualties.

The Canadians began regular trench raids and were soon recognized as experts in the technique, which became standard practice in all armies. The French, who had hitherto accepted a policy of live and let live with the enemy between major battles, now asked for Odlum; but he preferred to remain with his fellow Canadians. In February 1916, Joffre sent an officer to Currie's headquarters to learn at first hand how the Canadians did it.

Victor Wentworth Odlum was a curious specimen. The men in his brigade were infuriated by his teetotalism. They called him "Peasoup" Odlum because, when neighbouring brigades were warming their bellies and stiffening their resolves with the daily tot of rum, they had to be content with mugs of broth. That finally ended in February 1917, when tensions began to rise over the coming battle; Odlum himself later regretted the puritan strain inherited from his Methodist father.

A missionary's son, born in Cobourg, Ontario, schooled in Tokyo and Vancouver, and shuffled around the world, he had been brought up to believe that strong drink, card games, and the theatre were all devices of the devil. Since these were among the chief diversions of the soldier, it is possible to believe that Odlum fought a personal war within himself, especially in the mess where he was always a little apart from his fellow officers, never quite one of the gang. They called him "Old Lime Juice" and, more affectionately, "Victor of Vancouver."

Like his staff officers – a lawyer, a politician, a miller, a mayor – Odlum was a militiaman, a civilian in uniform, whose interests were far broader than those of the regulars who confined themselves to polo, pigsticking, or ragging in the mess. Odlum had studied political science at the University of Toronto before becoming a reporter on a Vancouver newspaper. Such were his abilities that he rose in three years to become its editor. By the time war broke out, he was owner and editor of the *Vancouver Star*, but that did not consume all his energies. On the side he sold bonds and insurance.

He was also a bookworm who would later boast that he managed to get through a volume every day of his life, a passion he could scarcely indulge in the hurly-burly of Vimy. But he came from a military family – various of his ancestors had served with William of Orange and Wellington and fought in the Upper Canadian rebellion of 1837 and the Fenian raids. Warfare fascinated him. It was said that he had taken to peacetime soldiering because it presented an interesting problem, that he had set himself the task of mastering the psychology of war. It is more than probable that this preoccupation led to the idea of the trench raids, which were really miniature battles, fought in minutes instead of hours, but combining all the characteristics of the more ambitious set pieces.

By the time he reached Vimy – an austere, thirty-seven-year-old brigadier-general with a lean, hawk's face, piercing blue eyes, and a hard, scarred body – Victor Odlum had seen a good deal of battle in South Africa and France. He had been wounded five times, had seen his own brother blown to bits by his side, had won the Distinguished Service Order, the army's second-highest decoration, and been mentioned in dispatches half a dozen times. He never ordered his men to do what he himself was not prepared to do. He refused to wear a steel helmet because he believed his men should be able to recognize him at all times and know where their orders were coming from. Like Lipsett, Odlum preferred to stay up front. He himself led some of the night raids for which he was famous and that were his chief contributions to the Vimy victory.

In the four months before the assault the Corps launched at least fifty-five raids on the German positions. The earlier ones were carried out by a handful of men; the later ones involved as many as seventeen hundred. The smallest took place on New Year's Eve, 1916. Two brash Canadians crept out into No Man's Land, wriggled under the enemy wire, jumped quietly into one of the forward German trenches, seized two sentries, and somehow managed to drag them back to their own lines for questioning.

The Canadians felt, with good reason, that they owned No Man's Land. The scouts of the 2nd Division grew so confident that they treated it as their private playground, standing up and taunting the Germans, daring them to come out, and tossing bully beef tins into their trenches wrapped with notes urging them to come over and enjoy some good food. The game was played all along the Vimy front: on one raid by the 4th Canadian Mounted Rifles two officers actually nailed up a sign in one of the enemy trenches: "COME ON OVER AND WE WILL TREAT YOU RIGHT."

The 46th Battalion, a particularly aggressive unit made up of Westerners from Moose Jaw and Regina, raided the Germans every time they moved into the line; but the Germans rarely raided and when they did, the raids were small – sometimes *very* small. There is a comic opera flavour to the image of one German patrol, consisting of a lone and bewildered Bavarian seen stumbling about No Man's Land by three amused Canadian scouts, into whose waiting arms he eventually blundered.

Because the trenches were as little as thirty-five yards apart, the Canadians were able to creep to the very rim of the enemy's defences to report on the condition of his wire or the presence of new machine-gun posts. The Germans fired flares and star shells in a vain attempt to seek them out, but every man had been trained to freeze into immobility when the flare exploded. As long as they didn't twitch, as long as they held their position – no matter how grotesque – and stayed that way until the flare faded, they were simply part of the moonscape.

The raids were vicious because the weapons used – the Lewis gun and the Mills bomb – were vicious. The common image of the Great War soldier is that of a man in a steel helmet carrying a rifle and a bayonet. In reality the helmet gave little protection while the rifle and bayonet were all but obsolete. Few soldiers were well enough trained to fire the Lee Enfield with any accuracy. On the range, men lay on their bellies under perfect conditions and banged away at stationary targets. At Vimy, they blundered forward in the gloom, firing on the move at indistinct figures that popped up for a moment, then vanished. Too much oil in the barrel or a slight breeze could deflect the fire of the steadiest marksman. It's safe to say that most of the enemy killed or wounded by rifle bullets were killed by snipers using the Ross or were hit at close quarters in the hand-to-hand fighting that took place in the trenches. But even here the rifle was an awkward weapon to handle in a narrow ditch full of struggling opponents.

The bayonet only added to the problem: a man was just as likely to gash a friend as an enemy. There were few bayonet wounds among the men treated in the Regimental Aid Posts and Casualty Clearing Centres. As one British general put it, "No man in the Great War was ever killed by a bayonet unless he had his hands up first." It was an excellent tool for opening bully beef tins, toasting bread, or prodding those who had already surrendered, but as an offensive weapon it was about as useful as a cutlass.

All of this makes the long political battle over the rival qualities of the Ross and the Lee Enfield seem beside the point. The rifle was a psychological weapon, not a practical one – "the soldier's friend," whose presence certainly gave him a sense of security. In the monotony of trench life, the infantryman worked out his frustrations by banging away at an elusive enemy. But in the trench raids across No Man's Land, it was the light machine gun and the hand grenade that did the job.

The Lewis gun was light, easy to carry, and could be fired like a rifle from the shoulder. It weighed twenty-six pounds and was only four feet long. It could get off all of its forty-seven rounds in a single devastating five-second burp, though the gunners were trained to use shorter bursts of five rounds. It gobbled ammunition hungrily: in major battles half a dozen men in the Lewis gun section were detailed simply to carry the panniers of .303 cartridges to feed it. But, with the Mills bomb, it could clear a German trench in seconds.

At close quarters, the Mills bomb was deadly. Shaped like an egg and about the size of a tennis ball, it had a shell constructed of cast-iron segments, which explains why Chicago gangsters later dubbed it a "pineapple." As long as the spring lever was pressed down the grenade was safe. The bomb thrower removed the pin, kept the lever down with his hand, straightened his arm and lobbed the bomb or simply dropped it into a dugout or trench. Four seconds later it exploded. More often the grenades were fired from a cup-shaped launcher attached to the muzzle of the rifle and propelled by the gases released by the explosion of a blank cartridge (a real bullet, of course, would have mangled the launcher and destroyed the barrel).

The Germans, whose equipment was superior in almost every instance to that of the Allies, had developed grenade launchers that had twice the range of those of the British. This bothered Lieutenant-Colonel Chalmers Johnston. The ingenious commander of the 2nd Canadian Mounted Rifles, better known as "Whizbang" Johnston, believed that the problem lay with the barrel of the Lee Enfield; it was just too long for the task. If the escaping gases could be confined in a shorter space, the thrust would be greater. Johnston proceeded to break the rules by sawing eleven inches off a rifle barrel, thus committing the heinous army crime known as "destroying government property." But the experiment worked; the shorter rifle hurled a grenade twice as far as the longer ones. Byng watched Johnston work with the new device and approved it, so that every rifle grenade section was equipped with sawed-off weapons.

Hollywood films have given the grenade awesome powers that it does not possess. It will not blow the tread off a tank, smash a building, or hurl a soldier into the air. What it does is quite gruesome enough. Dozens of bits of jagged pig iron whirling about and ricocheting can mangle everybody in a room, a dugout, or a section of trench. Seventy-five million Mills bombs were thrown at the Germans in the Great War. Like the trench raid, the grenade was not perfected until the war was two years old. It is hard to contemplate one without the other; they went together like bully beef and plum-and-apple jam.

2

Each raid was planned to the second. In some cases the raiders had to be back in their own trenches in as little as fifteen minutes from the moment they went over the top. This heart-stopping efficiency could produce dreadful tensions, as William Darknell discovered when he and twenty others were picked for a raid on the Prussian trenches below the Pimple early in 1917.

Private Darknell, English born, Alberta bred, was given exactly forty-five minutes to harass the Germans with Mills bombs and dynamite and to bring back as much information about the enemy lines as he and his fellow raiders could gather in that brief span. Well after dark, they hoisted themselves over the parapet and began crawling across the dead and silent world of blasted stumps, rusted wire, and stinking ponds until they reached the enemy defences, thirty-five yards away.

Darknell was flat on his belly, trying to squeeze under the massive rolls of wire that barred the way to the Germans' forward trench. He couldn't make it; entangled in the barbs he could move neither forward nor back. The clock was ticking. Darknell was painfully aware of his deadline. If a man didn't get back within the allotted minutes, others would endanger themselves by returning to No Man's Land to find him. But Darknell, at nineteen a veteran of almost two years and a survivor of the Somme, didn't panic easily. He began to snip methodically at the wire with his cutters until finally he was free. He found the German line, pulled the dynamite sticks from his pocket, helped to blow up a machine gun, and was gone, almost before the enemy knew what had happened. With the others he scurried to safety and reported to his company commander on the dot of the deadline.

Happily, on that night there were no casualties, but on most raids there were. When the same Calgary battalion (the 50th) sent one hundred men on another raid, only thirty-five came back.

It wasn't always easy to bring casualties back in the time allotted, especially when the wounded were as bulky as Lieutenant A.A. "Gonkie" McDougall of the Princess Pats. This massive officer, who weighed 230 pounds, was badly wounded on a ten-man raid in early December. When he rushed two German sentries on the lip of a crater, one managed to trigger with his foot a mechanism that dislodged a grenade from the parapet. The blast left McDougall terribly mangled and presented his comrades with a problem. They had only fifteen minutes for the entire raid. It would take at least four of them to drag him back. In spite of that encumbrance the raiding party made it home in the required time, having destroyed the post and killed the sentries. It was a point of honour for officers to scoff at adversity. "I shall be able yet to play nine holes of golf," McDougall remarked gamely as he was hoisted to safety. A week later, the wounded man wrote to his C.O.: ". . . my left leg is off, my right leg is shattered below the knee, my left arm is broken, I have some shrapnel in my hip, but otherwise I am jake."

The strict timetable made the raiders ruthless. When 150 men of the 26th (New Brunswick) Battalion punched a hole in the enemy's front line, thirty shell-shocked Germans fled to a dugout in the rear. The Maritimers had no time for niceties. When the Germans refused to come out, they sealed them in forever.

But it was attacks like these that achieved another purpose of the raids: to keep the Germans off balance, nervous, and jumpy, never knowing what was coming. The troops in the line could sense these jitters. A single bomb thrown close to the enemy trenches would often touch off the warning blast of a sentry's whistle; the Germans, their sleep disturbed, could be heard thumping along the bathmats to stand to in case of an attack that never came.

The heaviest casualties of the trench raids were probably suffered by the Japanese Canadians from British Columbia, who were determined to prove they were as good as or better than their fellow Canadians. Victor Wheeler of Calgary noted that of twenty-five Nisei assigned to his company in the 50th Battalion, only two or three survived. They were, in the words of the company sergeant-major, "a bloodthirsty lot of chaps especially in hand to hand combat." The trouble was they either ignored or forgot about the timetable and ended up casualties. One, a Sergeant Kaji, finally got permission to carry into battle the sword and special dagger used in ritual suicide that his father had carried in the Russo-Japanese war. Over the parapet Sergeant Kaji went, naked sword flashing in the moonlight, the dagger at his belt. He never came back.

It was part of the Canadian tactics to stage a raid at a time when the Germans least expected it – in broad daylight, for instance, or on Christmas morning. While other battalions were planning to meet the Germans in No Man's Land for a Yuletide truce, the lst CMRs – more than half the battalion – were pouring out of hidden tunnels on the attack. The raiders fought hand to hand with the enemy (who hadn't expected anything so diabolical), destroyed twenty-seven dugouts, a supply dump, and a machine-gun emplacement, and brought back fifty-eight prisoners, some of them lugging Christmas parcels. The whole affair lasted forty-five minutes. Six CMRs were killed, twenty-two wounded.

Another unexpected raid was carried out by the 50th in January. The Calgarians had learned from a prisoner that the Prussians were about to enter the line. "They'll show you what real soldiers are like," the POW boasted. The 50th immediately organized a raid to catch the enemy just as the changeover took place. The disorganized Prussians were still moving into position when the Canadians struck, seizing more prisoners for the intelligence staff.

The raids paid off. By March, Corps intelligence had accurate figures on the strength of the enemy as well as his intentions, the character of the reserves, times and places of relief, and the physical features of the German positions. Moreover, the men who would attack the ridge knew in advance every detail of the ground before them because they'd been over it time and again.

By March, too, the reinforcements were becoming battle seasoned, thanks to three months of trench raiding. Every raid was, in a sense, a rehearsal for the big moment. The techniques that would be used to capture Vimy Ridge were honed and polished in the careful training that preceded the larger raids. As early as December, five officers and ninety men of the 3rd Battalion from Toronto had trained for a week using a replica of the enemy trench system located by aerial photography. These practice trenches were actually dug and the men trained to leap into them, first with dummy grenades and later with live ones. Scouts who had been over the ground guided the attacking parties to within fifteen yards of the enemy wire. The attackers flung bathmats over this obstacle and were in the German trenches in just eight minutes. In that time they killed or wounded one hundred Germans, cleared one hundred and thirty yards of trench, and suffered thirty-five casualties. These were not seasoned veterans. Two thirds of the party were new men who had arrived just in time to be trained for the job.

3

The British, who had adopted the techniques of the trench raid, began to compete with the Canadians as if trench raiding were a kind of Olympic contest. When one Canadian unit captured a record hundred prisoners in a single raid, the British, a few days later, sent news from the Ypres salient that they'd taken one hundred and twenty.

Over the winter the raids grew more complicated. On January 17, Burstall's 2nd Division mounted a massive two-pronged attack involving more than a thousand men. It was preceded by a ten-day bombardment and consisted of two raids, fifteen hours apart. It devastated two parallel lines of German trenches spread over a mile of front.

In this way, the various elements that constitute an army corps learned the complicated art of working together. For the larger infantry raids involved all the elements of a set-piece battle: artillery support, creeping barrages, box barrages, indirect fire by machine guns, and all the supporting services, from the engineers who blew up mineshafts and emplacements to the stretcher-bearers and lorry drivers.

By February entire brigades were involved in trench raids. On the morning of the thirteenth, 870 men of the 10th Brigade, their faces blackened with soot, jumped off before dawn behind a pounding barrage. They included 200 infantrymen from each battalion together with pioneer troops and engineers. The raid had been carefully rehearsed; each man knew

122

his exact job. The raiding party smashed its way for almost seven hundred yards through the three parallel lines of the enemy's forward trenches, killing or wounding 110 Germans and capturing 50 prisoners. The raid was counted a success: Haig himself came down to inspect and congratulate the survivors. But the cost was high: the Canadians lost 150 killed, wounded, or missing.

The value of the raids as a training ground for other branches of the service was becoming obvious. That same February morning, the Canadian Black Watch of Montreal decided to take a signaller and an artillery observer with them on an attack against the German trenches. The signaller, who volunteered, was a tough little private from Brantford named Harry Coutts. The artillery observer was Lieutenant Conn Smythe of the 40th Battery, field artillery – the same Conn Smythe who would one day build the Maple Leaf Gardens in Toronto and become one of the best-known figures in Canadian hockey.

The Germans and the Black Watch faced each other from the rims of the craters that lay in front of their forward trenches. For several days the Montrealers had pounded the enemy with that all-purpose piece of trench artillery, the Stokes mortar, which could be fired from behind the security of the parapet, its range corrected by the use of a simple periscope. At 9:13 A.M., nineteen rifle grenadiers stationed in the forward craters opened up with a barrage of Mills bombs. Two minutes later, the artillery barrage began, and fifty members of the battalion headed across No Man's Land with Coutts and Smythe right behind them. Coutts carried a phone, stringing wire as he went, so that Smythe could report the effect of the fire close at hand rather than from an observation post farther back.

The first salvo looked too high. Smythe called back on the phone: "Drop two hundred." Immediately he saw white puffs of smoke among the attacking Black Watch. "My God," he thought, "I'm killing my own men."

Smythe had no wish to return to his own lines if that were true and so, drawing his revolver, he ran down among the raiders, peppering away at the Germans up ahead – a wiry bantam cock of a man, determined to expiate his error and sell his own life dearly.

At that point he discovered to his relief that the puffs of white were caused not by his telephoned correction at all but by German stick bombs bursting around him. He jumped into the nearest enemy trench, banged away, hit two of the enemy, ducked around a traverse, and ran straight into a huge German standing behind the parapet, his rifle aimed at the advancing Canadians. Smythe jammed his pistol into the German's belly, fired, and had the satisfaction of seeing the man slide to the ground, cursing him. Now, with Lieutenant Gillingwater, the leader of the Canadians, wounded and out of action, Smythe led a fighting withdrawal back to the Canadian trenches. He didn't use his revolver again until he reached the relative safety of his own lines. Then, in an act of defiance, he turned about, levelled his revolver at the enemy trenches, and squeezed the trigger. To his horror it gave only a click. A chill rippled down his backbone as he realized that he hadn't fired a shot since he'd hit the big German in the enemy trench. If he had got off just one more bullet in the wild dash before that fateful meeting, that click would have meant his own death and he, not the German, would have slid into the mud uttering one final curse.

From raids like this one the gunners gained practical experience in forward observation and telephone communication. Conn Smythe earned the Military Cross. And, because of a single bullet, Toronto eventually gained a new National League hockey team and an arena to go with it.

4

Were the trench raids worth the cost? Certainly they served a multitude of purposes: they provided valuable information about the enemy, they kept the Germans in a constant state of tension, they prevented the Canadian troops from growing stale, they taught both men and officers how to act under fire, and they gave clear proof to the various arms of the service of the value of close co-operation.

To Arthur Currie, the main – indeed, the only – purpose of a trench raid was to get information that would help prepare for the battle to come. He thought nothing of cancelling one raid at the last moment when he discovered that he already had the information the raid would have brought in. "I'm not sacrificing one man unnecessarily," he told his disappointed officers on that occasion.

But if a raid *didn't* give him the needed information he could be ruthless with his senior commanders, as W.A. "Billy" Griesbach, the one-time "Boy Mayor of Edmonton," discovered after his brigade had failed on several occasions to capture a single German.

"I want a prisoner, not for curiosity's sake, not to see what he looks like," Currie told Griesbach acidly. "I want to get from him information that will be of some use in the preparation for the forthcoming operation, so naturally I want a prisoner before Zero Day." If the battalions weren't successful that very night then, Currie ordered, they would mount raids every three hours until they *were* successful. "I want results and I want them now!" He got them.

But Arthur Currie thought the big raids took too large a toll. He clearly believed that most of the purposes could be achieved by the smaller raiding parties that his own division mounted.

This brought him into open conflict with Byng, who was convinced that the large raids contributed to the morale of the troops. Currie's stubborn refusal to bend caused the first violent row between the two. Byng claimed that the 1st Division "was losing its go" and told Currie off. Currie held his ground as he vainly tried to search for a match to light his pipe; he was clearly shaken by Byng's tongue-lashing. Nonetheless Byng, who believed in giving his divisional commanders their head, let him have his way with his division.

In the last two weeks before the Vimy attack, the Canadians lost 1,653 officers and men killed, wounded, or missing – the equivalent of almost two battalions. Most of these casualties were the result of trench raids – a high price to pay for the results achieved. The raids were certainly necessary – but were they necessary on a grand scale? Against the educational advantages achieved through interservice co-operation must be weighed the weakening of the fighting battalions in the fortnight before the battle. The casualties in those last two weeks included seventy-one officers, all trained men, who would not be present to lead their units on April 9. And against the morale-building qualities, which Julian Byng extolled, must be balanced the morale *lowering* that occurred when a raid went sour or too many men were lost.

The largest raid attempted by the Canadians at Vimy took place on March 1, five weeks before the attack. The casualties were appalling and the raid itself was a ghastly failure, an object lesson in how *not* to conduct a raid, or, as it was called at the time, a "reconnaissance in force." A quarter-century later the same phrase would be used to describe the Canadian raid on Dieppe in the Second World War. The reasons for that famous failure bear a distressing similarity to the March 1, 1917, raid: postponement because of weather, leading to a lack of surprise; failure to soften up the target before the assault; the stubborn insistence by the High Command, in the face of repeated warnings, to carry on regardless of consequences; and lastly, the hollow justification – that valuable information and experience was gained.

The March 1 raid was a mammoth endeavour involving seventeen hundred men of the 4th Division, half of them plucked from the 11th Brigade, whose commander, Victor Odlum, was the chief exponent of the trench raid, which he'd developed in his days as a battalion C.O. with the 1st Division.

Their task was to reconnoitre and damage the German defences on the slopes of Hill 145, the whale's hump of Vimy Ridge, which Odlum's brigade was scheduled to attack on the morning of April 9. Surprise was to be the key. Since it was felt that a bombardment would alert the Germans, there was to be none. Instead, clouds of poisonous gas – chlorine and phosgene – would be released from cylinders in the Canadian trenches to smother the German positions. The wire would be cut by the attacking troops using tubes filled with ammonal, a high explosive.

It would all be a piece of cake – or so everybody was told. Jack Quinnell, the red-headed scout from Toronto who helped bring the tanks forward, was told that the new gas – phosgene – was colourless, noiseless, and completely deadly. "All you have to do once this blows across is just go as if you were on the parade ground," Quinnell was told. It was said that the gas would corrode every rifle and field gun on the enemy front line – that the troops' chief task was simply to snip the epaulettes from the uniforms of the dead for identification, then skip back home for breakfast.

This was mainly hokum. Yet those in charge believed the hokum, pinning their faith on the ultimate weapon, as commanders had before them and have since. Magically the clouds of gas would render the enemy impotent and allow the troops to saunter across the enemy lines unmolested. But it didn't work out that way. It is dangerous for generals to believe in magic.

The awkward gas cylinders, known to all ranks as "rats," were carried forward on the backs of sappers – "the frightfulness squad," as they were dubbed. The cylinders weighed 160 pounds each – as much as a middleweight boxer at the top of his class. Each was suspended from a long bar that banged against the tank as the back-packers struggled forward, braving the wobbling duckboards of the Zouave Valley and exposed to German fire for most of the four miles between the dump and the front line.

The cylinders, in batteries of four, would spew out their poison through the nozzles of rubber tubes, to be thrown over the parapet when the attack began. The idea was that the gas would blow across No Man's Land and penetrate for three hundred yards into the German lines. It did not seem to occur to anyone that the gas, being heavier than air, has difficulty climbing hills and has a tendency to drift into low-lying areas such as shell holes – the very depressions the assaulting troops would use for cover. Even if the weather were perfect for the occasion – a steady, gentle breeze blowing eastward –

the situation would be dicey. But the weather wasn't perfect; it rarely is in battle. The wind refused to co-operate: it was variable; it blew the wrong way; it became too strong to be effective. The attack was postponed for three days and then, when the weather remained variable, for another two.

The night of February 28 arrived. By this time there were several unfortunate complications. The troops, having stood out in the cold and the mud for several days, were weary, wet, and dispirited from the strain of waiting. The cylinders had been leaking gas, and some men became ill. Worse, everybody in the back areas seemed to know all about the coming attack. Jack Quinnell was asked constantly by the French villagers: "When's the gas attack coming off?" If they knew, surely the Germans knew.

Worst of all, the weather deteriorated. By now a strong wind was blowing *toward* the Canadian lines, and it was obvious, at the battalion level, that an attack would be suicidal. The battalion commanders realized this and protested. Lieutenant-Colonel A.H.G. Kemball, the crisply handsome C.O. of the 54th Kootenays, tried to convince the brass hats in the rear that the raid should be postponed or cancelled. The higher ups would have none of it.

If Kemball went through channels, as he must have, his protest would have been made to his brigade commander, Victor Odlum, the master of the trench raid. Thus Odlum must bear some of the responsibility for the carnage that followed, though David Watson, the divisional commander, is also not free of criticism since this was a divisional raid, involving four battalions from two brigades, only one of which was under Odlum's command. There is no evidence that either Watson or Odlum proposed a delay (although there are hints that the army command, under the British general, Henry Horne, continued adamant). But there is plenty of evidence that Kemball protested.

Why was the raid allowed to go on? Partly because of the distance of the generals from the front line. Few red tabs were ever seen in the forward trenches (though Byng was certainly an exception). Staffs fought paper wars with plasticine models, safe from the moan of the minnenwerfers or the whine of the whizbangs. Yet Odlum had the reputation of being a front-line brigadier-general, and Odlum let two of his battalions go forward to certain destruction. Why?

The answer has to do with the impetus of battle and the mind-set of the military. At certain points, events take on a momentum of their own that is difficult to arrest. A general hesitating on the eve of battle is like a bride who goes to the altar realizing at the last moment that she no longer loves her intended. Can she really undo all those weeks of planning, cause a scene that will humiliate her friends and relatives, and turn herself into an object of scorn and laughter? The logistics alone are complicated. What happens to all the wedding invitations, the plans for a reception, the food that has been ordered, the dresses the bridesmaids have paid for? Perhaps, after all, the marriage will work out – easier to go on than turn back! It takes a strong-willed and courageous woman to change her mind at this point – and a courageous military leader to cancel a complicated operation.

The will and the courage were lacking in the dark hours of the morning of March 1, 1917. Currie, who had a reputation for standing up to his superiors, might have averted the tragedy that followed. Watson didn't. Too much planning, too much effort, too much training had gone into the operation. Surely after all that brawn and brainwork it couldn't fail! No doubt the wind would change. Surely the Germans were ignorant of the impending attack. No doubt the troops would act as supermen and carry the day. And so the division gambled, as Mountbatten was to gamble at Dieppe and (to be fair) as Eisenhower was to gamble on D-Day, 1944. After all, Byng himself had said it was better to do *something* in a crisis than nothing; and if this attack came off there would be kudos and probably promotions for all.

So Kemball was ignored. That gallant officer – the adjective in his case is deserved – defied orders and refused to stay in the rear when his men were in peril. He led them personally on an attack he knew was futile.

For the Germans knew everything. They had heard the

clanking of the gas cylinders being brought forward days before. They knew the details of the plan from two of their own men, prisoners who had escaped from the compound and made it back to their own lines. They heard it from the chatter of the Canadians, caught on listening devices in the tunnels below the trenches. And so they set up new machine-gun posts, which they kept masked until the very moment of the battle. The young men from the Kootenays, the Seaforths from Vancouver, the boys from Mississauga, and the Highlanders from Montreal were mowed down almost before they left the security of their own lines. And when they tried to take cover in the shell holes they died horribly. The gas – the ultimate weapon, which was supposed to nullify all opposition – was waiting for them in the slime.

5

The human details of the gas attack are heart breaking. The poisonous clouds were released in two waves, the phosgene first at three that morning, the chlorine two hours later. It was more than ineffective; it killed the men it was supposed to cover. The first cloud hung heavy over the battlefield; the second was blown back in the faces of the advancing troops.

On the left of the line the Seaforths were badly mauled. They were supposed to jump off at 6:40 after the gas had saturated the enemy. But ten minutes before the assault, the Germans laid down a barrage on the Seaforth positions. The shells hit the gas cylinders, which exploded, putting half of "B" Company out of action. Because these men, strangling in the fumes, could not go forward, "C" Company behind them couldn't go either and had to abandon its part in the raid.

Behind the lines, in the 50th Battalion from Calgary, which was held in reserve, Victor Wheeler lay in his bunk of chicken wire, waiting for the order to move into the trenches and go over the top. It seemed to that sensitive young signaller that every vestige of humanity was perishing that dark morning.

130

Troubled and confused, he prayed for forgiveness for mankind even as the specialists nearby were discussing the details of releasing the gas from the cylinders. All Wheeler could think of was the young men who would soon die in agony. It did not occur to him that it was his own comrades who would succumb.

Not far away, in the forward trench of Lieutenant-Colonel Sam Beckett's Mississauga Battalion, the eighteen-year-old scout, Jack Quinnell, heard a tremendous roar and realized it was the sound of gas escaping from the cylinders. Quinnell ruefully remembered the briefing he'd received. "Where's all the quiet gas they told us about?" he asked himself. Was everything else they'd told him equally false? He peered over the top, saw the gas creeping into the shell holes, and realized he'd been sold a bill of goods.

Victor Wheeler, too, heard a frightening noise, like the sound of water rushing over rocks. But this was not the sound of escaping gas; it was far more horrifying. This was the noise of dozens of rats scrambling in terror into the entrance of the dugout, tails twitching, instinctively fleeing from the poison. They scurried under the blankets and ground sheets, hid under the signal boxes, and squeezed under any loose board. Unlike the troops, they sensed disaster.

The two battalions of Victor Odlum's 11th Brigade went over the top after the gas was released and following the briefest of barrages – a mere seven minutes of shellfire. Sam Beckett, the commander of the 75th, followed Kemball's example and insisted on leading his men personally in an attack that he too knew had little chance of success.

Kemball's Kootenay battalion was immediately mowed down by the German machine guns. These had been sited on the pathways through the Canadian wire, a task made easy by the presence of large battalion signs marking the attack routes. Only five men of the Kootenay battalion actually reached the enemy front line. Of these only three managed to scale the parapet, all dying in the attempt. The surviving pair miraculously escaped, crawling back from shell hole to shell hole, through their own gas and the enemy fire. Of the four hundred and twenty members of the battalion who took part in the attack, more than two hundred were casualties, including thirteen officers. Kemball himself had died, as he almost certainly knew he would, caught on the German wire.

The 75th from Mississauga, on the Kootenays' flank, was also badly cut up. When Jack Quinnell went over the top, gas mask firmly in place, he could see his friends dropping all around him. Then his vision blurred as his mask fogged. He flung it aside, dodged ahead coughing and choking until he found a hole to shelter him from the withering gunfire. The training program's orderly progress by section, platoon, and company bore no relation to the ragged and confused mob of men crawling and stumbling back and forth between the opposing lines. Quinnell's shell hole was already occupied by his own officer, who turned to him and said, "I'm going to make a run for it; you can do what you like." He stood up, started to run, and was felled by an enemy bullet.

Jack Quinnell had no intention of following his example. At eighteen he was an old soldier who'd enlisted at sixteen, young enough to be called "baby face" by his comrades. Now a veteran, he carried the more adult nickname of Quinnie. Wounded at the Somme, he knew enough to keep a low profile and so removed his steel helmet and crawled on his belly, nose in the mud, until he saw the sign marking the gap through which his battalion was supposed to advance.

This was one of the markers that had alerted the Germans, who had trained machine guns on the gaps. The closer Quinnell got to his battalion sign, the more corpses he encountered. He caught his breath: there, on a pile of dead, lay the body of one of his closest friends, George Meade; and there, too, was the corpse of his C.O., Sam Beckett, who'd been killed trying to collect his scattered troops. One of Beckett's men was trying to cut his way through the wire to reach his colonel's body, but the German machine-gun fire frustrated the attempt.

Meanwhile, Victor Wheeler, hearing the cry "Stand to!" had strapped his Lucas lamp to his belt, fingered his telegraph key, stuffed four grenades into his pocket, and prepared for the attack. The first wave of phosgene had been let off in the face of a terrible German barrage and now the second wave of the less deadly chlorine was ready to go. But the wind had risen and changed, and the phosgene was already blowing back in the faces of the Canadians. It made no sense to release any more. The Calgarians tried desperately to climb over the parapet; it was not possible in the face of the German barrage. The first six men to reach the top were killed instantly. Others were collapsing in the green clouds of phosgene blowing back upon them. But Wheeler and his comrades were luckier than most; they lived, those who were not gassed, to fight another day.

Jack Quinnell found himself in an apparently hopeless situation. Looking back he could see fresh troops being hurried into the division's empty front lines–a precaution against a German counterattack. Somehow he managed to crawl back under the wire, coughing and choking, his buttons and brass insignia green from the gas, his eyes in dreadful shape. It was daylight when he fell into the forward trench. Somebody handed him a large insulated jug of tea. He swallowed a mugful and immediately vomited over the man who gave it to him. He continued to vomit, and that probably saved his life. But for all of his years, his lungs would bear the scars they sustained before dawn on the first of March, 1917.

Others weren't so lucky. The dying and the wounded lay out in No Man's Land, waiting for help that never came. Phosgene is an insidious gas, eighteen times as powerful as chlorine. Its effects build slowly: breathing becomes shallow, the victim begins to retch, the pulse rises to 120, the features turn ashen grey; over the next forty-eight hours the victim drowns slowly as the lungs discharge pints of yellow fluid. As the day wore on, the suffering of those who had been gassed increased as the phosgene ate into their lungs.

Such scenes of adversity in battle are always illuminated by small epics of courage and endurance. Six hundred yards behind the German front, two privates of the Seaforths, Black and Debouchier, found themselves stranded, cramped and muddy, in a shell hole with a wounded comrade. They would not leave him and so lay out all through that long, hideous day. When dusk fell they drew lots to see which would go for help. Black won and somehow managed the extraordinary feat of crawling for six hundred yards right through the enemy trenches, dodging between groups of Germans, guided only by the stars. At one point, the sleeping enemy soldiers were so tightly packed that Black had to crawl up and down the back wall of the trench seeking a place to slip through. He made it at last to his own barbed wire, convinced the sentry that he was friendly, and then, in spite of the fact that he was grey with fatigue, insisted that he lead a party back to save his friends. His pleas were denied: any attempt that night would have failed. Black's comrade, Debouchier, was captured. The wounded man died. Black survived to be killed in the mud of Passchendaele.

Two days later, at ten o'clock on the morning of March 3, when the gas had dissipated and No Man's Land was a silent, corpse-littered waste, the Germans offered a truce to allow the Canadians to bury their dead. Representatives of both sides met under a Red Cross flag at a spot equidistant from both lines. The Germans – all picked men in smart new uniforms – carried the Canadian dead and wounded half-way across and handed them over to their enemies, who picked them up and carried them to their own trenches. The body of Lieutenant-Colonel Kemball was treated with great respect by his adversaries; one of the Germans who spoke English mentioned the commander of the Kootenay battalion by name, an indication of the laxness of security that had preceded the attack.

Lieutenant David Thompson, a bank clerk from Niagara Falls, was present at that truce. It gave him a queer feeling to be standing there in the broad daylight, not on his stomach but upright, without a shot being fired over that pock-marked field. It was almost as if he were in a dream. It was strange to see the Canadians exchanging cigarettes with the men they had tried to gas to death, but there they were, attempting to talk to any who spoke English. The German brigadier, who had been stationed at Esquimalt before the war, asked after old friends. He had words of praise for Travers Lucas, a Hamilton officer who had led his men gallantly to the wire – a practice uncommon in the German army. The officer, a Bavarian, spoke perfect English, having been educated at St. Paul's, a famous British public school. He didn't like the war, he said, hoped it would be over soon, and remarked how queer it would be to go back to the lines when the truce ended at noon, to, in his phrase, "pot at one another again." The whole affair was rather like the atmosphere in a public house after a football game, when the players of both sides gather for a beer to discuss the contest. It lasted two hours and was hurriedly cancelled when the High Command got wind of it and ordered the immediate resumption of hostilities. But the guns were silent for the rest of the day; no one on either side had any stomach for further shooting.

The losses in the raid were staggering – 687 casualties out of a total of 1,700 attackers, including the very serious loss of two seasoned battalion commanders. The abortive attack had greatly weakened the 4th Division, a tragedy that had its effect on the battle that followed five weeks later.

The press, of course, treated the raid as a victory, as the press always did. *The Times* reported that "the whole affair was carried out with great gallantry" and wrote of the heavy casualties inflicted and "valuable information gained."

Such reports incensed Captain Andrew Macphail, who confided his disgust to his diary. "Nothing could be more utterly false," he wrote. "The dispatch is the grossest and lowest form of journalism."

CHAPTER SIX

Not What They Expected

1

The news of the failure of the March 1 gas raid swept through the lines like a sour wind. The men of the 4th Division, especially, were shaken. If an attempt of that size and complexity could fail so dismally, what hope was there for a larger venture? But the trench raids continued. More men died or were wounded or went missing – captured by the enemy, or ground into the mud of No Man's Land to be lost forever, no more than a name on a post-war monument. By the end of March the total casualties would number the equivalent of two infantry brigades.

The men in the trenches lived with death – and slept with it. Jim Curtis of Calgary was so cold and so tired one night that he crawled under the blankets with a group of strangers only to discover the following morning that they were all corpses awaiting burial. It did not faze him. Will Bird's first task on arriving at the Vimy front had been to gather up in bags the legs and flesh of three men who had been shredded by the premature explosion of their own mortar bombs. A group of ten gunners digging a pit for a trench mortar in a French cemetery worked their way down through six layers of corpses and thought nothing of hanging their canteens on protruding shinbones: the dead were part of the landscape.

Fresh troops poured in to fill the gaps left by the casualties. In Canada, those who had once been rejected as unfit found themselves wooed by the army. Healthy-looking civilians were reviled as slackers. There was increasing talk of conscription.

Out of Halifax the convoys steamed, loaded with reinforcements bound for England and, after a few days of training, for the French port of Le Havre. Here, in the first week of March, a draft of new recruits disembarked, destined for the signals section of the 42nd Battalion, Royal Highlanders of Canada, better known as the Black Watch. Among them was a twenty-one-year-old Scottish-born Canadian from Sherbrooke named William Breckenridge. A quiet, down-to-earth young man, Bill Breckenridge had arrived in Canada at the age of nine and had completed a course at the Ontario Business College in Belleville when the war broke out. He'd been in training ever since enlisting in 1915, and at Le Havre the training continued for another ten days before the reinforcement draft was ready to move to the front. By this time Breckenridge and his fellow signallers were sick of training and eager (if a little nervous) to encounter the real thing. But first they had to suffer the usual pompous send-off. As they stood fidgeting on the parade ground, the commanding officer appeared, hoisted himself onto a box, and made the kind of speech that commanding officers like to make and private soldiers don't care to hear:

"Now men, you are going to the front. You are going to get your heart's desire – a crack at the Hun and a German helmet. . . ."

It began to rain. the C.O. kept it up over a chorus of taunts and grumbles.

"Tell it to Sweeney!" somebody shouted. "Let's get going." But they couldn't get going until the C.O. had finished and the padre had spoken a necessary word of prayer.

Breckenridge and thirty-nine others were herded into a boxcar marked 8 CHEVAUX OU 40 HOMMES—ARMEE ANGLAISE. For the next twenty-four hours, a rusty engine pulled its cargo at six miles an hour in a series of fits and starts to Doullens, where the guns of the Somme front could still be heard rumbling in the distance, and then on for another day, past shattered villages to Bruay in the heart of the mining district of northern France. This was the end of the line. As the Canadians tumbled off the boxcars, Breckenridge got his first glimpse of war – a German airplane directly above him dodging the black puffs of smoke sent up by the anti-aircraft batteries.

They slept that night in a barn, sheltered from a sudden

blizzard. The following morning, as the sun cleared away the snow, they set off on foot, a twenty-mile march to the battalion rest area near the town of Mont St. Eloi, some six miles behind the Vimy front. Long before noon, Breckenridge could feel the straps of his eighty-pound pack biting into his shoulders, as, one by one, the weaker members of the group fell by the wayside, exhausted.

As the others trudged on, the sights and sounds of war increased and the tension began to build. Observation balloons floated above the battle lines (''canteens for the aviators'' one old-timer told a gullible rookie). Little trains rumbled by on narrow-gauge rails, loaded with shells. Long lines of battle-weary men began to appear, their faces grey with exhaustion, their uniforms spattered with mud, their puttees protected by ragged sacking. More planes buzzed overhead; lorries and limbers jammed the roadway. The new men threaded their way through the increasing traffic until they reached what was left of St. Eloi. There they enjoyed a bit of food and an hour's rest before setting out again.

Suddenly, just past the ruins of Villers-au-Bois, there came a dramatic change, as if a gigantic but invisible hand had rung down a heavy curtain. All sound ceased. All signs of life vanished. The road was empty of traffic, for it was still daylight and the German positions astride the famous ridge were only six miles away. The marching men had come within the reach of the enemy guns and had entered the ribbon of stealth.

They had no choice but to continue. To keep casualties to a minimum, the draft was divided into parties of five, each marching at an interval of one hundred yards. In this fashion they reached the rest area, known as the Dumbbell Camp, unscathed. Here, in a swampy wood, the Black Watch was bivouacked – indeed, imprisoned. Because the entrance to the wood was in plain view of the German positions, no one could move out of the camp during the daylight hours.

Breckenridge and the other rookies spent the night in bivvies no more than three feet high, built of sandbags and draped with tarpaulins. To his dismay, the camp was a swamp.

The ground squished beneath a foot of water, and the troops waded through the resulting muck to their knees. Nevertheless, Breckenridge thought to himself, if the others can stick it here, then there's no use of me complaining.

That night the Canadian artillery opened a practice barrage to get the range of the German trenches. The noise was almost unbearable. Breckenridge felt as if he were in the middle of a blast furnace. In the distance, he could see the German flares go up, calling on their own guns to retaliate – a brilliant display of rainbow colours against the night sky.

What would war be like? he asked himself. He tried to picture the scene, with shells falling all about him, wounded comrades being carried from the field. He had heard that men were sometimes buried in their own trenches during a strafe. Could those stories be true? Thirty minutes after it began, the barrage ended, and the troops slept.

The rest period was over; orders came to move into the front line. One night at dusk, the battalion marched off by companies in single file through roads clogged with traffic, until the long communication trench that the French had named Pont Street was reached, and the files moved into the labyrinth of the Vimy trench system.

They had entered what might be thought of as the business section of a small city – a large city, in fact, by 1917 Canadian standards, as large as Vancouver and larger than any other Canadian community except Montreal, Toronto, and Winnipeg. In this eerie metropolis, silent by day, a-buzz and a-clatter by night, one hundred thousand khaki-clad citizens were hived.

Here a confusing network of trenches and sunken roads, more than two miles thick, so complex that men could easily get lost in the maze without a guide, wriggled and squirmed through the mud along the four-mile front. This was the heart of the city that Breckenridge's battalion now entered. Behind lay the suburbs from which they had just emerged, a land of billets, rest areas, and training centres, the haunt of heavy artillery and brass hats.

The city came complete with streets and avenues, each

with an identifiable name: Indian Trench, Border Lane, Stargate Street, Spadina Avenue, Tottenham Road, Gallows Gate. Most lay eight feet below the surface; some were not even open to the sky, for the city was underlain with tunnels and caves, some used from medieval times. Even as the Black Watch negotiated the trench system, thousands of men were slaving beneath their feet, chipping away at the soft chalk, probing closer to the enemy lines. The Germans, too, were hacking away underground, lengthening their own tunnels on the forward slopes of the ridge, seeking their enemy in a subterranean war of nerves that would last until the day of the offensive.

It was a gloomy world that Breckenridge entered, devoid of any hue, a monotonous, mud-coloured monochrome. The trenches were mud coloured, the water in the shell holes was mud coloured, the dugouts were mud coloured; the men themselves in their muddy khaki with their mud-coloured helmets, mud-coloured packs, and mud-coloured webbing blended with their surroundings. Everything – trains, ration boxes, guns, even the sullen skies above – was the colour of mud, and so were the rats that scuttled through the mud-coloured garbage.

The trench system was like a grid that had been squashed out of shape by a giant's paw. Three more or less parallel lines of trenches – forward, support, and reserve – faced the Germans, all linked and criss-crossed by the long communication trenches, such as Pont Street, down which the Black Watch sloshed and stumbled.

This cobwebby maze was never static. Many trenches were disused, others falling in, still others being obliterated by shelling. Lines that seemed firmly planted on the map scarcely existed on the ground. Dug and re-dug, battered and cratered, half filled in, they reverted to the mud and were abandoned or became part of another trench line.

As the battalion drew nearer to the front there came the faint rattle of machine guns and the whine of the occasional bullet directly overhead. All talking ceased as the troops in crouching position negotiated the wooden trench mats that lay in the slime beneath their feet. Occasionally a whisper was passed back from the company commander: "Step down, hole in mat," or "Wire underfoot." Sometimes the file would break and all would halt until it closed up. In the distance, Bill Breckenridge could see the sky light up as a star shell fell over No Man's Land.

As the company entered the forward lines, the only sound was the thud of heavy boots. The front lay just ahead. Beyond that were the great mine craters in which sentries were posted. Beyond that lay the dead world of No Man's Land, and beyond that, invisible in the darkness, the great bulk of the ridge.

The battalion that had been garrisoning the line was about to be relieved by the Black Watch. "Relieved" is the proper word, for relief was written on the faces of those who had survived a week of standing at the alert, eating cold food, sleeping in their clothes, twelve hours on and twelve off, never free of rats, lice, rain, snow, or mud and the constant hammering of the guns – the drumfire of their own artillery and, far worse, the roar, whine, crump, and moan of the German mortars, minnies, howitzers, and whizbangs plus the sharp stutter of the machine guns and the snap of the snipers' bullets.

Guided into the forward trench by old hands detailed for that purpose, Breckenridge could hear the nervous whispers around him: "Does he shell around here?" "What sort of place is this?" "Isn't it quiet?" And the varying answers: "It's a little hell at times," or "He hasn't made a direct hit yet," or "It's jake-a-loo around here."

As the battalion settled down, Breckenridge decided to wait and form his own opinion. Soon he had become an old hand, standing from dusk to dawn in his soaking boots, never changing his clothes or taking off his equipment for the six or eight days spent in the line, climbing up on the firing step when his turn came, clambering over the parapet at night to join a wiring party, learning to freeze at the burst of a flare in No Man's Land, and waiting his turn on that last nervous night for the new relief to arrive – a long, uneasy vigil, when the minutes seemed like hours and the guides, with their welcome group of followers, seemed to take forever to arrive.

2

By the time Bill Breckenridge joined the Black Watch in March the tempo of work and planning had reached a new pitch of intensity. The troops did not know the exact date of the attack – it had, indeed, been postponed for several days – but they knew it was coming soon. Those who were not shivering in the front lines toiled and sweated in the rear. For this was a drudge's war, and that had not occurred to those who rushed to the colours in the early days. Many had been raised on tales of derring-do in *The Boy's Own Paper* and in the novels of G.A. Henty: nothing there about hacking away in tunnels and gloomy caves, laying rails, toiling on road gangs, hauling back-breaking loads for miles over rough terrain, or swinging a pick or shovel for hours on end.

The Canadians hated pick-and-shovel work: many had joined the army to get away from it. They had come to fight, not to scrabble in the dirt. Once at the Somme, after they'd been ordered to dig in, aerial photographs revealed a line of ineffectual scratches rather than the well-sited and deeply dug trenches that were called for. Julian Byng examined one photograph, then turned wryly to a group of Canadian officers.

"You Canadians are a very brave people," said the general. "You would, I know, fight and die if necessary to the last ditch. But," and he raised his voice, "I'm damned if I can get you to *dig* that ditch."

They hadn't bargained on ditch-digging, nor had they contemplated burrowing underground like so many moles, squeezing through narrow, airless passageways, clawing away at the dripping chalk walls.

But if the ridge was to be taken the work had to be done. The army, which scorned euphemisms, called it "fatigue." It was especially fatiguing for those who had joined those branches of the service that seemed to be the least irksome and possibly the safest: the medical corps, the cyclist corps, and the regimental band. Most of these ended up with a shovel in their hands or a burden on their shoulders.

There was a great deal of this fetching and carrying in spite of the fifty thousand horses and the narrow-gauge railways. It irked a young staff captain in the 11th Brigade named F.R. Phelan to think of the hours used up in lugging ammunition from the wagons and railheads. Here were hundreds of soldiers, slogging along in pairs, each pair carrying two boxes of ammunition between them in a sling made with their rifles. Here were others, toiling through the mud, bowed down with heavy packloads of supplies biting into their shoulders. Surely there was a better way!

And of course there was. Like Whizbang Johnston, Phelan decided to build a better mousetrap. On camping trips in Quebec he had seen Indians loping through the bush with their backs straight, the weight of their packs distributed evenly by means of a broad strap supported by the forehead. After Captain Phelan demonstrated this Canadian tumpline, the method was adopted, special tumpline companies were formed, and thousands of man-hours were saved.

And every man-hour was needed if the Corps was to be ready by Zero Day. Like any other small city, Vimy required a network of supporting services. Unlike other cities it needed them in a hurry – and all at once. Water-mains had to be constructed, reservoirs dug, pumping stations installed. There were roads to be built, ties to be tamped, rails to be laid, tramways to be put into operation. Sweating troops buried twenty-one miles of electrical cable in trenches seven feet deep and strung eleven hundred miles of telephone wire, some of it carried on aerial supports, which also had to be erected. And all this work had to be carried out at night in the cold by men constantly slopping about in water or muddy gruel and under constant fire.

Water alone was a major problem. Every man needed five gallons a day, every horse ten gallons. That meant a total of one million gallons daily, but the planners, with grisly realism, cut it to six hundred thousand, knowing there would be daily casualties among both men and animals. The horses, tied in unprotected lines, were especially vulnerable and died by the hundreds.

The water came from springs behind the lines, but it wasn't easy to move it forward. Twenty-two pumping stations were installed and forty-five miles of pipeline built, every inch of which had to be buried three feet below ground level. Two reservoirs, each holding fifty thousand gallons, had to be dug by hand. And every piece of equipment – every nut, every bolt, every foot of pipe, every bracket – had to be brought in by road, hauled by horses or on the backs of men.

The engineers built, maintained, or improved thirty miles of road in the shadow of the ridge in full view of the enemy. Heavy guns dragged over a well-laid thoroughfare could pulverize it in a single night, destroying the work of weeks. Thus the roads were constantly in need of repair.

War had obliterated the old drainage system of Artois. In the Zouave Valley and in the farmland beyond Neuville St. Vaast, the ground was so sodden that no amount of rubble or metalling could have kept the roads from sinking into the muck. Here, the double plank roadway so familiar to frontier Canadians saved the day. Men who had once worked in the forests of the Maritimes or the timberlands of Western Canada were enrolled in a forestry company, felling old trees in the Bois des Alleux. Portable sawmills set up in that forest turned out one hundred thousand feet of rough planking every week – enough to build three miles of plank road and to supply timber for tramline sleepers and tunnel supports.

Without the main plank road, the problem of getting men, ammunition, and supplies forward before the battle would have been horrendous. Once twilight fell, the finished thoroughfare came alive with wagons and limbers threading their way between working parties and troops shifting positions at the front. No lights were allowed. If a driver dozed and his vehicle slipped off the planks and into the mud, the traffic jam lasted for hours.

Another unit, the Canadian Corps Light Railway company, operated the tramway system that the engineers had extended to a length of twenty miles. Concealed in the forest known as the Bois de Bruay, not far from Ecurie, a mixed bag of Canadian businessmen, train dispatchers, and Western railroad hands now turned soldier operated a hidden terminus twenty-four hours a day. Just after dark, the engines puffed off, loaded with shells for the gun positions, on a circular route from Byng's advanced headquarters north to the Zouave Valley and back. The tramway had another, grimmer task. Three hundred pushcarts were built to fit the rails so that wounded men could be trundled smoothly and efficiently to the casualty clearing stations when the attack began.

3

Long before the Canadians arrived, the opposing troops on both sides of the ridge had fought an underground war in the soft chalk that underlay the Vimy battlefield. The Canadians kept it up. By March the entire sector was a Swiss cheese of galleries, dugouts, subways, and narrow tunnels in which men toiled and scrabbled. The smaller tunnels that reached out from the front lines toward the enemy positions were known as "saps," a derivation from old French meaning "an undermining." The sappers' task was to undermine the enemy – to tunnel beneath him, eavesdrop on his plans, or plant an explosive charge and blow him up–in short, to sap his strength.

All along the front line in these claustrophobic passages, men were scratching away at the chalk, pushing farther and farther into No Man's Land, listening for the sounds of their German counterparts, fearful that the enemy's mines would explode first before their own were prepared or that they would unwittingly break through into a nest of armed Germans. It was heart-stopping work, as Will Bird discovered.

He would never forget a night he spent with a work party underground. For weeks afterward, whenever he thought of those moments his whole body would grow tense. For two years Bird had tried desperately to get into the war, after being turned down early in the game. Now, having finally made it, he found himself descending a dizzy ladder into the half-light of a fetid subterranean passage. The air was dank and close, and even before he flung off his greatcoat he was bathed in sweat. He and the others tied sacking over their boots to muffle all sound and then, crouching on their knees, began to spray the face of the chalk with vinegar. The sap was just four feet high and three feet wide, so tight that the men had to work in turns. One scraped away the softened chalk and passed large chunks of it back to his helper, who in turn passed it farther back. The last man in the crouching file laid it on a small trolley, which, when loaded, was hauled silently back on its rubber-tired wheels along a narrow track of two-by-fours to the hoist.

All night long the men worked, cramped, sweating, and wordless. Silence was mandatory, for the Germans were also underground only a few feet distant, chipping away.

Bird and the others had a second task: they had to get rid of the tell-tale chalk. If the German air observers spotted it – and it was easy to spot – they'd know the whereabouts of the sap. Some could be hauled forward and thrown on the trench parapets. Some could be carried to the rear and taken by rail to points beyond the lines. But the most ingenious method of concealment was no concealment at all. The spoil from the saps was dumped in the shell holes; from the air the white chalk in the pale light could not be distinguished from muddy water.

Like Will Bird, Leslie Hudd, the cyclist, was scared stiff all of the time he worked in the saps. His job was to place a geophone (similar to a doctor's stethoscope) against the chalk wall to find if the Germans were tunnelling near him. As long as he could hear the scraping of their knives or the gutteral whispers of their conversations he was content. But when the scratching stopped, the hair stood up on his nape and he sounded the alarm, for it meant that a mine was about to blow.

The geophone picked up the tiniest noises, as another cyclist, Dick Warren, discovered. Warren was assigned to keep watch in a tunnel under the twin Crassiers craters on the 1st Division front. This tunnel was already mined but was not to be blown until the moment of the attack. Thus it was necessary to patrol it in case the Germans broke through. It was, as Warren discovered, a lonesome and eerie job. Carrying

146

his candles, his flashlight, and his geophone equipment, he crawled up one branch of the tunnel only to find it was flooded. Suddenly his candle sputtered and died: *Gas!* He scurried back into a right-hand branch until more gas stopped him. He retreated again, cleared a space on the floor for the equipment, lit a cigarette, leaned against a pit prop, put the plugs in his ears, and listened to the enemy mumbling away on the other side of the wall. In the wavering candlelight he could see reflected the red eyes of his only companions, the scores of rats crouched just beyond his reach. Their squeaks, magnified by the geophones, sounded like high-pitched battle-cries.

At this point nature called, and Warren answered without moving from his spot. Suddenly, in his ears, came the frightening rumble of rushing water. Panic! He remembered the flooded tunnel branch and knew he was doomed to drown with the rats in this subterranean trap. He tore the earphones from his head and abruptly the noise stopped. Only then did it dawn on him that the flood had been of his own making, magnified by the listening device.

When Dick Warren's tour was over and he reported back to the engineer officer on the surface, he was grateful for the tot of rum that was always proffered. It was strong stuff. Any man who could choke out a thank you after knocking back the rum was allowed a second tot – a "door prize" it was called. But try as he might, the shaken Dick Warren was never able to put away a second.

These jobs were not quite what the young recruits had expected. George Henry Hambley, the pious young man from Swan Lake who had been shocked by the brothels in Neuville St. Vaast, had joined the cavalry, considered the most dashing branch of the service, yet he seemed to spend most of his time not on a spirited steed but deep in the bowels of the earth working ten-hour shifts until he turned ghastly white from lack of sun. And when his work party was sent out of the line for "rest" at Divion, he became a carpenter, rising at six and toiling until dusk, building horse troughs. After that there was cavalry drill. When Hambley forgot to remove

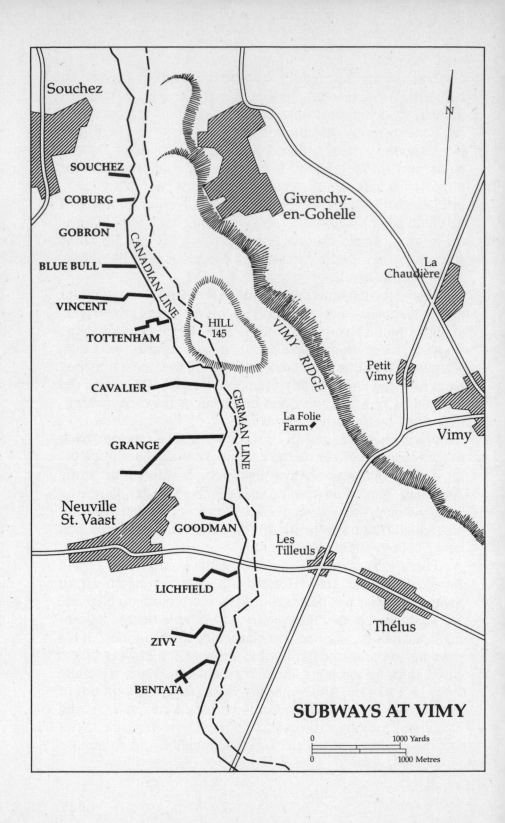

Souchez

SOUCHEZ

COBURG

GOBRON

BLUE BULL

VINCENT

TOTTENHAM

CAVALIER

GRANGE

Neuville
St. Vaast

GOODMAN

LICHFIELD

ZIVY

BENTATA

CANADIAN LINE

GERMAN LINE

HILL
145

VIMY RIDGE

La Folie
Farm

Les
Tilleuls

Givenchy-
en-Gohelle

La
Chaudière

Petit
Vimy

Vimy

Thélus

N

SUBWAYS AT VIMY

0   1000 Yards

0   1000 Metres

the heel strap from one of the animals he was exercising, the sergeant gave him extra fatigues cleaning the messroom. When the "rest period" was over Hambley faced a five-mile march back to put in another ten days in the saps.

To reach the sap, Hambley entered the vast Zivy Cave, half-way between Neuville St. Vaast and the front, and followed the Zivy Subway right to the edge of No Man's Land, safe from German shell and sniper fire. This was one of a series of large subways being built or extended by the British tunnelling companies in the Canadian sector to connect the back trenches with the front line. The tunnellers were aided by Canadian work parties, many of whose members were familiar with the coal mines of Nova Scotia or the railway tunnels in the Rockies and the Selkirks.

At first these great subways were seen merely as a safe method of moving troops into the forward positions. By January, however, the planners had become convinced of their tactical value. With the ends of the subways sealed off, the assaulting troops could be hived in the tunnels in the small hours before the attack. Then, at Zero Hour, the mouths of the tunnels would be blown out and the attackers would pour out into the heart of the battlefield.

By late March, the tunnellers had completed twelve subways to the forward line and in some cases past it. Their total length was 10,901 yards or just over six miles. Working at top speed, stripped to the waist in the dank and often suffocating atmosphere, the tunnellers achieved miracles. In one subway they managed to hack through forty-six feet of chalk in a single twenty-four-hour period.

The subways varied in length from the little 290-yard Gobron Subway in the northern sector to the vast Goodman and Grange Subways each with a mile of tunnelling. In most subways, with their six-foot-six-inch ceilings, the tallest man could stand erect. Most were three feet wide, some three and a half. Nine were lit by electricity from gasoline generators. All had telephone communication to the rear and many were equipped with narrow-gauge railways. The shallowest was twenty feet underground, so deep that the

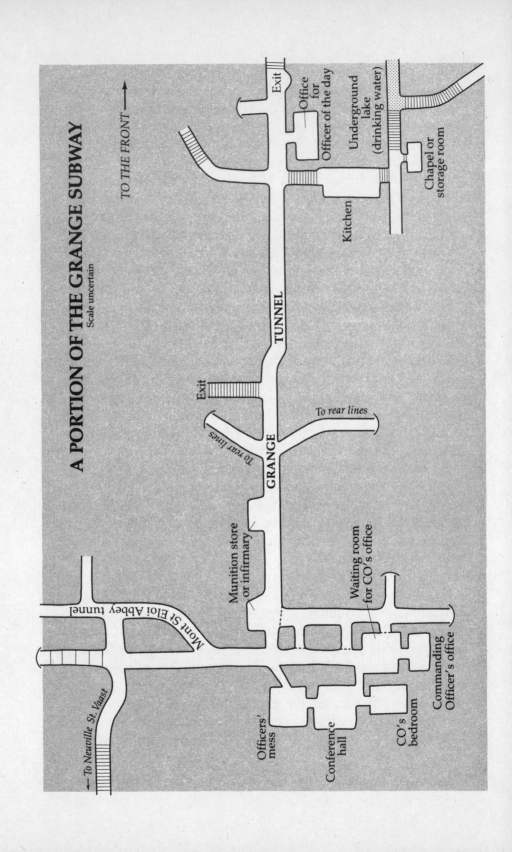

A PORTION OF THE GRANGE SUBWAY
Scale uncertain

TO THE FRONT →

Exit

Office for Officer of the day

Underground lake (drinking water)

Kitchen

Chapel or storage room

TUNNEL

GRANGE

Exit

To rear lines

To rear lines

To rear lines

Munition store or infirmary

Waiting room for CO's office

Mont St Eloi Abbey tunnel

To Neuville St. Vaast

Officers' mess

Conference hall

CO's bedroom

Commanding Officer's office

sounds of war vanished and only the trembling of the earth hinted at the shellfire above. At the northern end of the sector, where the ridge rose most steeply, some subways were fifty feet and more below the surface.

The subways were so labyrinthine, with lateral galleries and dugouts running off the main stem, that signs had to be posted and guides stationed to prevent troops from losing their way. The famous Grange Subway, first to be completed, provides a good example. The main stem of the Grange was 750 yards long, but the galleries that ran laterally totalled another 600 yards. Off these galleries were vast chambers, 80 to 150 square feet in size, housing trench mortar emplacements, ammunition stores, officers' dugouts, dressing stations, reserve ration dumps, even kitchens. In addition to the tramline and electric wiring, a four-inch water-main led to a 1,500-gallon tank beneath the floor of one of the rooms.

As the subways nosed their way toward No Man's Land, the tunnellers sometimes came upon existing caverns, some of which went back to the sixteenth century, when the Huguenots, fleeing from their Catholic persecutors, used them as hiding places. The old villages were underlain with a rabbit warren of caves and passages quarried from the soft chalk that had given Neuville St. Vaast the title of the White City. It was said that even in 1917 you could walk ten miles from the Grange Subway on the 3rd Division front to the Spanish caves near Arras without ever emerging into the sunlight.

The caves were earmarked as assembly points to harbour troops in the second wave of the attack as well as various headquarters staffs. The largest was the vast quarry known as the Zivy Cave, so big it could hold five hundred or more men. When he first saw it, Duncan Macintyre of the 4th Brigade staff, which would have its headquarters in the cave during the battle, thought immediately of Ali Baba and the Forty Thieves. At night when the generator was shut off and hundreds of candles guttered from ledges in the walls, it more than lived up to the Arabian Nights comparison.

More than ninety steps led down to the main chamber of the cave whose twenty-foot ceiling, supported on chalk pillars, was lost in the gloom. Hundreds of men working on the Zivy Subway that led from the cave to the front line or, like George Hambley, in the mine galleries that ran under No Man's Land, slept in the cave between shifts. Macintyre, who first visited the cave in February, found a company of infantry sleeping, cooking, eating, playing cards, cleaning rifles, and carving their names and regimental numbers on the chalk walls. Here were bunks, tables, cook stoves, telephones, and running water, everything essential to the day when two brigades and five battalions would have their headquarters here and half a thousand men, held in reserve, would wait poised to reinforce their fellows trudging up the slopes of Vimy Ridge.

4

When the saps were blown, new depressions appeared in No Man's Land, just beyond the forward line, to join the ragged succession of gigantic craters that ran the whole length of the Canadian sector. These water-filled hollows, some deep enough to swallow a four-storey house, seemed to have been carved out by meteorites or volcanic action. Many were legacies of the British, who had exploded earlier saps to nudge their front line a few yards closer to the Germans.

For the soldiers of both sides who clung to the opposite lips of the craters, sentry duty was particularly trying. One never knew what was going on below the ground. Was it the enemy boring away beneath your feet or your own people? It was silent work, squatting on the crater's edge, unable to cough or smoke. A sneeze could give you away. Wet, cold, and cramped after their tour, the sentries must then work their way cautiously back, crater by crater, to the comparative safety of their own front lines.

The crater line constantly changed shape as new cavities were formed and older ones refashioned. Each crater had a name and even a personality. The older ones had been named by the French and the British (Duffield, Durand, Crassiers);

the new ones bore Canadian names. Earlier that season, George Hambley had watched the Montreal Crater blown: "The whole earth shook and heaved and erupted, blowing up at least 50 yards of trenches." Unfortunately the sappers blew up more than they intended, burying a number of Canadians. Hambley, who helped dig some of them out, almost lost his own life in the shower of earth and stones thrown up by the explosion. A hand-to-hand fight followed for possession of the crater. When the Royal Highlanders of Montreal seized it and drove off the Germans, the crater was named in their honour.

The tunnelling companies had tried to make the craters easier to defend by consolidating and reshaping the old ones. The resulting explosions were Brobdingnagian. They had used eleven thousand pounds of the high explosive ammonal to create the Longfellow Crater out of four earlier depressions on the 3rd Division front. It was well named, being two hundred feet long and twenty feet deep.

The neighbouring Patricia Crater was named for the Princess Patricia's Canadian Light Infantry, the unit that had seized and held it after it was blasted out of the mud. Two parties of the battalion, each consisting of thirty men, dashed through lanes previously cut in the wire, ran across several smaller shell holes spanned by duckboards, and seized the lip of the new crater. The first man to reach it, Private Walter Scott, was actually under arrest for drinking too much rum. But all was forgiven when the seventeen-year-old Scott returned with three blood-spattered German helmets. A few days later, 1st Army headquarters honoured the unit by giving its name to the crater.

Battalion commanders had mixed feelings about the craters. They could be an impediment to the assault; they could harbour German machine gunners and snipers; and wounded men could (and would) drown in the water that collected in their depths. On the other hand, the craters could provide shelter for the advancing troops, who zigzagged forward from one depression to the next, and they could even harbour elements of the assaulting force before Zero Hour and –

if a safe entry could be found – signal crews and telephone lines as well.

The ingenious Captain Duncan Macintyre, who had been promoted to Brigade Major of the 4th Brigade, discovered such a safe entry by simple deduction. As he pored over a series of aerial photographs, his trained eye prompted an inspired hunch. Directly in front of the Zivy Subway he noticed the presence of the Phillips Crater, the product of a French mine explosion months before. It occurred to Macintyre that the French couldn't have blown that mine under the German lines unless they'd first dug a sap out from their front line in which to carry and place the explosive. The end would have been blown up when the ammonal was touched off, but the rest should still be intact.

Macintyre got the old records from the French, located the sap, and set his men to digging down to find it. Sure enough, the little tunnel was there, three feet wide, three feet high, still timbered. It ran for two hundred feet out into No Man's Land, its forward end still blocked by the debris of the explosion.

Working in absolute silence (for no one knew whether the Germans had a listening post above it), the tunnellers grubbed their way through the rubble, shaving off the chalk with their bayonets, scooping it up silently with their hands, and dragging it away in gunnysacks until, with a rattle of falling earth and timber, they saw a tell-tale glimmer of light at the tunnel's end. That night they returned to find that they had indeed broken through to the Phillips Crater, on whose far lip a German sentry was posted. This meant that the signals party, which followed the attacking troops, unrolling spools of telephone wire, could reach the crater from the reserve lines without being exposed to enemy fire.

Macintyre was typical of the young breed of civilian officers who were breaking new ground at Vimy. He came from pioneer Canadian stock. His grandfather was a Hudson's Bay trader and his uncle, the famous Walter Moberly,* had helped

* See *The National Dream,* pp. 156-64.

survey the original Pacific railway line through the Rockies. Resourceful and independent-minded, Macintyre was unfettered by the barrack-room mentality. He had been on his own since the age of seventeen on survey gangs in the Quebec bush and on the rail line north of Lake Superior. As a storekeeper in Moose Jaw and later a real estate salesman,* he'd watched the West develop from empty prairie to boom country. He'd had little military experience when he joined the army, but as Brigade Major he acted, in effect, as the general manager of a military corporation that employed several thousand men.

He set to work to wire the new tunnel, making sure that a heavy cable line should run all the way from brigade headquarters in the Zivy Cave to the new Phillips gallery, two hundred feet beyond the forward line. Here switchboards could be set up and surface lines run forward to follow right behind the attacking units on the day of the battle. Macintyre had hundreds of feet of cable and several telephones ready for the moment when the brigade punched through the German front defences. In that way, he hoped to avoid the snarl of surface wire that had frustrated communications in earlier battles.

Macintyre had written a booklet on communications with the help of an old school friend, Captain Talbot Papineau of the PPCLI, a grandson of the leader of the 1837 rebellion in Lower Canada. The Corps used the booklet, but its keenest student was Macintyre's own communications officer, Ken McKinnon, a young subaltern from Nova Scotia.

McKinnon was obsessed by the need to get back word from the front, both to brigade headquarters and to the artillery. In the confusion of battle this would not be easy. Because no single system could be considered foolproof, McKinnon came up with no fewer than *seven* ways to get word back: by runner, by semaphore, by pigeon, by aircraft signals, by telephone, by wireless, and by Morse buzzer. It was, Macintyre always insisted, a record in ingenuity, and it

* See *The Promised Land*, p. 323.

155

would be no more than enough. On the day of the battle, when the barrage deafened the ears, drowned out all speech, and inhibited communication, these seven options could help make the difference between success and failure. Useful though it would prove, Macintyre's plan held one hazard neither he nor anyone else foresaw: when the signalmen emerged from their haven far out in No Man's Land, the advancing Canadians might mistake them for the enemy.

CHAPTER SEVEN

Things Worth Remembering

1

In one of his handwritten memos to himself entitled "Things Worth Remembering" the methodical Arthur Currie had included as Item 3: "Thorough preparations must lead to success. Neglect nothing" and as Item 19: "Training, Discipline, Preparation and Determination to conquer is everything."

He could not accept the excuse given at the Somme, where entire brigades had advanced blindly in neat waves to vague spots on the map with no clear idea of the tactics or strategy of battle: the men, it was said, were not sufficiently trained for anything more sophisticated. To this alibi Currie had a blunt response: "Take time to train them."

As a result, the thoroughness and scope of the training that took place on the broad slopes in the back areas of Vimy that March were entirely new to the Western Front and, indeed, the British Army. Troops had rehearsed battles before, using tapes to represent enemy trenches, but never with such detailed, split-second timing.

Miles of white and coloured tapes and thousands of flags were used to mark out full-scale replicas of the German trench system. Suspected mine positions, buildings, topographical features were all pinpointed, thanks to the information received from the trench raiders and from the photographs taken by the Royal Flying Corps. Enemy forward, support, reserve and communication trenches were outlined with tape. Every stronghold, every pillbox, every redoubt, every barbed-wire entanglement known to the Canadians was marked and labelled. Big signboards named the German trenches; coloured pennants outlined the enemy positions – red for trenches, blue for roads, black for dugouts, yellow for machine guns.

By the end of March entire divisions were going through manoeuvres. The advance behind the creeping barrage had to be choreographed to the split second; men's lives depended on it. Officers on horseback carried flags to represent the advancing screen of bursting shrapnel. Behind them the troops walked slowly – not in line but in groups ("lumps," to use Gregory Clark's descriptive phrase) – carrying their rifles at the high port, bayonets fixed, ready to shoot or lunge when the red tapes were reached. Over and over again they practised the "Vimy glide," walking at the rate of one hundred yards every three minutes, while the instructors checked their watches, halting the troops to allow the barrage to lift, then ordering the advance again. Beside them other officers with megaphones pointed out strong points and suggested methods of dealing with them.

Perfect timing was essential. If the troops moved too quickly they would be killed by their own artillery. If they moved too slowly they wouldn't be able to pounce on the German dugouts before the enemy recovered. As Julian Byng put it, "Chaps, you shall go over exactly like a railroad train, on the exact time, or you shall be annihilated."

Officers were under orders to grill their men to be sure they knew exactly what to do and where they were at every stage of the advance. Duncan Macintyre, during his brigade's turn at the tapes, picked one man at random during the practice advance and asked him where he was supposed to be. "On the Red Line, sir," came the reply, indicating the second objective of the division.

"Right," said Macintyre. "And what are you going to do?"

"Stay right here and hang on like hell."

The troops grew weary of the repetition. Harold Barker, the RCR scout who had joined the army from homesickness, pronounced himself heartily fed up with it; he was to change his mind on the day of the battle. A.E. Wright, a private with the 18th Battalion from Western Ontario, asked himself, "What are we doing?" and agreed with his friends that they were just playing games. Harry Wilford and his fellow soldiers in the 28th Battalion, all from the Canadian North West, treated the whole thing as a joke. Leslie Hudd found his boots wearing thin because his unit was an hour's march from the training area. The constant rehearsals added to the drudgery. Although Currie had insisted that troops in training be relieved of heavy fatigues and given as much rest as possible, there were still sandbags to be filled, dugouts to be propped up, and parapets to be repaired.

Nonetheless, as the training progressed, the men began to gain a sense of confidence. "We are going to give them a tremendous licking right here," one stretcher-bearer wrote on March 29. "[I] am absolutely sure of it; every tiniest detail is perfect . . . confidence is absolutely the limit – everyone is laughing and cheering like a bunch of kids." His enthusiasm is striking, for the weather that day was dreadful. In the training areas, only ground sheets rigged up as makeshift tents sheltered the infantry from a howling wind.

One reason for their high morale was Currie's insistence on a return to the pre-war tactics of fire and movement at the platoon level. The basic technique is easily described: while part of the platoon keeps the enemy occupied with heavy fire, the others sneak around his flank and rear to bomb him into submission. In the stationary war of 1914, these tactics had been discarded or forgotten, but Currie saw how useful they could be in dealing with isolated machine-gun nests or other pockets of resistance that might hold out during the advance. An old maxim was dusted off: reinforce success, not failure. If a brigade or a division was held up during the attack, the units on its flanks would not stop, as they had been ordered to do at the Somme. Instead they would defend their own flanks with machine guns but continue to push on, encircle and mow down the resistance.

For the first time, junior officers, NCOs, and ordinary soldiers would all be given specific responsibilities. On Currie's advice each platoon was reorganized into a self-contained fighting unit made up of a lieutenant, three sergeants, fifteen riflemen, eleven bombers, eleven rifle grenadiers, six Lewis machine gunners, two scouts, and a stretcher-bearer, all of whom could be interchangeable in the event of casualties. By the end of March, every platoon and every section had developed into a tightly knit group of cronies who knew each other well and knew exactly what their job was to be in the battle that followed.

There was more to this than a mere increase in efficiency, and no doubt Currie sensed it. For he had stumbled, perhaps unwittingly, on a principle that was only partially understood even in the wars that followed: the reason why men fight – why, in the face of all human logic, they continued, in that war as in other wars, to stumble forward into the whirlwind. They did not do it for patriotism or love of country. They did not do it for mothers, fathers, sweethearts, or wives. They did not do it for the colonel, the lieutenant, the sergeant, or even the corporal. They did it for their closest friends – the half-dozen private soldiers with whom they slept, ate, laughed, worked, and caroused, the men in their own section – grenade throwers or riflemen or Lewis gunners – whom they could not and would not let down because in moments of desperation and terror their virtual existence was woven together as tightly as whipcord.

Two generations would pass before the psychologists came to understand what Currie had sensed. Had they listened to the survivors of the Great War, who talked so wistfully, even longingly, about the comradeship of the trenches – a comradeship so intense they were unable to duplicate it in civilian life – they might have reached their conclusions far earlier.

The platoon system adopted at Vimy had broader implications. Claude Williams, writing home as early as January, had quoted Byng as saying that ''war in the future more than ever will be won or lost by platoon commanders.'' It was a prescient remark. In the peacetime army, the veterans who stayed in uniform taught the platoon tactics adopted at Vimy. In the next war they were the basis for what came to be known as ''battle drill.''

The Canadians had an advantage over their Allies. The social gap in the British army had led to a communication problem that affected the course of battle. On the first brutal day at the Somme, when officer after officer was mowed down, few rankers knew enough to assume leadership. At

Vimy, Currie and Byng were determined that no one would be kept in the dark.

Canadians were baffled by the haughtier members of the British officer class. Captain Andrew Macphail, McGill professor and medical officer at Vimy, wrote in his diary in March 1917 that a certain British quartermaster-general, Lieutenant-Colonel E.L. Hughes, "is as foreign to me as the Prussian is to the German." According to Macphail, Hughes "fails to conceal the contempt he feels for all who were not born in his own parish and attended the same school; but he is quite sure that they will accept that contempt as being perfectly natural and proper, and so take no offence."

It did not pass unnoticed, either, that the British Guards officers insisted on being saluted in the trenches – something the easier-going Canadians dispensed with – and that those Imperial officers attached to the Corps sometimes ordered extra fatigues or other penalties for soldiers caught with mud on their greatcoats. Such officers did not last long in the Canadian lines: those who weren't sent back to the British Army were shot in the back by their own men.

There was an easiness between the Canadian officers and men that was foreign to both the French and British forces. At times the Canadian Corps seemed like one big family where everybody knew everybody else – like William Klyne, a sixteen-year-old stretcher-bearer with the Royal Regiment who got into action only because the C.O. was his sister's boyfriend.

Any graduate of Sandhurst would have been shocked right down to his polished boots by a scene that Gordon Beatty, a gunner with the 5th Field Battery at Vimy, witnessed in the battery's orderly room. Beatty's driver, Private Dan Surette, asked to be paraded before the commanding officer on "a personal matter." Beatty marched him in, saluted smartly, and reported: "Driver Surette to see you, sir."

Whereupon Private Surette turned to the C.O., extended his hand, and said, "Got a chew, Colonel?"

"Sure," said the Colonel, reaching into his hip pocket for a plug. "Just keep it, Dan," he said as he handed it over.

161

The two men were old friends who had both worked for the town of Moncton, the C.O. as a city clerk, the driver as a garbage collector.

At 1st Army headquarters, Canadian sergeants and brigadiers rubbed shoulders as they clustered around a plasticine model of the Vimy sector, showing the German trench system and all the topographical features – every contour and fold in the ground – together with every strong point and pillbox. Byng himself often turned up to explain and to guide. "Make sure that every man knows his task," he would say. "Explain it to him again and again. Encourage him to ask questions."

The Corps commander had devised a catechism, which he handed out in pamphlet form at officers' training courses. The would-be subalterns were required to ask themselves a series of questions beginning: "No. 1: Do I know all the NCOs and men in my platoon? Do I know my snipers, bombers, Lewis gunners, scouts and rifle grenadiers? Have I practised with my platoon in getting out of their dugouts quickly to meet an attack, and does each man know where to go?"

That a junior officer should know all the men under him seems elementary today, but in the British Army in the Great War, the platoon commander was more often than not a vague and distant upper-class figure who spoke with a different accent and dealt with the men only through his sergeant.

"Are my men full of keenness and as happy as I can make them?" the eighth and final question in Byng's catechism asked. "Can I say that my platoon is one of the smartest, most efficient and most aggressive in the corps?" As the training period drew to a close and Zero Day approached, this keenness was evident. The knowledge that nothing had been overlooked had seeped down to the newest private soldier and contributed to the high morale of the Corps. In no previous British offensive had so little been left to chance. Every possibility, it seemed, had been considered. The Canadian gunners had been taught how to dismantle and use captured German artillery pieces. In a nearby wood, platoons took a unique course in bush-fighting, stalking hidden machine guns through the trees and knocking down dummy snipers with live ammunition. Byng, who had booby-trapped the Turks at Gallipoli, gave lectures warning men to shun attractive souvenirs. And the gunners were cautioned not to increase their fire in the hours before the attack because that might alert the Germans.

Four days before the assault, Andrew Macphail recorded his awe over the meticulous preparations for the battle: "For two months I have had the plan of the battle before me in as much detail as if it were the plan of a house which an architect proposed to build," he wrote. "The disposition of every man in the corps is settled and the moment for his movement arranged. Therefore every incident has its meaning for me and the significance of it is dreadful." For medical men like Dr. Macphail would have to deal with the by-products of battle, the maimed and the mangled, brought back from the shambles of the ridge, blood-caked and mud-begrimed, clinging desperately to life in the overcrowded casualty clearing stations just behind the field of slaughter.

2

While the foot soldiers rehearsed their roles in the drama to come, Andy McNaughton, the shaggy counter-battery officer, worked with his staff trying to nail down the position of every one of the German guns, sited along the ridge or hidden in the woods under the steep eastern slopes.

When McNaughton returned from his journey of inquiry at Verdun and the Somme, Byng had relieved him of all paper work and given him carte blanche to order all the guns and ammunition he needed to knock out the enemy batteries. His was a close-knit unit made up of men who had known each other in civilian life. His headquarters, by all accounts, was a lively place. What other senior officer on the Western Front kept a pet lion cub under the packing cases that did duty for his desk?

The animal had been brought back from Paris by Mc-

Naughton's staff captain, a former Prince Albert lawyer named Lennox Napier, who had clearly enjoyed his spot of leave. Napier and some friends, after a night on the town, saved the cub from execution at the Paris zoo; now it spent most of its day under McNaughton's feet and, in spite of the fact that it was in no way housebroken, became a fixture. Great hilarity ensued when the cub began to snap at the shins of an air intelligence officer named Davidson. Poor Davidson would leap on a nearby table to screams of laughter. When McNaughton and Napier toured the back areas by car, the lion sat between them in the back seat, attracting more than a little attention from the gaping troops along the road.

This gregarious and open atmosphere was bound to attract to McNaughton's circle those dedicated scientists who felt themselves less than comfortable working with the hidebound senior officers of the British Army.

The idea that you could actually pinpoint the position of an enemy gun and then knock it out was considered radical nonsense by the old-line British gunners. "Is there some kind of Free Masonry between the artillery of both sides?" Arthur Currie asked his artillery adviser in 1915. "They fire at the opposing infantry but never at each other." A young Canadian, Harold Hemming, a McGill graduate serving in the British 3rd Army, had been experimenting with flash spotting, a method of locating a gun position by triangulating its muzzle flashes; but his general was not impressed. As he put it to Hemming, "You take all the fun out of war."

But McNaughton was an old friend of Hemming's and, unlike some of the conservative gunners, was eager to listen to his theories. He was equally impressed by a remarkable trio of scientists whom he persuaded to quit the British and join his staff at Vimy. These three men – Lawrence Bragg, Charles Galton Darwin, and Lucien Bull – all became life-long associates. They left the British Army because they were tired of being ignored as dangerous radicals and because they knew that the conditions for their research would be much improved under a man who was himself a scientist and who rejoiced in an elastic and questing mind.

164

These men were experts in the new science of sound ranging – the companion to Hemming's flash spotting. Bragg, whose father was a celebrated physicist, was only twenty-seven but already held a Nobel prize for physics. Darwin was the grandson of the author of *On the Origin of Species*. Bull had invented the first sound-ranging recorder.

The key to sound ranging was the oscillograph, the same instrument that McNaughton had studied at McGill. But the novel idea of carrying a delicate device similar to an electrocardiograph into the lines, setting it up, and depending on a photograph of the vibrations to identify the enemy gun emplacements was, in McNaughton's own words, considered "treason, literally treason." The scientists were virtually ignored by the British. They had no real quarters, no dugouts, no friends. McNaughton changed all that, made them welcome, looked to their comfort, and encouraged their experiments.

Both sound ranging and flash spotting are complicated procedures. The latter required a series of posts all along the front, each equipped with telephones and surveying gear and a reporting system back to a panel of lights at headquarters. So accurate did this system of lights and buzzers become that the Canadian artillery was able to locate a German gun position to within as little as five yards.

The sound-ranging technique was even more complicated. When an enemy gun opened up miles away an entire sequence of events took place. A man in a listening post, often out in No Man's Land, pressed a key activating a recorder at McNaughton's headquarters. A series of microphones, placed all along the front a mile and a half back of the forward line, picked up the sound in turn as it travelled. From the time intervals between the microphones the gun's exact location could be spotted. Similarly, the sound waves sent out by a shell bursting on the Canadian side, and picked up by a succession of microphones, could locate the target.

There were many problems. Some shells travelled faster than the speed of sound, some slower. Heavy winds, temperature and pressure changes, the contour of the ground, the very condition of the layers of air above the battlefield – all these affected calculations. In spite of this, the scientific wizards who had joined McNaughton's team were able to calculate not only the position of the enemy gun but also its type, its calibre, and the target on which it was registered. Under good conditions they could do it in three minutes, spotting the location within a twenty-five-yard circle.

A steady flow of information from other sources poured into McNaughton's headquarters – from the men who raided the enemy trenches in the dark of the night, from sweaty documents and maps ripped from German corpses or liberated from captured prisoners, from the coded reports of secret agents, and finally from the young men of the Royal Flying Corps, winging as close as they dared to the enemy lines.

Aerial photography was in its infancy. The pilot shot his stereoscopic pictures using a cumbersome camera lashed to his cockpit directly behind the observer. It was dangerous work – each reconnaissance plane required a cover of five fighters – and it was exacting. Because the battlefield contained so few recognizable features, each photograph had to be carefully identified, otherwise it would be almost impossible for the gunners to string all of them together in an accurate pattern.

The observation balloons, tethered to the ground and manned by men with strong field-glasses, overlooked the ridge itself. From a mile up, the observers could see far behind the German lines; but they were not popular, especially with the red-tabbed staff officers who were unaccustomed to up-front warfare. The balloons were sitting targets for the Germans' long guns, and more than once a senior officer ordered their removal. Nonetheless, they provided the counter-battery unit with a stream of information.

McNaughton, who didn't like balloons, forced himself to spend hundreds of hours floating above the trenches, training his field-glasses on the enemy areas. He had some close calls. Yet his life would be saved and he would live to fight in another war because of his own scientific abilities and the knowledge he amassed at the Vimy front.

He was soaring four thousand feet above the enemy lines when a gigantic shell exploded not far from the basket in which he and the balloon commander crouched. A few feet closer and both would have been blown to bits. McNaughton realized that it was the first of a salvo, and so the pair lowered themselves gingerly over the side of the basket, preparing to parachute to earth. At that point, McNaughton froze. His hands refused to loosen their grip. Both men decided there and then that a drop would be more terrifying than the German shelling. They pulled themselves up by their shins and fell back into the basket.

McNaughton knew that he had to get the gun before the gun got him. He began working feverishly to locate its position from its flash, timing the arrival of the shells by their explosions and telephoning the information to his counter-battery staff on the ground. It must have given him enormous satisfaction to see the Allied long-range guns bombarding the German position and to realize that because of his expertise the shelling of his balloon had stopped and he was safe.

Once the hidden guns were located, the trick was to hit them, blow them up, force the enemy to repair or move them, hit them again and again, and during the final assault, to make things so hot that the enemy gunners couldn't operate. This all required stunning accuracy – the same accuracy that would be essential when the troops moved forward under a canopy of flying steel, exploding only a few yards ahead. If the range was slightly off or the shells faulty, men could die at the hands of their own gunners. All generals in the Great War expected a certain number of casualties from friendly fire; it was the artillery's job to keep these to a minimum. The French, it was reckoned, lost fifty thousand men killed by their own shells, the result of faulty arithmetic. Discarding obsolete methods, the Canadians brought science to bear on the art of gunnery.

Though they did not look it, these huge artillery pieces were sensitive weapons. The old hands didn't treat them that way. Corrections for wind, weather, and barrel wear were primitive. As McNaughton later put it, anybody who tried to develop greater accuracy in shooting "was looked on as somebody who ought to have his head read – this wasn't war at all, this was some sort of fandango going on."

But McNaughton persisted. To a layman, his meticulous experiments are breathtaking. One example is his investigation into the problems of barrel wear. As a gun barrel wears from constant use, its muzzle velocity drops and the shells start falling short. This can mean in the case of an 18-pounder, firing at a range of eight thousand yards, a loss of three hundred yards during a gun's life – enough to kill all the troops moving behind the curtain of shells. Yet that is only an *average* barrel; some wear out faster than others. For this reason the tables showing gun corrections are not meticulously accurate.

Here McNaughton's scientific background came into play. He was familiar with a device known as a Boulengé electrical chronograph with which he could measure the time it took a shell to pass through two electrically charged wire screens. That knowledge enabled him to figure out the actual muzzle velocity of each weapon. As a result, every key gun in the Vimy battle would be individually calibrated.

The old rules of thumb were no longer good enough. At the outset of the war the British field gunners had laughed at the idea of making any allowance for weather. Even as late as 1915, when the Royal Flying Corps offered to pass on the details of wind velocities each morning to the heavy artillery, the staff reply was: "We cannot make use of this information." Astonishingly, the Somme was the first battle in which the artillery took weather reports into account.

Yet a falling barometer could make a difference of three hundred yards on a five-thousand-yard shoot, while a strong wind could push a big shell fifteen yards off target. McNaughton and his counter-battery staff changed all that, adjusting the range tables to correct for weather and revising the dangerously inaccurate French maps. This was another reason why air observation was so essential to the artillery.

Outworn ideas had almost deprived the army of its quintessential weapon, the 18-pound field gun. Before the war, many British gunners, looking back to the days of fire and movement, had wanted to standardize production on the lighter and more mobile 13-pounder, the choice of the nearly obsolete horse artillery. Only by the closest of votes – a tie broken by the British Prime Minister, Arthur Balfour – was the 18-pounder saved. In the siege warfare that followed it became the workhorse of the artillery. Sited close to the front, with its direct and wicked range, it could be fired like a peashooter to demoralize the enemy. It far outshone its lighter and more mobile cousin: for every shot fired by the 13-pounder, the Canadians fired seventy from the heavier gun.

Its companion was the 4.2-inch howitzer, absolutely essential for trench warfare because of its high, looping trajectory. Its barrel slanted upward at a 45-degree angle, and its thirty-five-pound shell dropped into a trench or onto a parapet could create terrifying havoc.

A heavier model, the 6-inch howitzer, placed farther back, weighed more than a ton. Firing from its wheeled carriage, it hurled its hundred-pound high-explosive shells for more than six miles into the German rear areas where McNaughton's wizards had pinpointed targets that nobody but an airman could see.

There were also heavier howitzers, set even farther back. The 8-inch lobbed a shell weighing 180 pounds, so heavy that only the strongest gunner could manhandle it in two lifts – one to the knees, a second chest high. The largest piece of ordnance in the Canadian Corps (the bigger howitzers and naval guns were under Army command by the British) was the gigantic 9.2-inch howitzer, so large that it travelled in three sections, each weighing four and a half tons and hauled by tractors. This gun, which took twelve hours to assemble, hurled a 290-pound shell that smashed pill boxes, gun emplacements, dugouts, and batteries into rubble.

To put any of these guns into action and keep them firing required a complicated infrastructure. Two hundred men were needed to handle one battery of four 18-pounders; these included mechanics, saddlers, blacksmiths, drivers, and cooks as well as gunners. Fifty men were always on duty at the guns. Caisson drivers came up at night, halting several hundred yards from the gun positions in order to leave no revealing tracks for the German air observers. Though it was safer to be a gunner than an infantry man, the work was hard. It took stamina and training to manhandle a three-hundred-pound shell and fling it into the breach with shrapnel bursting all around. In battle the emphasis is usually on the infantry; but at Vimy it was the gunners, stripped to the waist, sweating despite the wind and the sleet, labouring hour after hour without rest or let up, who were the real victors in the battle to seize the ridge.

3

Completing the arsenal of howitzers, guns, and mortars was the deadliest weapon of all – the one that had transformed warfare. The heavy, water-cooled Vickers machine gun and the more portable Lewis, with its cylindrical feed drum, spewing out bullets at rates that could exceed five hundred rounds a minute, had mechanized the science of killing. They dominated the battlefield. The firepower of each weapon exceeded that of a platoon of riflemen. Until the tank was invented nothing could stand up to machine-gun fire. Men were torn in two by its hail of bullets. Entire sections dropped like grain before the scythe. But it took a long time for the High Command to understand this truth.

The British thought of the machine gun as a kind of super rifle. It took the Canadians to demonstrate at Vimy that it could also be employed as light artillery. The man behind this innovation was another adopted Canadian, whose unorthodox views and keen mind had been honed on the frontier of the Canadian North West.

Raymond Brutinel, a twenty-three-year-old reservist in the French Army, had emigrated to Edmonton in 1905. For several years he roamed the West from Pembina to Fort Macleod, from the Skeena to the Peace. He was an explorer, a prospector, a land developer during the great boom, and, on occasion, a newspaper editor. In that yeasty era, Brutinel amassed a fortune. By 1914, still in his early thirties, he was living the life of a millionaire businessman in Montreal.

In his photograph, Brutinel looks as if Central Casting had sent him into the lines to play a comic Frenchman. With his neat little moustache, his pince-nez, his snapping eyes, and his smallish but definitely Cyranoesque nose, he is a caricature of an officer. In reality, he was a dedicated and dynamic figure who saw in the machine gun possibilities that others had overlooked.

One of the remarkable features of the 1st Canadian Motor Machine Gun Brigade, which Brutinel commanded, was that it was raised and underwritten largely by private money. Some of Canada's biggest industrialists footed the bill. It's significant that all were self-made millionaires, that most had had frontier experience, and that none had had a previous military background. They included Herbert Holt, the former CPR mountain contractor, J.R. Booth, the Ottawa lumberman, Clifford Sifton, the Western politician, J.W. McConnell, the Montreal broker, and, later, John Craig Eaton, the Toronto merchant, and "Klondike Joe" Boyle, the Yukon mining magnate. Boyle, for instance, raised an entire battalion of Klondikers, paid for it himself, and brought it out of the Yukon at his own expense. The least Sam Hughes could do was to make him an honorary colonel. Boyle, who went on to further adventures in Russia and Rumania, had his maple leaf lapel badges fashioned out of pure Klondike gold.

As a result of this remarkable demonstration of faith in the new weapon, and thanks to Brutinel's importuning, Canada entered the war with a machine-gun arsenal stronger than that of the British. In England, however, Brutinel met with incredible resistance. The machine gunner's enthusiasm was temporarily dashed by Kitchener himself, who announced that too many machine guns would throw the divisional fire power out of balance! Lieutenant-General Alderson, then in charge of the Canadians, tended to agree with Kitchener, but by the summer of 1915, when the machine-gun brigade joined the 1st Division in France, Brutinel was able to change

Alderson's mind. The Second Battle of Ypres and the brutal engagements that followed had opened the commander's eyes to the possibilities of the new weapon.

In Arthur Currie, Brutinel had an ally. With Currie's approval in 1916, he began to explore and test his ideas about indirect fire power. The supposedly inflexible Germans were also exploring this theory, but the British and French machine-gun schools discouraged the idea. "Indirect" means just that: instead of firing directly at the enemy, Brutinel believed the machine gun could also be used to fire over the heads of the assaulting troops, thickening the barrages of larger shells; that it could be used to harass road crossings, preventing enemy carrying parties from using overland routes; that it could fill in gaps left by artillery fire; and that by sweeping the forward lines of the enemy, it could prevent the Germans from repairing the wire destroyed by the 18-pounders.

In the Canadian West, tramping through the snow-covered forests of British Columbia, Brutinel had learned to act on his own. In the opening days of June 1916, in the battle of Sanctuary Wood in the Ypres salient, this experience paid off. The machine-gun brigade had, for the first time, been withdrawn from the line for rest. Brutinel was about to go on leave. But the situation made him uneasy, and he decided one morning to go forward to Corps headquarters. Suddenly at eight o'clock the Germans launched a four-hour barrage, which Brutinel miraculously survived. He went at once to the nearest headquarters, and there Brigadier-General L.J. Lipsett, then the commander of the 2nd Brigade, gave him the worst possible news: the 3rd Division on his left had suffered a devastating blow; its commander was dead; several brigadiers were either dead or captured; the front-line trenches had been blasted to rubble; entire units had been destroyed; communications were knocked out. Worst of all, the opening of a six-hundred-yard gap offered the Germans a breakthrough that could take them all the way to Ypres.

Brutinel offered at once to put his weary machine gunners back into the line to secure the flank of Lipsett's brigade and close the gap. By four the next morning they were in place. The gap was scarcely plugged when Brutinel received orders from Corps to withdraw at once. Had he done so, the Germans could burst through. He ignored the order. The next day a second order came through. Again Brutinel ignored it; the situation was still too critical to move his brigade back. On the third day a different kind of order came: Brutinel was to report personally to the new Corps commander who had taken over from Alderson – General Byng. Back he went, full of misgivings.

Byng was icy cold:

"Here is a map of the front. Please explain the present position as far as you know it."

Brutinel talked while the new commander listened.

Finally Byng spoke: "Now explain why you failed to obey my orders. A battle is in progress, and the only reserves I had were engaged without my knowledge."

Brutinel explained why he felt he had no other course but to stay and hold the line. When Brutinel had finished, Byng rose, laid a hand on the young colonel's shoulder, and declared, "Had you not done as you did, I would have had you court-martialled."

Byng agreed that the machine-gun brigade should stay with the infantry until the situation in the field was resolved.

"It's a good way to spend my leave," Brutinel remarked.

"Leave!" cried Byng. "What sort of fools have we got here? Officers with leave warrants in their pockets staying instead to fight battles!"

Brutinel explained that he did not feel this was at all unusual.

"I think we've struck it rich," said Byng, turning to his chief of staff.

It is doubtful that any other army would have given a junior officer his head in the way Raymond Brutinel was given his at Vimy. But in spite of critics within and outside the Canadian Corps, who worried about the expenditure of so much ammunition, his tactics were adopted. In almost every raid directed at the enemy lines, machine-gun fire was used to intensify the box barrages that held the Germans in a cage of exploding steel.

Soon the French became curious. Their chief of staff visited Byng at his headquarters and asked to be informed about the new technique. Byng by now was on familiar terms with his junior: ''You'll have to make a full report, Bruty, for our French friends.''

To which Colonel Brutinel replied: ''A report from me would be of little value. The report should be made by the Germans themselves. They, and they alone, can give first hand information on the subject from the business end of it.''

Brutinel had a questionnaire prepared for intelligence officers to use on captured Germans. The results were sent to the French without comment. The prisoners reported that indirect fire had made it difficult to repair at night trenches that had been destroyed by the big guns during the day. The machine guns hampered the delivery of supplies to the German lines. In the last days before the attack, they made it impossible. Moreover, when the machine guns were firing, no German could man a parapet or evacuate the wounded men.

By the time they reached Vimy, the machine gunners had become the élite of the Canadian Corps. ''I would not be an infantry officer for anything now,'' Claude Williams wrote home. ''I now understand the superior airs of the artillery. In our brigade, we are rated senior to the artillery even. In the advance, the machine guns on both sides are perhaps the most important branch.''

This élitism was carefully fostered by the Corps command, who were intent on making machine-gun work special and distinct. All machine-gun officers, like Williams, had horses. The badges were special – crossed machine guns supporting a maple leaf. Machine gunners didn't have to polish their buttons, which were a distinctive black. The salute was different, and so was the drill. Because of the narrow French roads, the machine gunners marched in threes rather than in fours. By March, no fewer than sixty-four machine guns were firing across No Man's Land at the German lines by day and another sixty-four by night. This drum fire continued until the barrels wore out and the firing had to be curtailed. And after the Battle of Vimy Ridge, indirect fire, scorned for so long by the brass hats, was adopted by all Allied armies.

4

The Germans knew something was up. How could they not? How could anyone hide the bustle and the build-up behind the lines, the monstrous piles of ammunition, the quickening activity of the Royal Flying Corps? Nonetheless, Julian Byng intended to achieve surprise. Instead of the usual lengthy bombardment in the hours preceding the attack, he planned to begin with a deceptively short burst of artillery – a sudden thunderclap before the guns lifted and the troops went over the top in what Canada would call the Battle of Vimy Ridge.

To the rest of the world it would be part of the collective battles of Arras, touched off by the attack on the ridge and by the British 3rd Army's assault on the right of the Canadians, known as the First Battle of the Scarpe. These twin attacks would be preliminaries to the much larger spring offensive being mounted farther to the south by three French armies under the new generalissimo, Robert Nivelle.

It galled Douglas Haig to be placed under French command for the newest push. He and Nivelle did not see eye to eye. Haig and Nivelle's predecessor, General Joffre, had originally planned a continuation of the Somme offensive to begin in February, 1917. But Joffre's incomprehensible neglect of the Verdun defences had forced his dismissal. Nivelle's brilliant successes in the closing days of that truly ghastly battle rocketed him, as Joffre's successor, into the post of commander-in-chief of the French armies.

Haig and Nivelle were opposites in almost every way. The impeccable British commander was aloof, stubborn and so uncommunicative that he found it difficult to get his ideas across orally, especially with politicians, whom he despised. He had about as much charisma as a carp. Nivelle, on the other hand, was eloquent, lucid, and easily understood for, thanks to his English mother, he spoke perfect, unaccented English. He was also a charmer. He even charmed Lloyd George, a considerable feat, for the pugnacious Welshman had little use for his own generals. Seduced by Nivelle's superb confidence and *élan*, the British Prime Minister scuttled the Haig-Joffre plans and agreed that Nivelle should have the supreme command of the spring offensive.

Though Haig and Nivelle were opposites in strategy as well as in personality, they had one trait in common – which seems to have been shared by most of the Allied generals in the Great War – they did not learn from past successes and failures. Once their minds were made up, they were inflexible.

Haig, who had overplayed the role of the artillery and dismissed the machine gun as "much overrated," found it hard to understand why determined troops needed to be held up by entanglements of barbed wire. The slaughter of thousands didn't bother him because he rarely saw a corpse. Haig had figured that since the Allies had more men than the Germans, they could lose more in the sure knowledge that Germany would be bled white before England and France. Now he hoped to punch a hole in the German line and achieve the breakthrough that would end the war.

Nivelle was a champion of the grand breakthrough. A national hero because of his recapture of the French forts at Verdun, he proposed to use the same technique on a larger scale against the German salient – that great bulge in the line south of the Somme and north of the Aisne. Under Nivelle's plan, the British Battle of Arras, to the north of the Somme, would be no more than a diversion to keep the Germans busy. A week after the British attack, three French armies would be unleashed against the bulge in the German line, squeezing the German defenders from both sides. In one swift blow of "violence, brutality and rapidity" they would punch a great hole in the German defences, break through, and end the war. "We have the formula," the confident Nivelle declared; ". . . victory is certain."

It did not occur to the cocky Frenchman that the Germans had learned something from Verdun; he simply assumed they would act the way he planned. They didn't. The French security was abysmal. The Germans, who knew all about the expected attack on the bulge, simply got rid of the bulge. They pulled back, leaving a desert of scorched earth, a belt of destruction from twenty to fifty miles wide in which every tree, every house and barn, every field, every road, was ravaged and flattened. Having straightened their line by some twenty-five miles and thus reduced their committed divisions by ten, they proceeded to construct a formidable defence in depth, which they called the Siegfried Line and the Allies later called the Hindenburg Line.

Nivelle was made aware of this German pullback in March, but, as in the Canadian gas raid, events had by then taken on a momentum of their own. Not by a jot or a tittle did the stubborn Frenchman change his now obsolete plan. Thus were sown the seeds of the disaster that followed. The assault troops would find that they were attacking a vacuum. By the time they reached the main German defences, the attack had run out of steam.

But the Germans did not pull back from Vimy Ridge; clearly they considered it too important a vantage point to give up. Nivelle and Haig did not agree on its significance. Haig wanted to seize the ridge at the outset of the Battle of Arras. Nivelle opposed him. He didn't believe the Canadian Corps could take the ridge, and his staff officers were almost contemptuous in their rejection of the Canadian plan. Once the breakthrough was achieved, so Nivelle believed, the Germans would have to vacate the ridge anyway. But Haig didn't expect the enemy to give it up so easily. As long as they dominated those ravaged heights, his entire left flank was in peril. Reluctantly, Nivelle gave in. As it turned out, the capture of Vimy Ridge would be the sole successful operation not only in the Battle of Arras but also in the entire spring offensive of the soon to be discredited Robert-Georges Nivelle.

The Germans had no illusions about the Canadians' abilities as fighting men. "The Canadians are known to be good troops and are, therefore, well suited to assaulting," a captured document signed by General von Backmeister reported. "There are no deserters to be found among the Canadians." But Colonel-General von Falkenhausen, the Bavarian commander of the Sixth Army at Vimy, was just as stubborn as his Allied counterparts. At seventy-three, he was not about to change the habits of a lifetime. What had worked at the Somme would work north of Arras, of that he was confident. His reserves were well to the rear, but the aged general was convinced there would be plenty of time to bring them up. He expected the battle to drag on for several days, probably for weeks. In vain, the ruthless Bavarian infantry commander, Karl von Fasbender, clamoured for more troops to help stem the attack that he believed would be launched on April 10. In vain did von Falkenhausen's commander, Prince Rupprecht of Bavaria, as well as the German quartermaster general, the coldly brilliant Ludendorff, urge the recalcitrant general to move up his reserves. The general insisted that there was no room for them in the forward areas. Besides, he declared, the attack would not come before April 15; better to send for them when they were needed.

But the Canadians planned to attack on April 9 and they intended to take the ridge not in a matter of days or weeks but in a matter of hours. The plan was simple. For the first time (and, as it turned out, the last) all four Canadian divisions would surge forward simultaneously to seize the crest by lunch hour under the curtain of the greatest artillery bombardment of the war.

They would do it in a series of carefully timed stages, the objective of each stage marked on the map by a coloured reporting line. At each stage the forward troops would consolidate, reporting their arrival to low-flying aircraft, while fresh troops leap-frogged through to the next objective.

The times allowed for these forward bounds were remarkably short. The troops had exactly thirty-five minutes to push right through von Falkenhausen's forward defensive belt, seven hundred yards deep. This the planners marked on the map as the Black Line. They were given forty minutes to dig in before the barrage lifted and the next wave moved through.

The 3rd and 4th Divisions on the left of the line had the shortest distances to travel. They were expected to be over the top of the ridge and into the woods at the bottom of the rear slope past the Germans' second defence line – the Red

Line on the planners' maps – in twenty minutes. It was a tall order. For here was a vast and carefully constructed trench barrier, supported by more parallel trenches, wire entanglements, concrete forts, and machine-gun nests. To reach it, one division – the 4th – would have to leap across Hill 145, enduring flanking fire from the Pimple, which was not scheduled to be taken until the following day.

In brief, by 7:05 Monday morning, just one hour and thirty-five minutes after the opening of the barrage at dawn, the two divisions on the left were expected to be dug in on the far side of Vimy Ridge.

The 1st and 2nd Divisions on the right had much farther to go. For them there were four reporting lines – Black, Red, Blue and Brown. Fresh troops would jump through the forward battalions consolidating on the Red Line to advance over the ridge, seizing the villages of Thélus and Farbus, both strongly fortified by the Germans. A British brigade, attached to the 2nd Division, would thicken that final advance. The last objective, marked as the Brown Line on the maps, ran along the eastern base of the ridge. The troops of Currie's 1st and Burstall's 2nd Division were expected to be there, digging in, at exactly 1:18 that afternoon.

In short, the Canadians were given less than eight hours to capture all of Vimy Ridge except the Pimple. All things considered, the French might be pardoned for scoffing.

CHAPTER EIGHT

The Final Days

1

In late March, the Royal Marine Artillery began to move its 15-inch howitzers into the rear of the Canadian positions – a sure sign that an attack was coming. These gigantic guns each weighed twenty tons and hurled a fifteen-hundred-pound projectile at enemy strong points and dugouts. It took nine tractors, each pulling one or two trailers, to haul the various parts of the weapons to the gun pits. Crawling forward at a sluggish eight miles an hour, they tore up roads and snarled traffic behind the lines.

The guns came up in pieces and were put together like a Chinese puzzle, bolted to an iron latticework in a pit twenty feet square. The assembling could occupy four days, the gunners working with only two fifteen-minute breaks each day, for dinner (bully beef soup) and for tea (bread and jam). They were all strong, powerful men, none under five feet ten inches, most well over six feet, and they slept on the ground beside their weapons.

Night after night, the ammunition trucks streamed along the main roads, piling up thousands of shells, like so many potatoes, in pits covered with earth and straw. At night, the shouts and curses of the mule-skinners turned the air blue. When the first phase of the artillery plan went into effect, forty-two thousand tons of ammunition lay piled up behind the lines. An additional twenty-five hundred tons poured in daily to feed the hungry cannon.

On a sunny afternoon at the end of March, Ed Russenholt, a Lewis gun sergeant from Winnipeg, climbed a small hill overlooking the Vimy sector to watch the guns firing below. The view was spectacular. The shoot, which had begun on March 20, would continue until April 2, by which time no fewer than 275,000 shells would have been hurled at the Germans. Yet only half the guns were allowed to fire at this early stage in order to conceal from the enemy the true strength of the artillery. Sergeant Russenholt sat with his back against the corner of a stone wall and began counting the seconds between a gun's muzzle flash and the explosion of its shell on the ridge beyond. He soon had to give up; there were too many guns, and they never stopped. Five hundred guns were firing that day – guns of every size, shape, and trajectory – a line of flame stretching from the Scarpe to the Souchez. The field batteries alone were under orders to fire five hundred rounds per day and the total statistics, as Russenholt shortly discovered, were staggering. He walked over to the 10th Brigade machine-gun battery where he was told the gunners were firing as many as three hundred thousand rounds per night per gun, changing barrels constantly and covering every enemy road junction.

The gunners lived more comfortably than the infantry, but they also lived in fear of premature bursts. A bad batch of 18-pounder ammunition had arrived in these last days before the battle. Ernest Black, a law student from Toronto, and his fellow field gunners feared it more than they feared the enemy cannon. Many of the time fuses were defective, the shells exploding as they left the muzzle. Black and his comrades, testing their ammunition, found two prematures in six rounds fired; one fell short and killed an officer and a sergeant on the Arras-Souchez Road.

By this time there were so many guns firing that Black found himself in a perilous position. His battery was in the front row of seven rows of guns, each of them firing a percentage of prematures. When such a defective shell burst it flung a pint of steel marbles directly in front of it, all travelling at top speed in a narrow cone twenty-five feet wide and one hundred feet deep. In this hail of small projectiles were two whirling chunks of brass, both lethal – the fuse that hadn't worked and the shell case that had blown off. All night and all day Black and the others were treated to the nerve-racking whine of these shrapnel bullets and the accompanying howl of the fuses and shell cases hurtling at them. Only a thick wall of sandbags at their backs provided any protection.

In those final days, the tempo of activity at Vimy quickened with the intensity of sound as events moved toward a final crescendo. The Canadians raided the enemy trenches every night, probing for scraps of information. It was a costly business. The raids and the German guns took their toll. In the fortnight before the battle, 327 Canadians died; another 1,316 were wounded or lost.

And some went sick. Will Bird was suffering from the early stages of mumps and didn't know it when, on the night of March 28, he was transferred to the sniping section and sent out with a veteran marksman named Harry Pearce, who had eighteen kills to his credit. As the bombardment thundered overhead, the two lay out on dry strips of brick and blocks, above the mud, concealed behind a slitted steel plate that had been camouflaged on the enemy's side with wire and rubbish. Two days went by during which each man took turns peering through the slit with binoculars, examining the enemy lines. Then, on the third morning, Bird saw a German rise waist high in his trench and look around. Bird got him in the cross-hairs at a hundred yards and shot him dead. Even as Pearce was recording the kill in his record book, a second German rose. Bird shot him, too. A third stood up, so sharply defined in the sights that Bird could count the buttons on his tunic. He shot him in the left breast. Two more of the enemy appeared, one of them carrying binoculars; when Bird shot him, the binoculars were flung in a high loop above his head. His comrade raised his rifle and pointed it in the direction of the snipers. Pearce gripped Bird's shoulder. "Shoot!" he said. "You won't get a chance like this all day."

But Bird couldn't continue. A wave of nausea swept over him. "Go ahead yourself," he said, "I've had enough." Pearce took quick aim and Bird saw the dark flush that spread over the German's face as he went down. Pearce shot two more Germans in quick succession, but for Will Bird the future novelist, his sniping days were over. Back in the trenches he told his sergeant he'd had enough of butcher's work. The following day, half delirious from his case of mumps, he was shipped by ambulance to Mont St. Eloi.

Tossing on his hospital cot, unable to sleep because the

sniping still preyed on his mind, he would miss the Battle of Vimy Ridge. But he would never forget that cold morning when he, William Richard Bird, aged twenty-five, late of Amherst, Nova Scotia, stared not only into the faces of the men he was about to kill but also into the deepest recesses of his own soul.

2

By April 2, every infantryman knew every detail of the attack except the date and the time. Every division had a thick, type-written volume, carefully guarded, each copy numbered, that covered every conceivable operation from the use of tram lines to the burial of the dead.

Now, the second phase of the artillery plan went into effect as the guns that had been concealed from the enemy came into action. For the next seven days, the Canadian and British artillery pounded the enemy positions until one million rounds had been fired. The Germans called it the Week of Suffering.

There had never been anything like it in history: fifty thousand tons of high explosives raining down on the demoralized and disoriented Prussian and Bavarian troops. For all of that time, the men in the German front lines had to stand to, unable to wash or shave, their rations heavily curtailed because supplies could not be brought forward under the intense bombardment. Ration trips that had once taken fifteen minutes now took several hours. Even the deep dugouts were not entirely secure, for the new armour-piercing shells with the delayed-action fuses could penetrate for twenty feet or more.

For the Germans, sleep, when it was possible at all, became fitful. The artillery carried out feints – creeping barrages, which seemed to signal an attack, or sudden intensifications in certain areas to throw the enemy off guard. These contributed to the Germans' confusion. Lulled by false alarms, wearied by constant orders to stand to, they grew complacent.

In vain, Ludendorff urged that more batteries be brought forward; his artillery was being outgunned three to one. But by the end of the Week of Suffering his extra batteries still weren't in position.

As the shelling intensified, so did the work behind the Canadian lines. The regimental tailors and their assistants were hard at it, sewing up canvas buckets for the bomb carriers. The pioneer companies were making wooden signs, each bearing a regimental shoulder patch to mark for the runners the quickest route back to battalion headquarters. Battalion scouts began to familiarize themselves with overland routes to avoid the clogged trenches and tunnels. Tools of every kind, from wire cutters to picks, were cached in underground storage areas. In one sap alone, the RCRs stored 46,000 rounds of rifle ammunition, 200 shovels, 150 picks, and great rolls of barbed wire.

On the night of April 3, the Corps faced an unexpected crisis: the RFC reported that the Germans were evacuating the Vimy front. If that were true, then all plans for the capture of the ridge would have to be abandoned. Front-line officers reported the situation normal along the line, but when the RFC reports persisted, the 29th Battalion (Vancouver) – known as Tobin's Tigers, after their original commander – was ordered to find out what was going on.

The Tigers were about to be relieved by the Royal 22nd of Montreal – the famous "Van Doos." Nevertheless, Captain Harry Clyne, who knew of a gap in the enemy wire, organized a patrol, crawled across No Man's Land, peered cautiously over the enemy parapet and, to his amazement, found the German trench empty. Water oozing from footsteps in the mud indicated it had been occupied only a few minutes earlier.

Clyne sent out scouts to the right and left: *nothing!* He and his men moved cautiously forward to the support line only to discover, to their astonishment, that it, too, was empty. They crept along the deserted trench and, as a flare shot up, huddled in a corner of the traverse. In the light they spotted a few German stragglers, unshaven, exhausted, their greatcoats caked with mud. All were high-tailing it to the rear.

What was going on? Had the Germans decided upon a ruse – to evacuate the forward areas and set up a new and stronger defensive line farther back, perhaps on the reverse slopes where they would be protected by the great bulk of the ridge? If so, all the planning and training, all the bombardment and split-second timing for the assault would be worthless.

Clyne, pondering the problem, made plans to seize at least one prisoner to confirm his suspicions. Then, suddenly, it seemed as if the entire German army was descending on his small patrol on the double. These were fresh clean troops in unsoiled greatcoats, leaping into the support trench on his right and dashing past his concealed patrol to occupy the forward line.

Clyne knew he had to get the message back as fast as possible. That wouldn't be easy. He gave each man the same message: "No retirement on the Vimy front – corps relief only." But how to get back with the fresh troops surrounding them? Clyne's only advice to his sergeant was to "go where the mud is thickest."

Through the mud they crawled, over the parapet of the trench to the very edge of a vast crater, fifty feet deep, two hundred feet wide. Their own troops held the far side, but two German sentries loomed up ahead, on the near lip, barring their way. Clyne sent his men in pairs, creeping around the enemy post with orders to race for their own lines even at the risk of being shot at by their own men.

Miraculously, they all made it. The Van Doos, who had already relieved the Tigers, had given the patrol up for lost. Now they couldn't believe their eyes: how could such a group get through the wire and the German trenches, remain for two hours behind the enemy lines, and return without a scratch? It was fortunate they did. The word went back to Corps headquarters that the enemy trenches were manned and there was no need to abandon the plan. The Germans, aroused now, shelled the Canadian front and had their revenge. Two members of Harry Clyne's bold little patrol were killed by shrapnel.

By April 6, Good Friday, senior officers knew the date of

the attack but not the time; it had been postponed for a variety of reasons from April 8 to April 9. The weather that Friday was bracing, ''the bluest of spring mornings, cold enough to be exhilarating, too cold to be delicious,'' in Andrew Macphail's notation. The news from across the Atlantic was equally exhilarating: the United States had declared war on Germany. Few had time to give that much thought: everyone's mind was concentrated on the coming battle. The sacred had to give way to the profane. When Canon Frederick George Scott, the senior chaplain of the 1st Division, tried to organize a Good Friday service, he was told everybody was too busy to attend.

It was a day of hard work and sober reflection. Over on the 2nd Division front, Major James DeLancey, the second in command of the 25th Battalion (Nova Scotia Rifles) – the man who would take them over the top – told a meeting of officers that if only one man was left alive their objective must be taken, and unless their plight was drastic they must not call for help from any other unit.

On the enemy side, the jitters were growing. At the far left of the sector, sentries of the 38th Battalion from Ottawa looked out across No Man's Land and, to their astonishment, spotted a lone German soldier, carrying his pack and rifle and walking directly toward them. He was a young private of the 11th Bavarians, short and blond and in good condition, apart from the mud caking his grey uniform, but the bombardment had been too much for him. The sentries shook their heads in amazement: something must be wrong if one of the enemy was allowed to walk into their trench in broad daylight.

That afternoon, the artillery obliterated the already badly shattered village of Thélus on the forward slope of the ridge, just below the crest. Its underground shelters were strongly defended by German machine guns. Now two hundred artillery pieces were turned on the ravaged community. Farther to the left the village of Farbus and Farbus Wood, on the far side of the ridge, received a similar battering.

The weather was so clear that Bill Breckenridge, detailed

186

for an advance party of the Black Watch, could see the smears of white chalk thrown up by the Germans in their trenches along the ridge. The rest of Breckenridge's battalion was again bivouacked in the Dumbbell camp, six miles behind the lines; the advance party's job was to prepare the jumping-off trenches for the coming battle. As they trudged past the old French cemetery, Breckenridge looked soberly at the long lines of crosses and asked himself: "Can the Canadians drive Fritzie from the Vimy Ridge after the French and the British failed?" It seemed to him an almost impossible task.

On the plank road that ran from Mont St. Eloi to the Arras-Souchez highway, the party stopped to rest. Breckenridge cast his eyes back to the village and the shattered twin towers of the old abbey perched on the hilltop. All around him the great guns lay in wait, guns of every calibre – row upon row – lined up on an old sunken Roman road that had once known the tramp of Caesar's legions. As the sun began to sink, the sky took on a deeper hue; Breckenridge had been here before, but now it seemed to him more beautiful than he'd ever known it. A phrase popped into his head: "Even in the jaws of death, life is sweet." He thought of his home in Sherbrooke and the turmoil that lay ahead. Who could survive? Who would fall? It occurred to Bill Breckenridge that *everybody* expected to survive, including himself.

By now, in the gathering dusk, the towers of the abbey had blended into a single spire. On that Good Friday evening, it seemed to Breckenridge that it had taken on the shape of a great monument, overshadowing the battlefield.

On this journey to the front line, everything would stand out sharply in Breckenridge's memory: the sight, for instance, of an artillery post disguised so well as a shattered tree trunk that it was hard to tell it from a row of real trees that lined the Arras road; or the scenes in Pont Street, flooded by April showers, where men continually slipped off the bathmats into the mud to the merriment of the others; or the sight of troops sloshing through the water of another sunken road known as the Quarry Line – as unconcernedly as if they were walking down the main street of their home village.

In the Grange Subway, labour battalions were still clawing away at the chalk, creating dugouts off the main subway to be used for the headquarters of various battalions. Here, Breckenridge vainly tried to find a place to sleep; the tunnel was so tightly packed with snoring troops that there wasn't a square inch of space to be had. He and the others moved up into the forward trench system only to be driven back by a rain of mortar shells. Finally, they returned to the Quarry Line to join a group from the field ambulance cooking a midnight dinner over a charcoal brazier. "I can't give you a bunk but I can give you a stretcher and a blanket," one of them offered. Breckenridge and his party accepted gratefully, flung themselves onto the ground, and dropped off to sleep.

Andrew Macphail had left the rear areas near Mont St. Eloi about the same time as Breckenridge to walk with his son, Jeffrey, to the Corps headquarters at Camblain l'Abbé. The road was good, but when he returned six hours later it reminded him of cream that had been churned into butter. Horses were fainting and falling, lorries spewing up stones, transport jammed for miles in both directions, a drizzle starting to fall – yet everybody was cheerful and punctiliously polite. As the guns gobbled the ammunition the traffic continued its snail-like pace, hour after hour. Workers at a YMCA coffee stand counted the three-ton trucks moving up the line, all loaded with shells, and figured that in a single twenty-four-hour period two thousand had passed that way.

Everywhere, as night fell, the work went on. The Zivy Subway was being rushed to completion. Tramways were being pushed forward as close to the front line as practical. Bridges were being thrust across the parallel lines of trenches so that the supporting troops would not be held up. The Canadian wire had to be cut to allow the attackers to go over the top and into No Man's Land unimpeded. Dumps were being assembled, dressing stations set up in the ruins of Neuville St. Vaast, and the great Zivy Cave made habitable for even more men. In the Vincent, Tottenham, and Cavalier subways, huge dressing stations were being completed. And out in No Man's Land that night, whole companies of infantry were silently digging away ahead of the forward line, building the shallow jumping-off trenches – three feet deep and no wider than a man's shoulders – that would give the first wave of attackers a head start at Zero Hour. But not all of those who dug trenches in No Man's Land that night would ever experience that moment. Even as they worked, the enemy shells exploded among them, destroying the sweetness of their youth.

Other men died that night and not all of them in No Man's Land. That same afternoon, Corporal Eric Forbes of the 6th Field Company, Engineers, stood beside the Arras-Souchez road watching the traffic. Up came an officer with a company of men. "Corporal," he asked, "do you know of any place around here my men could rest? We're a tunnelling company and we're going up to the ridge. We have to get some rest because we have to work all night." Forbes found a billet in a building behind the armoury where others were also sleeping. The tunnellers entered, slipped out of their equipment, and settled down on bunks of wire and netting. Fifteen minutes later a shell with an instantaneous fuse struck the building, killing twelve, wounding thirty. Just a few inches higher and it would have passed over harmlessly.

For Eric Forbes, this was a moment of horror. He was twenty-four, a Nova Scotian who had been studying engineering at Queen's. He'd joined a militia company of engineers because that would count as a credit toward his degree. He'd been working as purser on a boat out of Boston the summer war was declared. A telegram had ordered him into active service. Now here he was, standing outside a ruined building, his gorge rising as an old friend, the company driver William Stalker, staggered toward him, trying to stuff his guts back into the jagged hole in his belly before collapsing at Forbes's feet.

3

Saturday, April 7, dawned, another fine day, the kind of spring morning that makes a man feel good to be young and alive. With the battle only forty-eight hours away the attacking brigades began to organize their advance headquarters. As Brigade Major, it was Duncan Macintyre's task to make arrangements in the Zivy Cave. By afternoon the job was complete and the headquarters personnel of the 4th Infantry Brigade were sloshing forward with their kits and office supplies through the deep mud of the communication trenches, only to be halted by a flurry of shelling. One man died, another was wounded.

The cave itself was jammed with men, casting grotesque shadows in the candlelight as they played cards or brewed tea over small fires or carved their names on the chalk walls. A stream of humanity constantly shuffled in and out, splashed by water that dribbled from the roof above covering everything in an inch and more of grey slime. Stretcher-bearers staggered under wounded men whose cries punctuated the general buzz of voices. Carrying parties entered, dumped their loads, and went off for more. Mud-covered men stumbled in from the front to catch a few winks of sleep. To Macintyre, the stench of foul air, mud, cooking, sweat, urine, chloride of lime, and stale tobacco was nauseating. More than four hundred men had crowded into the cave, tracking in so much mud that a layer of wet ooze carpeted the chalk floor.

While Macintyre was setting up his headquarters, others were still out beyond the forward lines, preparing the way for the assault and probing the German defences. Two companies of 48th Highlanders had established themselves on the rear lip of one crater in broad daylight, as nervous a position as existed in the Vimy sector. One pair of scouts managed to work their way across No Man's Land and right into the German lines, so close they could hear the sentries chatting. Nothing would do but that the sergeant-major of one of the companies, Taffy Willis, should decide, against all orders, to attack a German post. He crept up to the enemy line, tossed three Mills bombs, emptied his Colt revolver and then, in frustration, flung his steel helmet at the Germans before getting back unscathed. It was not a healthy place to be; four of his men died that day in No Man's Land; six more were wounded.

190

Private Andrew McCrindle, a nineteen-year-old from Montreal, was also heading for No Man's Land early that afternoon with a work party from the 24th Battalion (Victoria Rifles) detailed to dig more jumping-off trenches. With his big glasses, his baby-blue eyes, his snub nose, and his smooth, innocent face, the skinny McCrindle bore little resemblance to the recruiting poster stereotype of the jut-jawed, gimlet-eyed fighting man. This would be his first battle, and so it gave him a good feeling to pass the hundreds of big guns lined up, almost hub to hub, and talk to the gunners, who boasted to him about the twelve-mile range that would drop shells far in the German rear to prevent reserve troops moving forward.

McCrindle was curious about the long ropes tied to the barrels of the big howitzers. The gunners explained that the trajectory was so high it was beyond the range of the usual mechanism designed to lower the barrel. Four men had to haul it down with ropes. But the German guns were still in action, as McCrindle's party found out when they worked with pick and shovel in front of their own trenches. The Germans spotted the chalk waste thrown up by the diggers and brought down a rain of shells. The work party scuttled to safety through the Zivy Subway and took refuge in the Zivy Cave.

The German aerial observers, floating in the cloudless skies above, had spotted the chalk and alerted the enemy batteries. In their frail sausage balloons they peered down at the mishmash of wriggling trenches, trying to make sense of the dun-coloured world below, seeking other tell-tale clues to pinpoint the date of the offensive they knew was coming. The balloons were under constant attack by the Royal Flying Corps – frustrating and dangerous work for the British and Canadian pilots. The Germans were able to winch their sausages to the ground faster than the airmen could manoeuvre to destroy them. It was a costly business: for every enemy balloon shot to pieces the RFC lost a flying machine.

Young Billy Bishop of No. 60 Squadron, Late of Owen Sound, became an official ace that day and also won his first decoration, the Military Cross. He had been given a specific balloon as a target, but just as he dived on it he heard the rattle of machine-gun fire and found himself in combat with the enemy. Fortunately, the German flew directly in line with Bishop's gun. Bishop shot him down but lost the target, which had been hauled to earth during the combat. Frustrated, he disobeyed orders to keep above one thousand feet, dived at the balloon and attempted to destroy it in its bed, scattering the crew and at the same time doing his best to avoid both the anti-aircraft guns and the balls of rocket fire that the British called "flaming onions."

Now he was in a real pickle: his steep dive had caused his engine to fail. Bishop went into a glide, heading for an open field, sick at heart, knowing that he would shortly be either dead or a prisoner. Like those of others before him, his thoughts turned to home. How his parents would worry when he was reported missing! But like most heroes and all air aces, Bishop was blessed with more than his share of luck. At fifteen feet above the battlefield, his engine kicked in and he streaked for home, so close to the ground that no ack-ack gun could get him and no pilot would dare dive on him. Below him in the Vimy trenches, the startled Germans missed their aim. Behind, the balloon he'd dived on was a mass of flames.

It was a bitter-sweet victory for Billy Bishop. When he got back to base he found that three other pilots from his squadron, all good friends, had been lost in a battle with Manfred von Richthofen's *Jagstaffel II*, giving the German ace his thirty-seventh kill and, coincidentally, a promotion to captain. "Oh, how I hate the Hun," Bishop wrote to his fiancée that night. "They have done in so many of my best friends. I'll make them pay, I swear."

On the ground that evening, the signals section of the Black Watch was ordered to bring up the battalion's rations from the dump on the Quarry Line. For Bill Breckenridge, these last few days had been a nightmare of fetching and carrying. The signallers seemed to be constantly on the move, night and day. And, in those last crowded hours, movement became more difficult. Breckenridge and his carrying party were

192

barred by sentries from using the Grange Subway, now restricted to one-way traffic forward. But no one liked using the trenches, which were by then waist-deep in water, so, after some discussion, the party decided to chance a route above ground.

Breckenridge was the first man out of the communication trench. Hunched well over, loping along at top speed, he willed himself to dodge the enemy bullets.

"Where are you going?" the man behind him shouted.

"Never mind where I'm going," Breckenridge panted. "Don't follow me unless you want to. If you know a better way, go to it. I'm getting out of here as quickly as I can."

When, at last, they tumbled into the Cross Street trench, Breckenridge felt as if a ton of weight had suddenly been removed from his shoulders. With the mud splashing over their uniforms they followed the trench to the Quarry Line. There they filled their ration bags and headed into the traffic stream moving up the Grange Subway. It was hard work, balancing the bags on their shoulders, trying to avoid stepping on the hundreds of men curled up on the wet chalk floor or simply standing, three deep. "Watch where you're going," Breckenridge heard one man grumble; and another: "What size boots do you wear?" Gingerly he and the others picked their way through the narrow subway, squeezed into the headquarters dugout, deposited their loads, and settled down as best they could.

As night fell and the rumble of guns continued and the occasional starshell illuminated the debris of No Man's Land, the Royal Flying Corps swept across the Douai Plain behind the ridge and bombed the Douai airport, where von Richthofen's *Jagstaffel* was quartered. Richthofen's own all-red Albatross barely escaped being blown to pieces, but as the last of the raiders droned off into the night, the German ace was able to get some sleep. It was a fitful slumber; he tossed on his cot, continuing to dream of guns firing above him. Suddenly the dream became a reality: he sat bolt upright in bed at the sound of a low-flying airplane directly above his hut. The noise increased until it filled his quarters.

The plane, he realized, could be no more than one hundred feet above him. Instinctively, in his fright, Germany's greatest pilot pulled the blankets over his head just as a bomb shattered the window of the hut. Von Richthofen leaped up, ran out onto the tarmac, pistol in hand, and fired a few shots at the vanishing British plane. Then he returned to his troubled sleep, awaiting the coming dawn.

CHAPTER NINE

The Final Hours

1

Easter Sunday dawned, another bright and beautiful spring morning with a breeze light enough to be balmy and strong enough to dry the roads. As far as the eye could reach, in the clear air, the kite balloons stretched in an unbroken line to the north and south horizons. At his observation post that Sunday morning, Lieutenant Jack Fairweather of No. 4 Siege Battery looked up to see the larks circling and singing, oblivious to the thunder of the guns, just as in John McCrae's famous poem.

Duncan Macintyre awoke, braced by the weather, and, like so many others that day, found his thoughts turning to home – to family members going to Easter service, his new wife, Marjorie, in her finery, the relatives gathering for the traditional Easter dinner. Macintyre found it nauseating on this final day before the battle to contemplate the horrors that lay ahead: two Christian nations tearing at each other's throats at the time of the great religious festival, each side convinced that it was right. The 4th Division's commander, David Watson, shared Macintyre's reflective mood. "What a contrast to the real object of this Holy Day," he wrote in his diary. "I never heard such shelling as last night."

Behind the lines, the French countryside was at prayer. As the fighting troops moved forward, streams of peasants in sober black walked to church. Bells rang. Mass was sung. A few soldiers, such as Dr. Robert Manion, took Holy Communion. Manion, a medical officer and a future leader of the Conservative Party, prayed for his family and scribbled a note in his pocket diary: "If anything should happen to me, I would like this book sent to Mrs. R.J. Manion, 300 Wilbrod Street, Ottawa."

Not many followed his example. Canon Scott, thwarted

195

in his desire to hold a service on Good Friday, tried again. In a back area occupied by one of the siege batteries, he commandeered a Nissen hut and tried to light some candles for his makeshift altar. Each time he did so, the blast from one of the 15-inch guns would blow them out. The only suitable shelter he could find was the YMCA hut, full of sleeping men. Few bothered to rouse themselves to pray.

It was a day of rest for most, but not for all. There was no rest for Sergeant Charles Evans of the 3rd Division's ammunition column. Evans had been looking forward to spending a full day flat on his back in a civilian billet eight miles behind the lines, far beyond the reach of enemy guns. His job was done; the mule trains of his unit had brought the final loads of ammunition to the gunners. But at 5:15 that morning, Evans was roused from his sleep and given new orders. He must saddle his horse and deliver a load of signal equipment – plus a full bottle of Scotch – to a captain with the 7th Brigade signals in the Grange Subway off the Quarry Line. The signal equipment, one suspects, was a camouflage; it was the bottle of Scotch that counted.

Off went Evans, his day of rest forgotten, loaded down with four heavy coils of telephone wire, two on each shoulder, two nosebags, one on each shoulder, each holding two field telephones, plus his haversack and gas mask, and last, but certainly not least, the bottle of Scotch. He rode to the horse lines, left his steed there, and mushed on foot through the mud until he reached a track leading to what had once been the hamlet of La Targette on the main road from Arras.

Here two M.P.s stopped him. The track was closed; overland travel was out. He would have to use the communication trench. Obediently, Sergeant Evans climbed down into the trench and for the next three hours splashed slowly forward, knee deep in a muddy gruel, with the haversacks, telephones, and coils swinging wildly about him, threatening the safety of his precious bottle. But when finally he reached La Targette corner he could go no farther, for he found himself stuck fast in the gumbo. It was now nine o'clock on Easter Sunday morning, and as Evans called wildly for somebody to come and pull him out, he realized it would be some time before the signals captain got his Scotch.

While Evans was struggling to reach the Quarry Line by way of La Targette, Bill Breckenridge and a dozen signallers were trying to reach the big reserve water tanks not far away on the same Arras-Souchez road. There seemed to be no rest for Breckenridge. He had managed a few hours' sleep after one carrying job; now the medical officer had sent him back on another, this time for water. War is a thirsty business.

Like Evans, the signallers had opted again for an overland journey, since the trenches were almost impassable. But with the Germans only half a mile away it had been a nerve-racking trip. When at last they reached the tanks they came upon a chilling spectacle. There lay the mangled corpses of three men like themselves who had also been sent for water and were killed by German shells – grisly evidence that the enemy had the range of the tanks and was doing his best to frustrate any attempt to use them. The party scrambled to fill the buckets; but the tanks were in poor condition, and the water dribbled slowly from the taps. Just as the job was done, a whizbang burst fifty yards away. Breckenridge and his friends dived into a ditch, hugging the cobblestones. A second shell exploded. Off they all scurried for the safety of the Pont Street trench, heedless of the M.O.'s precious water supply splashing out of the swinging buckets.

Meanwhile, in the forward lines of the 10th Battalion, the adjutant, Major Daniel Ormond, was a worried man. Seven huge craters lay between the battalion's position and the enemy lines. The Germans had wired the intervening gaps heavily, and Ormond couldn't be certain that the wire had been destroyed. The artillery's ground observers assured him that it had; the air observers differed. What to do?

Arthur Currie had no doubts at all. Take no chances, he advised: get out there and find out. And so the battalion launched one final raid on the Germans and discovered that the wire still stood, hidden from the ground by masses of earth thrown up by the explosions that produced the craters. Currie ordered the trenches cleared for one thousand yards, moved the troops back a quarter of a mile, turned the guns on the wire and pulverized it. Thus was the 10th Battalion from Calgary saved from almost certain destruction.

Billy Bishop had crossed the lines that morning at nine, about the time that Bill Breckenridge and his fellow signallers were trying to fill their water buckets. He came out of a running fight at eight hundred feet above the German support lines to see the hundreds of grey-clad reserves moving forward, preparing for the coming battle. Separated from his squadron, Bishop that morning took on in succession no fewer than eight German aircraft, damaging several and shooting down two. At one point he fought off five planes single-handed and was down to his last round of ammunition when they dispersed. One bullet had grazed his helmet, another had cracked his windscreen. No wonder his commanding officer told him to take the rest of the day off when he returned to base! In just three-quarters of an hour on a sunny Easter morning, Billy Bishop had done the work of an entire squadron.

For most of that day, Private William Pecover, the Manitoba school teacher, had lain stretched out enjoying the warmth of the sun in the St. Eloi woods, well behind the lines. His battalion, the 27th (City of Winnipeg) was the reserve battalion in the reserve brigade – the Iron 6th as it was called. It would not go into action with the first wave at dawn. For Pecover it was a real day of rest. The men sat around under the trees in small groups, laughing and singing together, although, as Pecover noted, there was an undercurrent of anxiety, almost of sadness, as each man asked himself what the next day would bring.

All that afternoon, in the rear areas, as the troops got ready to move forward, the regimental bands played lively tunes designed to banish unspoken questions from everybody's minds. They played ''Mademoiselle from Armentières,'' ''Pack Up Your Troubles,'' and ''Take Me Back to Dear Old Blighty,'' and they played ragtime and jazz as the troops sang and adjusted their equipment and drew their Mills bombs and extra rations, packed away their bully and biscuits, and wrote letters home, carefully avoiding any suggestion of the possibilities the dawn might bring. But in his little khaki memo book, Pecover wrote down the unspoken question: "I wonder?"

As Pecover and his friends were taking their ease, Andrew McCrindle was sitting outside the Zivy Cave, taking a breather from his work party and chatting with his corporal, a former McGill theological student named Jarvis, better known by his nickname, "The Reverend." The Reverend felt it might be a good idea in view of the approaching battle if the entire party all went down into an old dugout, read aloud from the Bible, and indulged in a short prayer. Everybody agreed to go, but when Jarvis reached the dugout he found that only four had actually turned up. "What the hell," he said. "It's no use of us having a meeting. I'll just read a couple of verses and say a short prayer and then we'll bugger off back to the cave."

As dusk fell and the Easter afternoon darkened into night, the setting sun, a glowing fireball, reddened the khaki world of Vimy. The last airplanes droned homeward. The balloons, caught in the dying light, swayed languidly, like ungainly monsters. Blue smoke curled from the chimneys of the cook-houses near the gun positions. The sun went down and a chill, wet wind sprang up–an omen of things to come. In the shadowed woods, Private Pecover and his chums shivered in small groups and wished they were through with the bloody business they'd come to carry out for Canada.

2

As darkness began to cloak the trenches from the enemy and the long lines of men prepared to move off, the sound of martial music again filled the twilight hours in the rest areas at Bois des Alleux and Château de la Haie. Brass bands, bugle bands, pipe bands, fife and drum bands played their units forward and into history.

Thousands of men were moving through the gloom, wading through the long communication trenches, the reserves heading for the subways, the assault troops for the jumping-off trenches and shell holes well out in No Man's Land. As they passed they called greetings to each other: "There go the 13th! Good old 13th!" and the answering greeting: "Good luck, Toronto!" For the first and the last time all four Canadian divisions would be attacking in line, British Columbia side by side with Calgary, Ottawa next to Vancouver, the Van Doos of Quebec shoulder to shoulder with the Highlanders of Nova Scotia. Off they went, slopping through the mud and water, their paths marked out by luminous stakes, until, cramped and cold, they reached the assault positions scraped out for them in the mud and the chalk of No Man's Land.

For many battalions, especially those trudging through Death Valley on the far left of the line, the move forward was fraught with hazard. The 44th Battalion from Winnipeg found itself exposed to heavy German shellfire, which blew more than one man off the duckboards and into the mud. Fortunately the mud was so deep that the shells exploded well beneath the surface, smothering the troops with filth but not with shrapnel. Private Jack Spears, who had never been under shellfire before, was one who tumbled off the duckboards into mud to his waist. Another man pulled him out by grasping his rifle. Ahead, in the dark, Spears could dimly see a hole in the side of the ridge – the Cobourg Subway. He breathed a sigh of relief at the sight and, with the others, was soon scrambling about looking for a place to sleep. There was none. The floor of the subway was so wet no one could lie down. Spears, who was just twenty – another English immigrant from the West – philosophically turned his steel helmet upside down and sat on it with his feet in the water. He had a long wait ahead of him, since the 44th would not do battle until the following night. For twenty-four hours, Spears and the others sat or stood ankle deep in the muddy gruel of the subway.

The mud was so bad that some men couldn't be extricated by simply grasping their rifles and pulling. It took several men to save the orderly-room sergeant of the 20th. He was so firmly stuck that he couldn't be hauled out by hand.

In the end, the party stretched a pole across the top of the trench, made slings of their belts, and finally tugged him to safety, minus his hip rubber boots.

Most trenches were in ghastly shape. The 48th Highlanders moved up Douai Avenue, which had once been a narrow communication trench leading to the front. Now under constant battering by the German 5.9s, it had been mashed into a gaping, dish-shaped quagmire, fifteen feet wide. To get past the support trenches, known as the Music Hall Line, attacking troops of the 4th Division had to wade through waist-deep water and then stand all through the cold night in the jumping-off trenches – soaking wet, crammed so tightly together in their full battle kit that for most sleep became impossible.

Conditions were the same all along the front. While Jack Spears of the 44th was treading warily along the duckboards crossing Death Valley, Lewis Buck, a former Ottawa lumberjack, almost four miles to the south was also moving forward with the 4th Battalion from Western Ontario, trying his best not to look scared. Like Spears, Buck and his brother Billy, both stretcher-bearers, spent an uncomfortable night in a filthy dugout with water pouring in from the main trench, a foot of mud on the floor, and so many rats crawling over their heads that they too were unable to sleep.

The troops of the 13th, shivering in their cramped positions, waited for hot soup to be brought up from the field kitchens in the rear. Many waited in vain: the cooks bringing it forward were killed by shellfire.

In the Goodman Subway on the 3rd Division front, there was a near disaster. Private Alfred Thomson, working by candlelight, was trying to clean mortar grease off his hands with gasoline. His hands caught fire from the candle, and in his excitement he knocked over the entire can of gas. To his horror, young Thomson saw the flaming fluid racing toward a pile of ammunition. In a few seconds the entire tunnel would have been blown. Fortunately, the man closest to the flames had the presence of mind to seize a blanket and beat them out, saving the battalion for the dawn assault.

There were other, grislier accidents. In an underground

fort, twenty-five feet below the chalk pits behind the 3rd Division lines, David Moir of the 7th Machine Gun Company heard a sudden retort from a neighbouring gun crew and saw a man fall dead. The accident was the result of a breach of discipline. The orders were that all guns be half cocked so that they could be fired by a single pressure on the trigger. Since a mistake could lead to trouble, performing this ritual was reserved for the No. 1 man in the crew, and for him only. But here the No. 2 man had taken it upon himself to cock the gun in the belief that his superior hadn't done it. The gun fired, and a sergeant who happened to pass by the muzzle was instantly killed. It was too late to bury him, and so the corpse was put in the storage dugout. The gun crew lay down to sleep beside it.

Not far away at the neighbouring Grange Subway, Sergeant Evans, his day of rest now totally ruined, had finally reached his destination, loaded down with the signal equipment and carrying the precious bottle of Scotch. The subway at this point was like a scene from Dante – hundreds of men from the 7th Brigade, stumbling about in the dim, smoky light, some trying to sleep, others attempting to scribble a last letter home, or, like Evans, trying to squeeze through the narrow passageway to find a resting place or deliver messages or equipment. At this moment, the gas alarm sounded and the entire, squirming mass began to vibrate as men struggled with their respirators. Evans's own eyepieces misted so badly that he couldn't find his way and ripped off the mask in disgust. He found he had gone too far and retraced his steps once again, squeezing between protesting men until he reached the Brigade Signals room. ''Did you bring the Scotch?'' he was asked. Evans nodded wearily, handed it over, and, being too exhausted to return to his lines, finally found a place to rest. To cap it all, Evans learned the Germans had already put up a large sign reading ''WE HOPE THE CAPTAIN GOT HIS WHISKY.'' The water-soaked chalk was an easy conduit for clandestine listeners.

The Grange Subway was the connecting link between the front line and the dressing stations and ration dumps set up along the sunken road known as the Quarry Line, some five hundred yards to the rear. At eight that evening, as Evans moved up the Quarry Line to deliver his Scotch, Bill Breckenridge was squatting on the floor of one of the dressing stations playing poker, thankful that his long work day was at an end. Alas for him, it wasn't; once again, the M.O. was calling for three men to fetch more water.

The nine card players separated into groups of three to flip a coin, the losing man from each group to join the work party. Breckenridge tossed a franc into the air, looked at it, sighed and mumbled: "It looks like me for it." He had mistaken a head for a tail on the unfamiliar coin, and no one was about to point out his error. So off he went with two others heading for the wells at Neuville St. Vaast.

The shattered village was in turmoil. German shells were falling without let-up. In the moonlight, Breckenridge could see black clods of earth mixed with the debris of broken buildings hurled high into the air. He and the others stayed in the trench until the shelling stopped, then made a dash for the well. By a miracle it was still operating. Unfortunately, twenty men had reached it ahead of them; it would be hours before they could hope to fill their pails.

They knew there was another well some distance away, near the YMCA hut. For the next half hour they waded along the trench, waist deep in water, then struck out overland only to find a longer queue ahead of them and the well almost dry. It was growing late. The battle was only a few hours away now. All felt the need of sleep. They trailed back to report defeat, then, plastered in cocoons of mud, rolled onto the dugout floor and slept.

While Breckenridge was moving to the rear in search of water, Lieutenant-Colonel Cy Peck, the popular commander of the Canadian Scottish, was setting out, at 9:30 P.M., in the other direction to inspect his forward battle headquarters on the 1st Division front. Peck was known as one of the most belligerent battalion commanders in the Corps—a bulky, black-browed British Columbian with an enormous walrus moustache who believed that senior officers should not hang back in battle; indeed, it was his custom to move forward with the assaulting troops. "She's a bear, boys!" Peck would shout over the noise of battle. "She's a bear!"

Peck was accompanied by his artillery officer, his adjutant, S.G. Johnston, and three runners. The Bentanta Subway was so crowded they, too, decided to chance an overland journey. The C.O. wasn't well. Shaking with fever, plagued by a splitting headache, he should have been in hospital, but nothing was going to keep him from the coming battle.

All his life Cy Peck had trained for moments like this one. He had taken every militia course available and had even gone overseas before the war, intending to enlist in the British Army, a decision he found easy to abandon on closer inspection. For Peck was the quintessential Canadian, born in the Maritimes of United Empire Loyalist stock, schooled in Toronto, lured to the Klondike during the gold rush and later to Prince Rupert. Now a proud, if ersatz, Scot who wore the glengarry cocked over one bushy eyebrow, he insisted that no fewer than five pipers accompany him into battle – one for each of his companies and one for himself. He was nothing if not resourceful in his adopted Highland calling. Asked to speak Gaelic at a Hogmanay dinner, Peck extolled the haggis with a five-minute speech in Chinook, the West Coast traders' pidgin. Few present knew the difference.

The Colonel's chills were not helped by the mud. It grew so bad that one of the party had to unlace his boots, climb up the bank of a sunken road in his stocking feet, and pull his footwear after him. The continual shelling was less of an aggravation to Peck, who was used to it. Badly wounded at Festubert, he had insisted on returning to his battalion weeks before his doctors felt it was safe. But now tragedy struck. The little group had been out for only a few minutes when a shell exploded among them. The adjutant, Johnston, was tossed high in the air. The artillery officer and two of the runners were killed outright, the third was seriously wounded. Bleeding heavily, Johnston tried to carry on but was soon a stretcher case. Peck, unscathed, kept on going alone and finished his inspection.

As the evening hours ticked by and the moon went down and the shells continued to fall, the men who would face death the following day slept, talked in whispers, or went on with small, necessary tasks. Major D.J. Corrigall of the 20th arranged for 150 scaling ladders to be placed along his assault trench during the night to enable the troops to scramble out quickly when the barrage began. Lieutenant-Colonel Jack Clark of the Seaforths crawled on his hands and knees along his own assault trenches to speak to every one of his men waiting for Zero Hour. Frank Ormiston of the 44th, sent back to bring up the officers' rations, stole a gallon of their rum and proceeded to drink most of it. Private Lester Giffin of the 85th, carrying bags full of bread and bully beef to the assault troops, emerged from the Tottenham Subway into No Man's Land and came face to face with a new corpse draped over the wire. He would see many more in the hours that followed.   ·

In the Cobourg Subway, on the 4th Division front, Lieutenant J.E. Tait told himself that it was surely no weakness at that time to think of home – of canoes and guns, of trails threading through the woods, of the camp on the river and the smell of woodsmoke in the twilight and the sunset on the lake. In the chill of those last hours, Tait conjured up memories of another kind of cold – of the snowclad trails of winter, the yelps of the huskies, the howl of the Indian dogs. How far away it all seemed! How different, that fragrant world of his boyhood, from this world of mud and starshells, of continual thunder, of endless days and restless nights, of the crump of mortar and rum jar, of devastation, unspeakable misery, and death!

On the 2nd Division front, Lieutenant William George McIntyre, battalion machine-gun officer for the 29th Battalion (Vancouver) – better known as Tobin's Tigers – was writing a long letter to his mother.

"I hope not, but this may be a note of farewell," he wrote, "for we attack tomorrow morning. If this must be goodbye I must try to acknowledge the unrepayable debt I owe you for love and tenderness, encouragement and sympathy, and high ideals all through my life – you have been the best of mothers to us – and to ask forgiveness – I know it has been granted already – for the pain and trouble I have sometimes cost you. God bless you for all your goodness!''

McIntyre was typical of the very best the country had to offer. His family had homesteaded in Manitoba; he had studied under George Munro Grant at Queen's. A good rugby player, he'd been president of his Alma Mater Society, had two seasons' experience as a teacher in Saskatchewan, was working on his M.A. when the call came. When the war ended, he intended to become a minister.

''. . .I feel very cheery,'' he wrote, ''and if my feelings are an index I should get through this alive, but one never knows. I trust humbly in God, whichever way the issue goes and ask success for our arms, forgiveness for our sins and rest after much toiling.''

For William McIntyre that rest came too soon. The following day he was felled by a burst of German shrapnel. He lingered on during the hours of the battle. By ten that evening, he was dead.

3

Midnight passed. It was now Easter Monday. Lewis Buck, the stretcher-bearer, lay beside his brother Billy waiting for the dawn, looking periodically at his watch. He came from a family of twelve who had emigrated from Birmingham to the Ottawa Valley. The watch was a cheap timepiece, long since thrown out of kilter by the reverberations of the guns. But Buck kept looking at it anyway. He couldn't sleep and it was something to do.

F.C. Bagshaw, paymaster of the 5th Battalion from Saskatchewan, lay quietly, trying to sleep, when he heard the voice of his friend Dave McCabe boom out: ''Bag, I'll tell you what we'll do. I'll recite Robbie Burns and you recite Shakespeare.'' For the next three hours they did just that while the entire battalion listened.

At about the same time – 2:30 A.M. – a company of the 262nd German Reserve Regiment, facing the 3rd Division front, reported that the Canadian assembly trenches were filling up. The news came too late. The Canadian artillery had already destroyed the German telephone cables. By the time a runner made his slow way back to the German artillery batteries, the battle was on.

Meanwhile, David Moir and his machine gunners, roused from their sleep in the chalk pits, had left the corpse of the dead sergeant behind and were making their way forward through the Grange Subway. It was not an easy passage, for they were loaded down with guns, tripods, spare parts, and ammunition boxes, and the tunnel was full of sleeping members of the PPCLI. Moir tried to avoid stepping on the sleeping men but couldn't avoid one, who awoke with a grunt. The oath died on his lips when the two recognized each other. He was an old friend from Winnipeg named Anderson, whom Moir hadn't seen for years. Led by guides, the machine gunners crept out into craters half-way between their own lines and the Germans. There they took cover until dawn. Just before daylight a bold sergeant named Catherwood crawled out to bring them a bottle of rum. A German machine-gun crew spotted him creeping back and opened fire, but he managed to roll into his forward trench unharmed.

Not far away in the Bentanta Subway, Gordon Tupper of the Canadian Scottish, a scion of one of Canada's most notable families, had finally convinced his C.O., the indomitable Cy Peck, that he should be allowed to fight that day. With his headquarters staff gravely decimated, Peck had sent word back to battalion headquarters that Tupper should take over as second-in-command. Since Peck meant to lead his men in battle, that meant that Tupper would have to stay behind. "Sir, if you order me to do so I will," said Tupper, "but otherwise I want to stay with my boys." Peck relented, and now Captain Tupper was writing home to his father, Sir Charles Hibbert Tupper, the son of one of the original Fathers of Confederation, Canada's seventh prime minister.

"If I am going to die," young Tupper wrote, "this is

worth it a thousand times. I have 'been over' two or three times before but never with a company of my own. Think of it–150 officers and men will follow you to hell if need be! . . . . I have seen this game for two years and I still like it and feel my place is here. . . . The war has done wonders to me and makes me realize a lot of things I would not have done otherwise. . . .''

He was an attractive young officer, barely old enough to vote but already mature beyond his years, strong and supple, erect of carriage, a company commander of poise and judgement, ''as proud as Punch on the most glorious day of [my] life.'' It was the third time that he had written what he called ''one of those 'in case' letters.'' Unhappily, it would also be the last.

The dark hours of the morning moved leadenly toward their climax. At three o'clock, Andrew McCrindle moved out of the Zivy Cave with his battalion and entered the front line trenches. Suddenly, seemingly out of nowhere, came cartons of chocolate bars and chewing gum. As he munched gratefully on a Lowney's bar, thinking how odd it was to be enjoying a Canadian confection under these tense conditions, a vagrant thought popped into McCrindle's head: if only somebody had thought to bring a camera, what an advertisement *that* would make for the Toronto chocolate firm!

McCrindle's unit was to be in the second wave of the assault, which meant that he and his friends had to move back to allow the first wave room to get a footing and climb over the parapet. McCrindle stripped off his overcoat to give himself more freedom of action. Like so many others he would spend the hours before dawn standing in a sea of mud.

At 3:40 A.M., ''C'' Company of the RCRs reached the jumping-off trenches. Lieutenant Robert England's immediate task was to lead a work party out into No Man's Land to cut the Canadian wire. His best wire cutter was a tough Russian-born private, too impatient to use gloves, who simply rolled the wire aside with his bare hands and uprooted the steel stakes. Suddenly a sniper's bullet struck one of the party, and to everybody's consternation the wounded man let out a shrill cry. Had the enemy been alerted? Flares went up from the German trenches as England and a fellow officer carried the man back. There a stretcher-bearer did his best for him. It was no use. The man was dead before dawn, but fortunately the German line was silent.

At about the same time, Bill Breckenridge and his fellow signallers in the dressing station on the Quarry Line were awakened to the corporal's shout: "Stand to! Get up soldiers and prepare for breakfast in the Zwischen Stellung!"

The men threw off their blankets, crawling with lice, and began to talk about their prospects in the coming battle.

"I'm going over this morning and I'm not looking for a blighty," the corporal declared. "If I'm with the boys after the battle, I'll be satisfied."

"I differ," said another. "A nice little bit of shrap right there"—pointing to his arm—"and I'll pat myself on the back."

And so, joking uneasily, they moved forward through the Grange Subway. The pipe band of the Princess Pats moved with them, ready to play the battalion over the top. Another battalion had nine footballs to place on the parapet, ready to be kicked across to the German trenches when they went over the top—another bit of morale-building bravado. Ahead, silhouetted against the moonlight, Breckenridge could see the line of troops moving into the jumping-off positions.

By this time, the entire Canadian Corps was in position, twenty-three battalions in the forward line, thirteen more waiting directly behind, and another nine along with three British battalions in reserve, waiting to leap-frog through—more than thirty thousand men stretched out over nearly four miles of front, the leading troops already half-way across No Man's Land, lying flat in shell holes or shallow ditches. Clouds began to obscure the bright moon, and as the minutes ticked by, a light, cold drizzle started to fall.

Tensions rose as the officers checked and re-checked their watches. "You're three seconds out, Cooper," Arthur Currie had told one of the Princess Pats' company commanders. "Now I don't want that to occur again."

Whizbang Johnston, commander of the 2nd CMRs—the

same man who had tinkered with the grenade launcher – found these last hours terribly trying. Did the Germans suspect anything? Would an enemy barrage come down suddenly on the masses of men waiting so quietly and so patiently in the cold? The wind had sprung up. The drizzle turned slowly into rain mixed with snow. Johnston stood at the parapet, watching, waiting, praying.

At 7th Brigade headquarters Archibald Cameron Macdonell grew increasingly restive. Time after time he sent his twenty-eight-year-old intelligence officer, Hal Wallis, forward to make sure everything was all right with the troops crouched in the front line. Macdonell was known as a front line soldier; indeed, Wallis was to say he spent as much time at the front with his brigadier as he had in his days as a private. Not for nothing did the men of the 7th call Macdonell "Fighting Mac" and sometimes "Batty Mac" because of his eccentricities under fire. Everybody knew the story of how he'd gone so far into No Man's Land that a sniper put a bullet in his arm. Instead of ducking, Batty Mac had stood up swearing, shaking his unwounded arm angrily at the sniper, who immediately put another bullet in his good arm. And everybody also knew that Macdonell, at the Somme, had insisted on walking among the wounded after the attack on the Regina Trench, unmindful of the enemy shells, to salute the corpses of the Black Watch. A sentimental Scot who sometimes swore in Gaelic in moments of great pressure, Macdonell stopped at every corpse and said: "I salute you, my brave Highlander," until Wallis managed to pull him to safety.

He was a seasoned spit-and-polish veteran, a professional soldier who had served with the Mounted Police in the North West and the Canadians in South Africa. He had endured moments like this before many battles, knowing from long experience that it was the waiting, not the action, that tried men's nerves. He had a sad, Celtic face, but he knew how to hide his emotions, never allowing himself to appear downcast even when things were going badly. When one of his battalion commanders gave him a gloomy response in a corpse-filled dugout during the heat of a Somme battle, Fighting Mac took him around a traverse in the trench and gave him a tongue-lashing: "Smile, man! Smile!" he said. "If you don't I'll do something to you that will make you." After Vimy, Macdonell would replace Arthur Currie as commander of the 1st Division.

But now, with dawn approaching, he could no longer contain himself. Wallis had come back to report everything in good shape, but the Brigadier-General had to see for himself. "We must go up!" he said suddenly. He gathered a party together and set out overland, peering ahead trying to make out shapes in the gloom. Suddenly a German shell exploded a few yards away. Even Fighting Mac was shaken. "I'll go down now," he said to Wallis, rather like a small boy whose mother had caught him outside the yard. But he refused to climb back until the others had made their way to shelter.

By this time a sharp frost had set in, hardening the mud and covering the subway floors with ice that cracked under foot like broken glass. Some men had been standing in the jumping-off trenches for twelve hours in full battle kit, up to their knees in freezing water.

William Pecover, his day of relaxation at an end, crowded into a shallow, muddy ditch, suddenly found himself aware of a strange and ominous silence hanging like a blanket over the trenches after a week of thunder. The guns had ceased, for they had to be rested like spirited animals, tested, and cleaned while new stocks of ammunition were brought to the batteries.

To Canon Scott, who had climbed a hill behind the lines, a tin of bully beef in his pocket, it seemed as if the war had gone to sleep, so heavy was the silence. Zero Hour was approaching, and to him "the thrill of such a moment [was] worth years of peacetime existence," a curious thought for a votary of the Prince of Peace. The luminous hands of his watch crept forward as the sky grew lighter and objects began to appear in the fields below. To the padre it was as if nature herself was holding her breath. It was five minutes to Zero.

The snow was increasing to blizzard intensity – a bitter contrast to Easter's glorious weather. In the distance a German starshell shattered the twilight before it sizzled out in a shell crater. In the assault trenches men were already dying. Harold Barker, the scout with the RCRs, noticed a man from Toronto making holes in the parapet to help his footing when going over the top. Alas, he reached too high. Struck by a sniper's bullet, he tumbled dead at Barker's feet. "No noise," said Barker's officer. "Roll him back." Thus, the first man to go over the top was a corpse.

Three minutes to go. A barrage of gas shells landed in the German rear, killing hundreds of horses. In the 1st CMRs' jumping-off trench, narrow and only thirty inches deep, Private George Johnston sat with his back to the enemy, his knees scraping his chin. Suddenly a dud shell killed the man next to him, spattering Johnston with his blood. Nobody budged.

Two minutes. Now came the whispered order to fix bayonets. The sound of the loose locking rings, rippling all along the miles of trenches, was like the humming of a thousand quivering bees.

Silence. Thirty thousand men held their breath, tensing their cramped muscles for the moment that some had been awaiting since November.

One more minute ticked by, and then a single gun fired. One second elapsed, and then the world exploded as the greatest artillery barrage in the history of warfare burst upon the unsuspecting Germans and the Battle of Vimy Ridge began.

BOOK THREE

The Battle

Moving forward in the full light of that clouded
April morning, we learned full well the nature of the
great modern battlefield. This was war.... The
wounded, friend and foe alike, lay everywhere about
in the cold, wet mud, silent and helpless in their
agony or crying out for help to the stretcher-bearers
who fanned out behind the attacking waves. And just
ahead of us roared the barrage and all the fury of the
fight – the death rattle of the machine guns, bursting
overhead, shrapnel and counter fire from the enemy
guns – all of the fiendish implements of death that
man had devised. In contrast, the conquered area
through which we passed seemed strangely quiet.
Here death reigned, and the agony of pain.

From the unpublished memoirs of
Private William Pecover, 27th Battalion.

CHAPTER TEN

The 1st Division

1

In the apparent chaos of the Vimy battleground there was order of a sort – more order, in fact, than in most battles. Each division had its objective, and within the brigades, each battalion, each company, each platoon – indeed, each man – knew exactly where to head, when they should reach each objective point (marked on their maps by coloured lines), exactly how many minutes to stop before moving forward again, and at what point to dig in and allow reserve troops to leap-frog through.

For each of the four divisions the style and method of attack differed, depending on the frontage, the distance to be covered, and the state of the German defences. There were four simultaneous mini-battles on the Canadian front that morning, all interconnected.

Arthur Currie's veteran 1st Division held the extreme right of the line and had the longest advance of all – four thousand yards to its final objective of Farbus Wood, the small forest just below the eastern slope of the ridge, where so many of the big German guns were hidden. On Currie's right was a British unit – the 51st Highland Division. Its commander, Major-General G.M. Harper, a venerable British regular, was Currie's antithesis. A hidebound commander of the old school whose men nicknamed him "Uncle Harper," he had opposed the use of machine guns by infantry soldiers and had little use for the newfangled tanks. Slavishly devoted to his own division, he was often blind to its flaws.

As they rose from the shallow assembly trenches the Saskatchewan troops on the right of the line could see Harper's Highlanders on their own right. It was important to keep in touch. All battles are confusing enough, but on this particular spine of mud with few identifiable features it would be

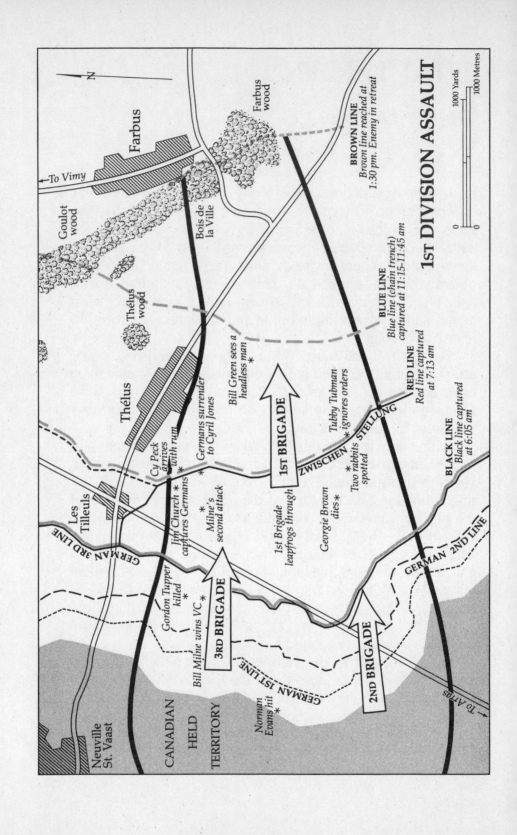

1ST DIVISION ASSAULT

N

To Vimy →

Farbus

Goulot wood

Bois de la Ville

Farbus wood

Thélus wood

Thélus

Les Tilleuls

GERMAN 3RD LINE

Neuville St. Vaast

CANADIAN HELD TERRITORY

To Arras

GERMAN 1ST LINE

GERMAN 2ND LINE

BROWN LINE
Brown line reached at
1:30 pm. Enemy in retreat

BLUE LINE
Blue line (chain trench)
captured at 11:15–11:45 am

RED LINE
Red line captured
at 7:13 am

BLACK LINE
Black line captured
at 6:05 am

ZWISCHEN STELLUNG

1ST BRIGADE

2ND BRIGADE

3RD BRIGADE

Bill Green sees a
headless man *

Germans surrender
to Cyril Jones *

Cy Peck
arrives
with rum *

Jim Church *
captures Germans

Milne's *
second attack

Gordon Tupper *
killed

Bill Milne wins VC *

Norman *
Evans hit

1st Brigade
leapfrogs through

Georgie Brown
dies *

Two rabbits
spotted *

Tubby Tubman *
ignores orders

1000 Yards
1000 Metres

easy for groups of men to wander out of their sector and find themselves tangled with the wrong units, leaving a gap in the line for the Germans to exploit. At Vimy members of each platoon kept their eyes on the men on each flank who carried signs of coloured metal to let their neighbours know who they were. But all attempts by Currie's men to get any information on the intentions of Uncle Harper had been frustrated. This stand-offishness would have serious consequences within a few hours.

Currie's orders were to reach the outskirts of Farbus and Farbus Wood by early afternoon. The division would do this in two stages, each stage consisting of two bounds, although "bounds" is scarcely the right word, for the men were loaded down with at least forty pounds of equipment. The ordinary private carried his rifle, 120 rounds of ammunition, two Mills bombs, five sandbags, forty-eight hours' rations, a waterproof sheet, gas mask, smoke helmet, a ground flare, a filled waterbottle, and a pick or a shovel. Sweating in their heavy greatcoats, stumbling and falling into shell holes, some drowned in mine craters while their comrades struggled to keep up with the barrage as it blasted its way forward.

And some carried considerably more. Norman Evans, the strongest man in the division, found himself burdened with a 225-pound box of Lewis gun ammunition, which he was persuaded to carry on his back, using a tumpline. Evans had actually joined the army to escape hard work, but the members of the 48th Highlanders soon learned that no one else could lift such a load. He had demonstrated his incredible strength on more than one occasion. As a youth working on the railway in Saskatchewan he had shown he could lift six hundred pounds. On the boat going over he had encountered some husky Scots trying to hoist a four-hundred-pound anvil. They sneered at Evans when he offered to help: "What's a little bugger like you think you're going to do?" one asked. Evans hoisted it easily and since that time had been given all the heavy jobs.

Now he stuck close to his friend Joe Lafontaine because Lafontaine never seemed to attract a bullet. It didn't help. Evans was scarcely out of the trench before he felt a hard thump in the groin that knocked the breath out of him. A shrapnel ball the size of a ten-cent piece had entered his groin and emerged just above his hip. Evans went down, throwing off the box of ammunition as he fell, and then waited patiently until the stretcher-bearers dragged him to shelter. By this time his clothes had frozen to his body and had to be cut off. Later his friend Lafontaine turned up, still unscratched.

"How come you got hit and I didn't?" Lafontaine asked.

"I stopped it before it hit you," said Evans wryly.

The first bound would take the division right through the German front line system of forward, support, and reserve trenches. The forward line was as little as seventy-five yards away, and much of it had been pulverized beyond recognition. But farther on the going was harder. By the time the troops had penetrated the entire seven-hundred-yard labyrinth of crumbling ditches and dugouts, some battalions had lost almost half their men.

On the division's left flank, Cy Peck's Canadian Scottish had trouble fighting their way around the clusters of old French mine craters that blocked their advance. The craters were twenty feet deep with slippery sides that led down to six feet or more of slime and water. As the Scottish squeezed through the gaps between the hollows, German machine guns on the far lips fired on the leading companies. The troops paused, then put Currie's platoon tactics into practice, attacking the machine guns from the flanks. The cost was heavy, but the battalion managed to get through the craters into the German forward positions. It was here that Gordon Tupper, leading his company in the running fight that followed, fell dead.

When the attackers reached the second of the three German trench lines, resistance stiffened. Men rushed from shell hole to shell hole, attacking strong points with grenades and bayonets. It wasn't hard to spot them: a mound of corpses indicated their position. Officers were hit; NCOs were hit; but the advance never slackened as juniors took over. Here, a young Scot from Moose Jaw, Private William Johnstone Milne, won the Victoria Cross by acting on his own initiative as he'd been taught. A machine gun on the left was doing fearful damage. Its crew fought off all attempts to capture it.

A fan-shaped heap of corpses was piling up in front of the gun when Milne leaped from a nearby shell hole, crawled on his hands and knees through the mud, and managed to destroy the Germans with a grenade.

Currie's division captured the entire German forward defence system – all three sets of trenches marked on the maps as the Black Line – in just over half an hour, knocking the Germans off balance. To the north, the 2nd and 3rd Divisions were enjoying equal success. All three arrived on their objectives almost to the second, just as they had on the training fields. They would continue to do so; it was one of those occasions in which a battle has gone almost exactly as the planners wanted it to, without the confusion and disarray that has accompanied most set-piece attacks, from Cannae to the Somme. Only the embattled 4th Division, more than three miles away on the extreme left, was in trouble.

The enemy trenches were so badly obliterated that some troops didn't recognize them: the standing barrage had reduced them to a muddy pudding. Yet it was so brief that, as Byng had planned, those of the enemy who survived underground couldn't believe it signalled an attack; they had been used to much longer periods of softening up. When they stumbled from their dugouts, stunned by the fury of the bombardment, they weren't prepared to find thousands of Canadians rolling over them.

2

As the forward platoons of the 1st Division reached their objectives, they searched the sky for the RFC reporting aircraft, identified by black bands and streamers attached to the struts. Right on time, a plane buzzed low over the battlefield, its klaxon blaring over the noise of the barrage. The troops waved flags carrying the divisional symbol – the famous red patch – to show they'd reached the Black Line. Back at divisional headquarters, Arthur Currie got the word that his division was precisely on schedule.

Now, as the division dug in, the barrage moved forward by two hundred yards to hammer the Germans' second defence system half-way up the slopes of the ridge. All along the Canadian front, the troops enjoyed a breathing spell. The leading wave, which had borne the brunt of the 1st Division's attack, moved back to allow the rear wave to come forward and lead the next phase of the assault to the Red reporting line. Behind them, on the ground just captured, the mopping-up platoons attacked small pockets of resistance and, in the army's coldly euphemistic phrase, "neutralized" them. The canopy of steel arced over the heads of the assault teams for thirty-eight minutes. Then, at exactly 6:55 A.M., the barrage began to creep forward once more, and the division advanced, right in its wake, as it had been trained to do.

The troops had almost half a mile of torn ground to traverse before reaching the next objective – the great transverse trench the Germans called the Zwischen Stellung. On the reporting maps this was the Red Line. The ground here was a honeycomb of shell holes in which could be discerned dugout entrances about one foot square. Apart from these and some ruined emplacements there were no observable features; the terrain had been wiped clean of any other signs of human habitation.

The advance to the Red Line was punctuated by small tragedies, blunders, triumphs, and the occasional surprise. As the 7th Battalion approached the shattered copse known as the Nine Elms (the Red objective), a British Columbia officer, Arthur Pollard, was astonished to see two rabbits hopping across the exploding battlefield and equally astonished to see two of his platoon taking pot shots at them instead of at the enemy. True to their training, they didn't stop but banged away on the move. The rabbits got away.

George Alliston, a young bugler with the same battalion – the 7th – also followed the rules even though it cost him many a heartsick night. His closest friend and fellow bugler, Georgie Brown, who had lived next door in Glasgow before the two emigrated to the Canadian West, keeled over and fell into a mine crater. Alliston ran to the crater to pull his friend out, but before he could do so an officer pointed his revolver directly at him and then skyward. The meaning was clear: don't stop for casualties. Alliston trudged forward, leaving his friend dying in the muck.

Resistance was crumbling, yet some of the German machine guns were still firing from the Red Line. Here the indomitable Bill Milne of the Canadian Scottish clinched his hold on the Victoria Cross with a second feat of daring. Vicious fire was holding up the battalion's advance. It seemed to be coming from a haystack directly in front of him. What was a haystack doing in No Man's Land, where every other object had been ground into the mud? Milne crawled forward and discovered, with no surprise, that the haystack was a cover for a concrete machine-gun emplacement. His throwing arm didn't fail him. The first Mills bomb put the gun out of action and terrified the crew, who looked up to see Milne charging directly upon them. They surrendered in a body and the advance continued. The V.C. was posthumous. Milne was killed later that day.

Some hundreds of yards to the rear the reserve battalion – the Little Black Devils of Winnipeg – had a worm's-eye view of the scene on the slopes just above them. Lieutenant Clifford Wells would never forget the spectacle: the dark, scarred remains of Nine Elms in the distance – the battalion's objective – the curtain of bursting shells creeping slowly toward the trees (like a flock of dragons, Wells thought) and the ragged line of khaki figures following close behind. Suddenly the sky darkened and a blizzard raged briefly. It seemed to Wells, peering through the veil of snowflakes, that the men in the advance paid no more attention to the shells and bullets thinning their ranks than they did to the white flakes whirling around them.

At this point the entire battlefield from the Souchez Valley to the banks of the Scarpe was humming with life – a scene of absolute confusion to the unmilitary eye. The three waves of steadily advancing troops, guided by scouts wearing green arm bands, were limned against the white and black puffballs of smoke and earth thrown up by the barrage.

Moving behind them and sometimes through them, often apparently at cross purposes, were other clusters of men: the moppers-up, with their white arm bands and their short grenade launchers; the carrying parties marching stolidly forward, wearing yellow arm bands and lugging mortars, picks, shovels, ammunition, water, and bombs. Threading through this maze of men came the runners, wearing red arm bands, their messages tucked in the right-hand tunic pocket with another red marker on the lapel to signal that the message was there. Above the fray, the occasional low-flying aircraft swooped by, sounding its klaxon, seeking the flag wavers who would report another objective had been achieved. And in the face of this constant forward motion came another line of soldiers, these in mud-stained grey, their faces dejected, their weapons and watches confiscated, traipsing through to the Canadian lines across a terrain that had, until a few moments before, been in their possession for more than two years.

The fight had gone out of the Germans. The dreadful barrage, climaxing their week of suffering, had crumbled their trenches, shattered their guns, wrecked what little morale was left, and reduced them to impotence. They seemed pathetically eager to surrender. Gordon Chisholm, a former Toronto bank teller, heading back to have a wound dressed, suddenly found himself faced with six of the enemy, who seemed to spring out of the ground. As Chisholm limped back to his lines he found the Germans meekly following him like sheep.

Cyril Jones, a subaltern with the Canadian Scottish temporarily separated from his mopping-up crew, suddenly saw twenty Germans emerge from a dugout and beat their way toward him. They surrounded Jones like a swarm of bees, crying "*Kamerad! Kamerad!* Mercy!" and began to pull off their wristwatches and other possible souvenirs, which they pressed on the bemused lieutenant. Jones began to howl with laughter at the spectacle. He pointed helplessly to the Canadian lines and they loped off obediently.

Those Germans who survived had remained in their dugouts, twenty, sometimes forty, feet below the ground. These could not be left alive to attack the advancing troops from the rear. As they passed over the dugouts, the Canadians tossed Mills bombs into the openings and moved on while men were mangled beneath their feet.

If one of the enemy showed the least sign of resistance, he was shot at once or dispatched with a grenade. But few wanted to fight, as Jim Church discovered when he reached the Red Line. Church was only seventeen, a bullet-headed, firm-jawed Slav from Saskatchewan. Just ahead, in a crater, he saw a group of some sixty Germans. This was what he'd been trained for. He reached into his sack of Mills bombs, pulled the pin on one, straightened his arm as he'd been taught to do, and was about to hurl it when an officer shouted, "No! Don't throw it!" The Germans had raised a white flag and were pouring out of the crater, forming a tight circle around their commander who stood on a ration box in their midst, waving the flag and pleading to surrender.

Church protested. The Germans, all armed, outnumbered his small group. But even as the officer spoke they began to throw down their rifles. Church, however, had a problem: he was clutching an armed grenade. Once he released his grip it would explode in four seconds. He tossed it as far as he could; it exploded, and suddenly another crater came alive with surrendering Germans, many of them bleeding from the results of the explosion. They seemed relieved to be out of action. "Me good to go over there," one of them told Church, pointing at the Canadian lines.

The prisoners were a problem. As the battalions couldn't afford to waste men to guard them, they were sent back without escorts, often under the fire of their own guns, which were pouring shrapnel on the old Canadian lines. Others were used as stretcher-bearers and many more were given shovels and told to help their former enemies dig in.

Again, the intensity and brevity of the barrage had caught the Germans off guard. Many were still asleep when the attack took place. So swift was the Canadian advance that some surrendered trouserless. The Canadians were delighted to find that the officers' dugouts, at least, were stacked with food.

Cyril Jones, who had burst out laughing when the Germans surrendered, now found himself in sole command of his company; all the other officers had been killed or wounded. When the Red Line was reached, Jones proceeded to enjoy the privileges of command, establishing himself in a comfortable bed in an officer's dugout lit by electricity and supplied with cases of fresh eggs, soda water, and wine.

3

The forward battalions of Currie's division had reached the Red Line from the Black in twenty-eight minutes. Then the barrage lifted and moved two hundred yards beyond the Zwischen Stellung trench to pour a rain of hot steel on the Germans' defence in depth. It was 7:13 A.M. The leading waves had advanced a mile beyond the Canadian forward line, and for them the battle was over. They had two hours and twenty-two minutes to dig in, consolidate, mop up, and rearrange themselves to allow the 1st Brigade to take over and continue the second stage of the assault.

Over the roar of the guns came a faint but familiar sound – the skirl of the pipes. Looking back to their own lines, the kilted troops of the Canadian Scottish spotted a small group of officers and men stumbling forward toward them. In the lead was the stocky figure of their commanding officer, Cy Peck. The events of the previous night had not helped Peck's illness. He was suffering terribly from stomach cramps, nausea, and diarrhoea, but it is doubtful if any of his men were aware of that. With Peck were his regimental sergeant-major and two batmen, one of whom carried a jar of rum under each arm. At that sight, a ragged cheer went up and became a roar as Peck distributed the rum and set up his headquarters in the captured German trench.

From their vantage point high on the slopes of the ridge, the men of the 1st Division could survey the battlefield. On their right, the British 51st Highland Division was toiling up the slopes and into position. On their left they could see the blue patches on the shoulders of the men of the 2nd Division, also digging in, and beyond that point, through the smoke, two miles away, some of the 3rd Division troops who had also reached their objective. Above and to the left, almost on the crest, the remains of Thélus village could be seen, a haven for German machine gunners. Suddenly a Canadian barrage descended on the already shattered town, and what was left of it was blown to bits.

Just before 10 A.M., the barrage that had been pounding the German defences lifted and began to move forward again. Now the 1st Brigade passed through to take their turn in the front lines, the men laughing, smoking, and calling out to the cheers of the others. And there, strolling along with the final wave, to the consternation of his C.O., was Lieutenant Leslie ''Tubby'' Tubman of the 2nd Battalion, an Eastern Ontario unit. Tubman was in full battle kit, but he had no business being on the field; he'd been given strict instructions to stay back in the transport lines. In army parlance he was ''L.O.B.'' – Left Out of Battle with other officers to form the nucleus of a restored battalion in case of severe casualties. Reproached for disobeying orders, Tubman blandly replied that he was merely on hand as an ''adviser.'' His sergeant was in full command. The eager Tubman survived the Vimy battle but not the war. Not long after, he was killed in action.

The brigade had to go six hundred yards to reach the next objective – a German strong point known as the Chain Trench because of its resemblance to a linked cable. This was to be the Blue reporting line. Once it was taken, the brigade would be given one hour and ten minutes to consolidate before moving on to the final objective.

The damaging fire originating at Thélus had been neutralized by the artillery barrage. Now as the men of the three fresh battalions – all from Ontario – toiled up toward the crest of the ridge, some began to be hit by their own guns: too many shells were falling short. There are certain grisly moments in battle that happen so quickly and so unexpectedly they cannot be absorbed at the moment of impact. All over the battlefield that morning men were experiencing such moments, scarcely comprehending, in the confusion and terror of combat, what they had just witnessed, numbly filing away the horror in the recesses of memory to be retrieved at a later time when it could never again be discarded. Such a moment came to Private Bill Green of New Hamburg as he struggled upwards with his battalion. Suddenly a dud shell whizzed past, barely missing him. It sliced off the head of the machine gunner beside him and took the leg off a lance corporal. The severed head flew through the air like a football, struck another man and nearly felled him. And the headless corpse, blood spouting from the severed arteries, actually took two steps forward before toppling into the muck.

It all took place in an instant, like a scene caught and frozen by a lightning flash. Green had no time to think about it; like everybody else, he had been trained to keep moving. But the incident was seared into his memory to return again and again over the next seven decades. Other scenes would blur and fade, but for Bill Green that brief, explosive incident would never lose its hideous clarity.

In less than an hour, the reserve brigade had reached the windswept crest of Vimy Ridge. Almost at that moment, the sun emerged briefly from the scudding clouds and bathed the countryside to the east in a warm glow. The effect was mystical. The sleet had ended. The smoke of the barrage was gone along with the fog of early morning. Now, spread out before their astonished eyes, the troops were offered a panorama that had been hidden from them for all those months. Here was mile upon mile of verdant countryside, virtually unscarred by war. In the woods just below, the trees were sprouting into leaf. Patches of green appeared in the farmers' fields beyond. The enemy had fled the crest and could be seen below, grey-clad figures, moving eastward, limbering their guns and dragging them along.

But there was little time to stop and stare. The Blue objective lay half a mile away below the crest. Three quarters of a mile beyond that the Brown Line ran directly through Farbus Wood. The troops burst down the ridge, seized the Chain Trench, which was not wired, before 11:15 and signalled to the reporting aircraft that they'd reached the Blue Line. As they dug in, the barrage began to soften up the German lines ahead.

At this point, the division faced a problem. The British on the right of the Canadian Corps weren't keeping up. Currie's right flank, held by the Eastern Ontario battalion – the 2nd – was therefore exposed to German machine-gun fire. The British had encountered great rolls of wire that had not been destroyed by their own barrage or discovered by their forward patrols. Unlike Arthur Currie, who had insisted on checking the wire in front of his own sector and had immediately pulled his troops back so that it could be obliterated, their commander, "Uncle" Harper, hadn't taken this precaution. The 51st suffered heavily because of Harper's oversight and so did the troops from Eastern Ontario, who were forced to put Mills bombers on their flanks to hold back any German attempt to attack with enfilade fire.

In spite of this, the advance of the 1st Division continued with remarkably few casualties. The Germans were in no position to rally their troops for any counterattack. Without waiting for the British, the Canadian 1st Brigade left the Blue Line at 12:25 as the barrage crept eastward to shatter Farbus Wood. The eastern side of the ridge was steep – almost clifflike in spots – and thick with underbrush. Down the Canadians scrambled, wondering how the Germans could have allowed themselves to be pushed off such a promontory. By 1:30 they had seized the German battery positions in the wood. So hasty was the enemy retreat that in one officer's dugout, lunch had been abandoned untasted on the table. The forward platoons of the 4th Battalion devoured it greedily.

All in all, the reserve troops who fought the final stages of the 1st Division's battle had had an easier task than the first wave that jumped off at Zero Hour. In spite of the threat to its flank, the 2nd Battalion, being in reserve, lost only 108 men killed, wounded or missing. By contrast, the 7th from British Columbia, which was in the vanguard of the forward brigades, lost 364 – more than three times as many. And yet in the neighbouring 2nd Division, the opposite proved true. There it was the reserve battalions that suffered most, the leading waves that escaped. War, like life, is as random as a roulette wheel.

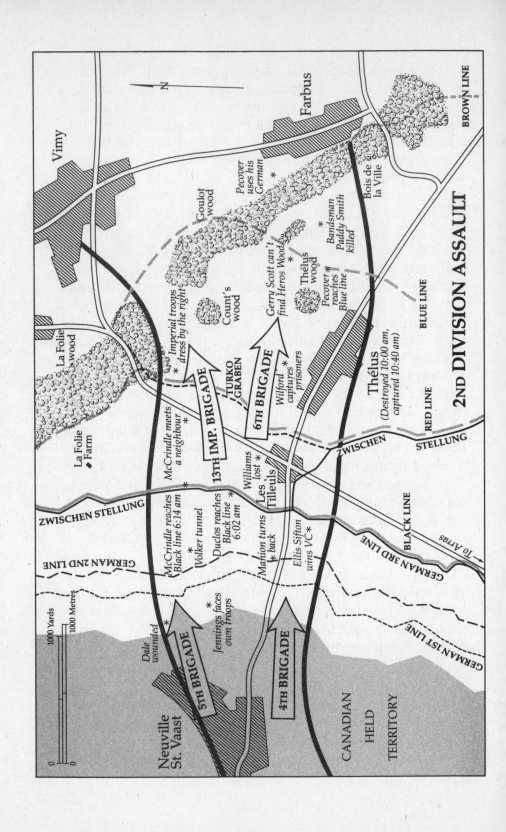

2ND DIVISION ASSAULT

N

Vimy

Farbus

BROWN LINE

Goulot wood

Pecover uses his German

Bandsman Paddy Smith killed

Bois de la Ville

Imperial troops dress by the right

Count's wood

Gerry Scott can't find Heros Wood

Thélus wood

Pecover reaches Blue line

BLUE LINE

La Folie wood

TURKO GRABEN

13TH IMP. BRIGADE

6TH BRIGADE

Wilford captures prisoners

Thélus
(Destroyed 10:00 am, captured 10:40 am)

RED LINE

La Folie Farm

McCrindle meets a neighbour

Williams lost
Les Tilleuls

ZWISCHEN STELLUNG

McCrindle reaches Black line 6:14 am

Volker tunnel

Duclos reaches Black line 6:02 am

Mahron turns back

Ellis Sifton wins VC

ZWISCHEN STELLUNG

GERMAN 2ND LINE

BLACK LINE

GERMAN 3RD LINE

To Arras

1000 Yards
1000 Metres

Dale wounded

5TH BRIGADE

Jennings faces own troops

4TH BRIGADE

GERMAN 1ST LINE

Neuville St. Vaast

CANADIAN

HELD

TERRITORY

0

CHAPTER ELEVEN

The 2nd Division

1

On the 2nd Division front that dawn – to the immediate left of
the 1st – William Pecover had a ringside view of the opening
stages of the battle. His battalion was in reserve; it wouldn't
go over the top until nine o'clock. Standing in the trenches
with the other Winnipeggers, Pecover watched the forward
elements of his division – the Ontario regiments, the New
Brunswickers, and the Victoria Rifles from Montreal – launch
the attack.

In front of him the sea of mud seemed to stir into life.
Out of the maze of dark shell holes and bits of jumping-off
trenches, thousands of khaki-clad figures suddenly emerged,
some leaping, some crawling in the mud, some stumbling
and lurching forward against a lurid background of flame
from the belching guns. Pecover could not contain his awe at
the spectacle unfolding before him: the desert of No Man's
Land lit by the stark flashes of red; the wet, grey dawn beginning to streak across the sky; and, later, the lines of prisoners stumbling back toward him, a scattered few at first,
then greater and greater numbers. How, he wondered, could
they have survived? It seemed that no inch of ground held by
the enemy could have escaped that rain of death.

Unlike the 1st Division, the 2nd had only two miles to go
to reach its final objective, the belt of woods that ran for a
mile and a quarter along the base of the ridge on the German
side, concealing more of their guns and reserves.

If the momentum of the attack could be maintained, the
division would roll over what was left of the hamlet of Les
Tilleuls and the ruins of Thélus, from whose cellars and dugouts on the ridge's crest the Germans were harassing the attackers. Then, at the half-way point, fresh troops would sweep
down the far side of the escarpment, through the stumps of

Thélus Wood and Heros Wood to reach the gun positions hidden in the long forested belt at the base – the Brown Line on the maps.

Tactical and logistical considerations dictated the strange wedge shapes of the two divisional sections. The 2nd Division's front was narrow at the outset – about half a mile wide, or less than a third of the breadth of the 1st Division's front. It conformed almost exactly to the contours of Neuville St. Vaast, directly in the rear, from whose caves and subways the attackers would emerge. But, unlike the 1st Division's attacking sector, which narrowed as it reached the ridge, that of the 2nd Division broadened out to a mile and a quarter at the Brown Line, to conform to the shape of the slender belt of trees – Bois de la Ville and Goulot Wood – that ran between the captured villages of Farbus and Vimy flanking the divisional boundaries.

Obviously, an extra brigade would be needed at the half-way point – the Red Line near Les Tilleuls – to fill the widening gap. The additional troops would be British – supplied from the 5th Imperial Division, now seconded to the Corps reserve.

As Pecover watched and waited for his turn, he could see that a weird kind of shuffle was taking place up ahead. Into the ghastly limbo of exploding debris, the clumps of attacking Canadians advanced and vanished. Out of it, moments later, straggled other clumps of men – endless groups of shaken Germans.

One of the first Canadians into the maelstrom was a young New Brunswicker, Charles Norman Dale. He stumbled forward behind his sergeant with two others filing after him. None made the German line. Almost immediately a shell hit the ground two yards away, buried itself four feet in the mud, and exploded, knocking Dale off his feet and breaking his right leg at the top of the thigh. Dale stuck his rifle in the ground, shucked off his equipment, crawled to a dugout, and waited more than six hours before a German prisoner came along and carried him to a dressing station. It was his first time in action – and his last.

As Private Dale slumped into the mud, an unforeseen problem arose at the mouth of the sap that Duncan Macintyre had discovered leading into the Phillips Crater in the heart of the battlefield. Macintyre had his signals crew installing telephone lines and rolls of surface cable in the sap ready to jump out of the crater and keep up contact with the rear as the assault rolled forward. Now, as the attack began, the Divisional Signals Officer, Major D.C. Jennings, climbed to the surface facing his own lines only to see his own troops advancing upon him, hurling grenades. As far as they were concerned, anyone that far forward had to be a German. Jennings popped quickly back into shelter. After the first wave passed over their hideaway, the Pioneer section sprang out and began to dig a six-foot trench to hold the cable while the signallers, moving right behind the advancing troops, unrolled the telephone wire.

Meanwhile, Andrew McCrindle, the baby-faced nineteen-year-old with the reserve platoon, Victoria Rifles, waited his turn to go over the top. Already McCrindle could see men falling – not in the dramatic way they did in illustrations or in the silent films of the day, flinging their hands in the air or clutching their hearts before toppling forward; here on the slopes of Vimy they just seemed to sink disconsolately into the earth. The dead did not distress McCrindle as much as the wounded who were left groaning and bleeding in the mud without help while the battle swept on past.

Almost as soon as McCrindle went over the top he fell into a shell hole, up to his knees in mud and water. He felt like crying: there he was, floundering helplessly in the muck while everybody else shuffled past him. At that moment another youngster spotted him, leaned over, and with his rifle pulled McCrindle out. The smell of cordite was strong in his nostrils as he hurried to catch up. Shells were bursting all around him; but it seemed to Andrew McCrindle that some good fairy had equipped him with an invisible shield, for while others fell, he survived.

A machine gun opened up on the left. McCrindle's platoon sergeant deployed his men, just as in training, to attack from three sides with rifle grenades. One lone German survived the tactic; they sent him back on his own to the Canadian lines.

Ahead lay the great Volker Tunnel, too deep within the ridge to be damaged by the Canadian artillery. It was packed with Germans armed with machine guns, waiting for the first waves to go by before attacking the second waves from the rear. But McCrindle's company didn't stop – the task of clearing the tunnel would be left for others. Up ahead they spotted a German officer leading a group of men, firing his pistol directly at them. One of McCrindle's platoon mates, Arthur Abbey, rushed at him, knocked him down, took his pistol, forced the others to surrender and, for that deed, won the Distinguished Conduct Medal.

The objective lay dead ahead. Not far away the troops could see the captain of a neighbouring company, V.E. Duclos, turning about and throwing open his overcoat so that the men of his company could spot the white lining and keep their alignment. Duclos was already wounded but kept going until his men had punched their way through the enemy's forward defences to reach the Zwischen Stellung trench. This was the Black Line. Duclos's men reached it at exactly 6:02, ahead of schedule. McCrindle's company arrived twelve minutes later. Behind them a furious fight was taking place for the Volker Tunnel, which had been mined. Fortunately, the Canadians discovered the trap in time and cut the leads before they were all blown up. At 6:25 the soldiers, digging in, heard the sound of a klaxon above them as a British biplane swept past to see by the flag signals that the objective had been reached.

In this first advance, the casualties had been remarkably low. Again the fury of the barrage had unnerved and surprised the Germans. McCrindle and his section rounded up one astonished officer still in his pyjamas. Piqued at having to surrender to mere private soldiers, he vainly demanded the presence of an officer. McCrindle stole his epaulettes as a souvenir and hustled him back to the Canadian lines.

Over on the right, Sergeant Ellis Sifton's platoon was digging in with their fellow units, all from Ontario. During the advance Sifton had performed an act of conspicuous gallantry, hurling himself at a machine gun that was mowing down his men, charging directly at its crew, clubbing some with his rifle and slashing at others with his bayonet. He didn't know it, but that act would win him the Victoria Cross. Nor would he ever know it. As he supervised the capture of the prisoners, a wounded German managed to reach for his rifle, point it at the sergeant, and squeeze the trigger. Sifton was dead before he hit the ground.

The enemy casualties were catastrophic. Entire battalions were wiped out. One of the battalions of the 79th Reserve Division, directly across from the Canadian 2nd, was so badly cut up that only one man escaped. This was Musketeer Hagemann, a quiet and sober farmer from the Lüneburg area of Germany. At first, Hagemann's battalion held fast and Hagemann was reassured to see rows of the Canadian attackers felled by his machine gunners on the flanks. But the German artillery proved useless, firing over the heads of the Canadians and falling on empty areas in the rear. On the other hand, Hagemann noted, the Canadians directed their own artillery to points of resistance by means of Very light signals from their aircraft. Soon men began to topple all around him. The machine gun next to him, which had created such devastation, was put out of action, the entire crew dead. As the Canadians committed fresh troops to the attack, the Germans moved back from crater to crater, dying and bleeding as they retreated. It seemed to the stolid Hagemann that there wasn't anybody left on his side who wasn't hit. He himself was bleeding from three wounds. His right arm was paralysed. He could fight no longer and so fell back, the only man in his entire battalion to reach safety.

2

On the 2nd Division's Black Line, the troops were being shuffled, the rear waves moving forward to take over from the leading waves in order to continue the next stage of the assault, following the creeping barrage to another great German trench known as the Turko Graben, just below the crest of the ridge. This was the Red Line; some of the troops would have to travel a mile to reach it. But the German resistance continued to crumble, and in a little less than half an hour the Turko Graben was in Canadian hands. Here, in a large shell hole, the troops were treated to a sight that might have been affecting had it not seemed so ludicrous: a dozen Germans, every man jack of them on his knees praying.

The Germans, meanwhile, were shelling the ground just ahead of the Canadian trenches, long since vacated by all but the staff officers moving their battle headquarters forward over captured territory.

Stranded in No Man's Land, half-way between the old Canadian front and the Zwischen Stellung trench, Captain Robert Manion, the future politician, thought his last hour had come: his wife, back in Ottawa, would receive his pocket diary, but she would never know the details of how he, the Medical Officer of the 21st, had met his end, huddled in a trench with shells exploding all about him, a wounded colonel clinging to him and a padre on his knees beside him.

For that was all that was left of the thirty officers and men who had set out that morning at 7:30 to establish a forward headquarters in the captured Zwischen Stellung trench. Shrapnel had sent all but this trio scuttling back to safety, and now the colonel was bleeding from wounds in the arm and the leg.

To Manion it made more sense to go forward than back. It wasn't easy. His wounded C.O. stumbled and fell to his waist in the mud. Manion pulled him clear. As they blundered forward again, the wounded man toppled into a shell hole. Clearly he couldn't go on; they would have to turn back. Manion tried to carry the C.O. When that didn't work, he dragged him for 250 yards to the shelter of another shell hole. They threw away their equipment and began crawling from hole to hole in a zigzag pattern toward their own lines. Miraculously, they made it.

Captain Manion, who won a Military Cross for his efforts, finally reached the Zwischen Stellung by another route, passing on his way a group of tanks bogged down in the mud. They were supposed to support the advance of the division in its attack on Thélus, but they hadn't even reached the Black Line. The mud was too thick, the shell holes too deep, the ground too treacherous, and the High Command too uncertain that these devices should be used. They looked awesome enough with their great snouts heaving over the lips of the craters, their engines snorting, and their treads rattling. But now, as Manion passed them, all were immobilized.

Up ahead, on the Red Line – the Turko Graben – the barrage lifted and came down on the German positions two hundred yards farther on. The troops dug in, the moppers-up did their work, and fresh units of the 6th Brigade – "The Iron Sixth" – held in reserve until this moment, moved out of their positions and prepared to push through to the next objective.

Back on the old Canadian front line, William Pecover's battalion was the last to go over the top, since it was the reserve battalion in the reserve brigade. Standing at his post, both horrified and enthralled by the spectacle before him, Pecover felt a strange elation. As the short word of command was passed along the trenches, he and his fellows clambered out into the mud. Here he came face to face with the horror of war: wounded men sprawled everywhere in the slime, in the shell holes, in the mine craters, some screaming to the skies, some lying silently, some begging for help, some struggling to keep from drowning in the craters, the field swarming with stretcher-bearers trying to keep up with the casualties. As Pecover trudged forward over the broken wire and the pocked terrain, he struggled to ignore the human agony around him.

Captain Claude Williams's machine gunners were also pushing off at almost the same moment. Williams had won the coin toss with a fellow officer to take them over the top. They lurched forward under back-breaking loads, heavily encumbered not only with normal kit and weapons but also with guns, tripods, ammunition belts, water, and spare parts.

The machine gunners had no sooner set out than a German gas shell landed among them. The six-foot Donald Fraser heard a "pop" close to his face and suddenly found that he could no longer exhale or inhale; his breathing was paralysed. With a celerity that astonished him, he slipped on his respirator and his breathing was at once restored. Soon he was stumbling across what had once been No Man's Land, passing a series of shell holes full of dead Canadians.

It occurred to Williams, as it had to others, that the scene of the attack was nothing like the popular conception of a line of soldiers racing forward and bayoneting the enemy. What he saw instead were clumps of men, scattered over the entire front, toiling slowly up the ridge. The scenes of death on all sides were not heroic but sickening. Williams passed one man lying in a deep shell hole crying "Water! Water!" The top of his head had been blown off, exposing his brains. Fraser noted it too, and couldn't help thinking that the brains looked rather like fish roe. That sort of thing was never shown in the Victorian paintings of gallant officers expiring slowly in the arms of their comrades, a small pink stain on the shirt front, a hand raised languidly in a kind of greeting as if the hero were sinking into a peaceful sleep. Such scenes, if they had ever existed, were obsolete. Never again would war be referred to as "noble."

3

Having reached their position on the Red Line, the forward battalions of the Iron Sixth watched the bombardment of Thélus and waited for their turn to move. Their task was to seize the blasted village, then head for the next objective – a series of German support trenches marked as the Blue Line on the maps.

On their left, the fresh British brigade had also moved into the line. One of the regiments, the King's Own Scottish Borderers, formed up in front of the Nova Scotia Rifles. To the astonishment of the Maritimers, taking cover in the trench, the Scotsmen stood tall, following the sergeant's command to "right dress ranks," as if on a parade-ground, totally oblivious to the presence of enemy snipers. It was magnificent, of course, but it was not war as the twentieth century was coming to know it.

At 9:35, right on schedule, the barrage again began to creep forward. All across the battlefield, observers in the rear could witness a spectacle they would never see again: the wall of exploding steel sweeping up the slopes of Vimy Ridge like a rainstorm with the youth of Canada following directly in its wake.

There is, alas, no such thing as a perfect battle. Tragedy mars the best-planned assaults. Some of the so-called silent batteries of Canadian field guns, pushed forward at the last moment and concealed until now from the enemy, opened up, only to fall tragically short. In that short advance toward Thélus more men were killed by their own shells than by the Germans. The survivors soldiered on firing their Lewis guns from the hip.

This was Harry Wilford's first battle. He was a twenty-two-year-old Englishman who had come to Canada in 1904 to join the Barr colonists in the North West. War was in his blood: his ancestors had come to England with the Conqueror, and some member of his family had been in the armed forces since that day. To get to France Wilford had dropped his reserve commission and reverted to the ranks. Now, as he moved forward with the men of the 28th Battalion, all recruited in the Canadian North West, he spotted a group of Germans holding out in a crater directly ahead. Wilford dived head first into a smaller shell hole, pulled the pin on a Mills bomb, and to his horror fumbled it. The live grenade tumbled to his feet; he had four seconds to get rid of it or be blown to bits. Wilford took a running kick at the bomb, booted it out of the shell hole, and then straight-armed a second one at the Germans, only to discover that they had unaccountably vanished.

Where had they gone? He found a small opening at the bottom of the crater that turned out to be the rear entrance to a chalk pit. Without a thought, Wilford squeezed down the narrow passage until he came to a turn. Now he cursed himself for a fool. There he was, all alone, with nobody behind him and God knew how many of the enemy lurking just around the corner. Gingerly, Wilford pushed his rifle around the corner and pulled the trigger. It was pitch black; all he could hear was the report of the gun. Back he squirmed into the crater, only to discover the Germans streaming out of the main entrance to the chalk pit. Fortunately, they were surrendering. One man who'd been hit in the stomach was carried out, and Wilford realized with a pang that it was his own blind shot that had done the job. For the rest of his life Harry Wilford was bothered by that incident. It was all so unnecessary, he realized: the Germans had been going to surrender anyway.

By ten that morning, the forward battalions reached the outskirts of Thélus. Within forty minutes, the entire village was in British and Canadian hands. The town was a shell; no wall stood higher than six feet. Only in the medieval caverns beneath was there evidence of enemy life – a bedroom complete with wallpaper and a feather bed with real sheets, a fully equipped bar, a table set for a meal with no fewer than five waiters in attendance. Back they went to the POW cages.

Above ground, all familiar landmarks had vanished under the battering of the artillery. Claude Williams felt lost. He and his encumbered gun crew had trouble keeping up. Williams had plotted his route carefully to take him through the hamlet of Les Tilleuls on the Lens-Arras road – not far from the Red reporting line on his map. But he could find no trace of it. At last he came upon a military policeman and asked him where Les Tilleuls might be. "You're in the middle of it, sir," the M.P. told him. Williams looked about: nothing. Not even a stump to mark the passing of the scented lindens.

Up ahead, Gerry Scott, a sniper with the 29th, searched vainly for Heros Wood, which lay beyond Thélus on the German side of the ridge. He'd been sent forward to scout the wood for signs of the enemy, but he couldn't find any wood and he couldn't find any enemy. He had a good map and knew he was in the right square, but there was no longer any wood. It had been smashed out of existence; here, too, the very stumps had been destroyed.

Scott finally found a wood. He recognized it as Bois de la Ville – the division's objective. It was supposed to be bristling with Germans, but Scott saw no one. He searched about, picked up some souvenirs, entered a German tunnel running under the ridge, and came face to face with an active howitzer whose crew, waiting apparently for any excuse to get out of action, fled immediately. Scott went back to his battalion to report that the objective was clear.

Meanwhile William Pecover's platoon had also reached the obliterated village of Les Tilleuls and was trying to get across the Lens-Arras road in order to reach their jumping-off position on the Blue Line. All Pecover could see ahead of him was bursting shrapnel. The Germans were trying to block the fresh troops from crossing the road. It seemed impossible that anyone could make it through that hail of steel balls. "We've got to get through," cried Pecover's officer. "It's every man for himself. Keep the line as well as you can. When you get close to the road run for it."

Pecover dashed forward, men toppling all around him. Somehow he made it. At 11:30 the battalion was in position on the Blue Line, the men working their way forward through the old German support trenches, crawling between the dead and the wounded and through the swarms of prisoners and the moppers-up with their white arm bands. Officers and NCOs scurried about straightening out the line. Pecover and the others crawled into the shell holes about 150 yards ahead of the new position, just short of the next barrier of enemy wire. There they waited for the barrage to move ahead and the last stage of the attack to begin.

4

On the right the barrage was already lifting and the 1st Division was starting to push forward. The 2nd Division troops could see the red patches on their neighbours' shoulders, bright as new wounds. At 12:42 the barrage began to lift on the right of the 2nd Division, exactly as planned. By one o'clock the whole line was in motion. Bandsman Paddy Smith of

Pecover's unit went forward with the assaulting troops, piping a regimental march on his piccolo. The notes came through the rumble of the barrage, sweet and clear, a haunting reminder of older, gentler wars. Then suddenly the music stopped. Paddy Smith was dead.

A machine gun opened up on the left of the Winnipeggers. Two rifle grenades blew it out of action. On the right, a battery of German 5.9s stood fast, the crew firing point blank at the advancing troops. One of the company commanders, Captain Lane, rushed forward, seized the guns, and killed those of the crew who refused to surrender. Later those same guns would be turned around to fire on their former owners.

The barrage, which had been concentrating on Farbus and Farbus Wood on the 1st Division front, now lifted as the troops seized the Brown Line and began bombing the German dugouts. Again the cry of *"Kamerad!"* was heard. When no one came out of one dugout, William Pecover tried out his high school German. *"Kommen sie hier, Herr Fritz,"* he called at the top of his voice, and out they came, apparently delighted to be steered toward the rear.

The Winnipeggers dug in on the lower east slope of the ridge, waiting for a counterattack that never came. It was bitterly cold, so cold that Pecover took a chance, climbed out of his funk-hole, and began to walk briskly up and down the sunken road that ran across the ridge. Suddenly a gas shell exploded a few feet away. He raced back to the security of his hollow, only to find that another soldier had appropriated it. A moment later a second shell blew the new occupant to pieces.

Claude Williams, meanwhile, had sited his four machine guns on the eastern side of the ridge to protect the front against counterattack. With that job done he found a dugout, climbed down its twenty steps, and proceeded to eat his iron rations. His batman miraculously produced a loaf of bread. Williams wanted to know how he got it.

"Did you notice that stiff near our headquarters?" the batman replied. "He had a loaf in his haversack. It was a bit bloody so I cut out that part." The two hungry men munched it without a second thought.

On the crest of the ridge, Andrew McCrindle, with other Victoria Rifles, was guarding a large group of prisoners. To McCrindle, the captured Germans had a strange, sour smell, and he wondered if it came from eating too much liverwurst. "Maybe we smell like bully beef to them," he thought.

At that moment, one of the Germans spoke to McCrindle in excellent English.

"24th Battalion," he said, indicating McCrindle's cap badge. "The Vics, eh? I knew where your armoury was – on Cathcart Street?"

McCrindle was taken aback. "How did you know?" he asked.

"I used to work in the restaurant in the Windsor Station," the German said. "We used to go over to Mother Martin's for a quick one."

McCrindle, who didn't drink, had never heard of Mother Martin's, a well-known Montreal watering-hole.

"I guess you're too young to know that joint," the German said. He explained that his father had wired to him to come home as soon as the war started.

His officers had warned their men, he said, not to be taken prisoner as the Canadians were all Red Indians who would scalp them. "I knew better," he said. "So I thought it would be a good idea to be in a place where the Canadians would take me, so here I am."

McCrindle accepted all this, as he had accepted everything that day, without much thought. Only later did the oddness of that encounter begin to seep in.

Duncan Macintyre had more time to reflect. The Brigade Major of the 4th left the Zivy Cave at three that afternoon and walked across the battlefield, surveying the scene around him. Everywhere he looked, men were digging in. Telephone lines and light railways were already being laid, and special parties were picking up the dead and taking them to the cemetery grounds. Some of the corpses were sadly familiar. There, lying with his pack still on his back, was Major Frank Thompson, who had played basketball with him in Regina and had eaten dinner with him just before the battle. Now Thompson lay crumpled, his pack giving him an odd, humpbacked look, as if he'd pitched forward from the weight of the load, face down, his knees buckled beneath him, his hands spread out in front.

Macintyre turned away, saddened, but he could not escape the hideous concomitants to battle – a dead German spread-eagled on the back wall of a trench, his arms flung wide as if crucified, his head crushed to a red pulp like a mashed strawberry; others lying as if sleeping, their clothes torn from them by the shell blasts; still others ripped open, their entrails spilling into the mud. In that drab landscape, a new and brighter hue had been added: the water in the shell holes was now red with blood.

All along the ridge men could be seen staring in astonishment at the pastoral scene to the east, marred only by one incongruous spectacle: a shell had struck a German freight train as it crossed a bridge over the road from Arras to Lens, and one car hung precariously over the side. The whole of the Douai Plain was wide open, with the enemy in full retreat; but the sudden collapse of his defence lines could not be exploited. Ironically, the very fury of the Vimy barrage had made that impossible: the ground was so badly broken that the guns could not be hauled forward between the shell holes.

The men on the ridge stared helplessly at the enemy soldiers, fleeing out of their reach to the rear where no barrage could reach them. "Jesus Christ Almighty!" cried a Forward Observation Officer with the 27th. "For two fucking years, I've been waiting for a chance like this and now I can't use it."

No one, it seemed, had expected such a sudden and overwhelming victory.

CHAPTER TWELVE

The 3rd Division

1

On the face of it, the 3rd Division had an easier task than the two divisions on its right. It had two objectives instead of four and it had little more than twelve hundred yards – about three quarters of a mile – to reach its final objective in the La Folie Wood below the steep eastern slopes of Vimy Ridge.

The division's two forward brigades swept through the triple defences of the Germans in half an hour, right on schedule. Some did not bother to wait for the barrage to lift but, in their eagerness, risked being raked by Canadian gunfire as they moved right through it. The second and final objective – the Red Line – was seized by eight that morning; there were no Blue or Brown objectives to attain because of the configuration of the ridge. And so, for the 3rd Division, the main attack was over in just two and a half hours. While the 1st and 2nd Divisions were still engaged in a fighting advance, the battalions of the 3rd were already over the crest, mopping up and digging in.

In spite of this, the division faced a hazard that no one had expected. Its left flank was in peril. Something had happened to the 4th Division, which was supposed to have seized the heavily fortified defences on Hill 145. They hadn't done it; the hill was still in German hands. The battalions advancing in its shadow – RCRs, Princess Pats, and especially the Black Watch – found themselves exposed to a merciless fire, raining down on their left from the highest point on the ridge.

The four battalions of the Canadian Mounted Rifles – former cavalry units now recycled as the 8th Brigade infantry – had an easier time on the division's right flank. At Zero Hour, Corporal Gus Sivertz, a twenty-two-year-old optometrist from Victoria with a pugnacious face and blue Icelandic eyes, was in the middle of the brigade front. He lay with his nose in

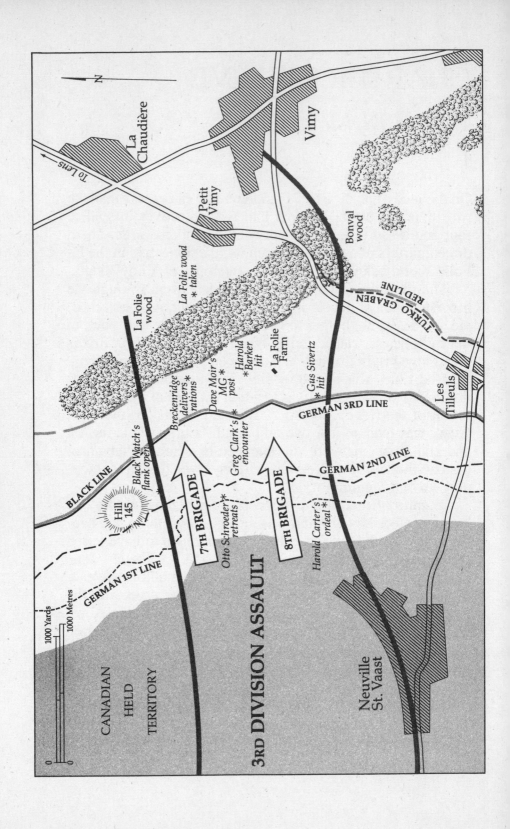

the mud, his backside pulled down as low as feasible so that his buttocks wouldn't be ripped by machine-gun bullets when the barrage exploded. Over the top he went at dawn and almost immediately tripped over some wire. At that very moment a German shell landed three feet from him, burrowed into the mud, and exploded. Sivertz felt a terrible blow on his helmet, which was pushed down over his ears. ''I'm killed,'' he thought, and was surprised to find himself alive. The shell had blown a huge piece of chalk out of the mud, and it was this that had struck him.

Suddenly he was all alone on the battlefield; already his little group of section mates had passed him by. Standing there in the carnage he felt that the entire German army was aiming at him. Like so many others that day he was swept by a helpless feeling of terrible loneliness. He wanted desperately to reach out and touch a friendly shoulder, to cry out ''Here I am!'' And so he stumbled forward, tottering in the debris, hunched under the weight of his equipment, blindly searching for his friends until, to his relief, he saw them ahead and caught up with them.

Not far away, John Alvis from Saskatchewan found himself in a similar fix. He was lost and he was scared – not of the enemy but of his reputation. He'd tried to help some machine gunners floundering in the mud of an enemy trench and got too far behind. Now he couldn't find the identification discs stuck in the mud by the advancing platoons. He wandered first to the right and then, trying to correct his position, to the left, where machine-gun fire drove him into a shell hole. There he sat and worried. Had he brought shame to his unit? Would he be charged with desertion? It seemed to him that an eternity passed while he strove to get his bearings, but it wasn't much more than a minute before he spotted the comforting figure of his company commander searching about for other lost men. In spite of his problem, Alvis went on to win the Military Medal and a promotion to sergeant.

From this point on nothing could stop the 8th Brigade. Gus Sivertz's battalion, the 2nd CMRs, was in the Zwischen

Stellung trench in twenty-five minutes, and there Sergeant Al Swanby ate the German commander's Easter Monday breakfast–three eggs with beautiful white bread. In a corner of the dugout Sivertz spotted a case of Carnation Milk, sent from Seattle and marked "Hoover Belgian Relief Fund."

Ahead Sivertz could see the barrage, which had moved 150 yards beyond the captured trench. In forty minutes it would begin to creep forward again as fresh troops pushed through to the Red Line on the far side of the ridge. But Sivertz's group couldn't hold back. Fred Selke nudged Sivertz and pointed ahead: "I believe there's a bunch of Huns in that dugout."

"Toss down a Mills bomb," Sivertz advised.

"No, to heck with it. I'll go down there and get them," said Selke.

He descended six feet into the dugout, turned a corner, and came face to face with a German officer who fired his Luger directly at him, missing Selke's heart by a mere two inches and crippling his arm. It was the German's last act. When he came out of the dugout, Selke's friends shot him.

Others followed with their hands up, but as one passed Corporal Jock MacGregor, he pointed his rifle at MacGregor's face and pulled the trigger. Sergeant Swanby, who'd just eaten the commander's breakfast and was a good amateur boxer, caught the motion out of the corner of his eye, swung his entrenching tool, sank it right through the German's helmet, and deflected the bullet.

Five minutes later a German machine gun began to chatter from a steel slit in a concrete pillbox on the right, threatening to hold up the advance to the Red Line. Sivertz offered to work his way around and attack it with grenades from the rear. He circled for sixty yards on his belly and then, growing impatient, stuck his head up to get his bearings. He felt a shattering blow, as if somebody had hit him with a mallet. There was no pain, just the stunning power of the blow.

The world had gone unaccountably silent. "That's funny," he thought, "what am I doing here?" He couldn't stop spitting for some reason, but it didn't help; his mouth kept filling up with a salty fluid. He put his hand to his face; it came away covered with blood. He felt the top of his head; it was swathed with bandages. He looked about for his comrades; there was no one there, no one at all. "By God, I've been hit," he realized. "I've got a blighty and I'm going to get the hell out of here."

Vaguely he remembered somebody turning him over – a stretcher-bearer – and then, on leaving him bandaged, dismissing him with the words: "It's a stiff." Semi-conscious, he had been unable to reply.

As the brigade plunged on down the steep eastern slopes of the ridge, as the battalions on his left continued to endure the German fire from Hill 145, as the fresh troops of the 1st and 2nd Divisions were nearing the Blue and Brown Lines and the embattled 4th tried vainly to fight its way to the highest point of the crest, Gus Sivertz, still bleeding from a four-inch gash across his temple, staggered back to the Canadian lines.

The world had reverted to slow motion. Sivertz felt like a man taking gigantic seven-foot steps, almost as if he were floating over the top of the ground. He felt hilarious; he wanted to laugh out loud, to speak to strangers. He threaded his way through reserve troops moving forward, maintaining a running conversation with the reinforcements as they passed by. He asked one man for rum. The soldier took one look at his head wound and told him nothing doing.

By this time the Germans, rallying from their initial shock, had put up a heavy artillery barrage on the rear Canadian areas to try to stop fresh troops from getting forward – the same shellfire that Dr. Manion and his C.O. were facing over on the right. But Sivertz, despite his light-headedness, was shrewd enough to notice something about the enemy barrage. McNaughton's counter-battery work had knocked out so many German guns that the artillery could cover only one divisional sector at a time. Sivertz got as close to the line of falling shells as he could, then waited for it to jump to the next divisional front. When it did, he made it through.

He had no idea where he was. The guns had obliterated

every distinguishing feature. At last he spotted a piece of white-painted wood with a two-inch triangle, sticking out of the mud. He pulled it out, wiped it clean on his pants, and saw that it read "Cross Street." With relief he flung it into the air. That was his trench – the exact point from which he'd started that morning at dawn!

A few moments later Sivertz spotted two big strips of red cloth and realized he'd reached the medical trench. He was sitting patiently with six other wounded men waiting for aid when a medical sergeant, picking out the haemorrhage cases, spotted him and dragged him through the door of a dugout. In the roulette wheel of battle, this arbitrary action saved Gus Sivertz's life. Just as they stepped down into the dugout they heard a sound above them like a freight train roaring across the sky. A moment later a shell exploded in the trench they had just quit. All that was left of the other wounded men were tatters of uniforms and bits of flesh.

He was moved back to one of the rear dressing stations, where he received an anti-tetanus shot and an indelible blue cross on his forehead. An eager YMCA officer, handing out cigarettes by the handful, was so excited that he kept pushing them into Sivertz's mouth one after another. It was no use; Sivertz had lost control of his jaws and couldn't hold them.

He was, in the army vernacular, one of the "walking wounded." Back he walked to his own artillery lines, where the turbaned Sikhs of the Lahore heavy artillery were manning the big guns. They had already moved forward to lengthen the range into the German back areas. Sivertz, now completely punch-drunk, oblivious to his surroundings, walked directly into the muzzles. He dimly heard an officer give the order to fire. Four gigantic shells screamed not more than a foot above his head.

Sivertz had lost all sensation in his knees. They seemed to have turned into rubber. As he stumbled down the cobblestones of Mont St. Eloi, like a fish thrown out of a stream, he spotted an Oriental in a Canadian uniform, one of the Japanese-Canadian volunteers. The Japanese had been blinded by shellfire. Sivertz could no longer walk. The blind man propped him up; Sivertz gave him eyes. The two crippled men, clinging to each other, managed to work their way to a dressing station where the wounded were queued up in droves waiting for attention. Two days later, Gus Sivertz was still there, the mud of the battlefield still caked on his clothes, the blood partially dried in his boots, and his long underwear stuck to his body hair.

By the time he was taken to the hospital train, Sivertz was all in. The dressing station had been so crowded there was no place to lie down. He climbed into an upper berth and didn't have the strength to pull off his boots. A nurse came by and gave him a package of Wrigley's, but he couldn't move his jaws to chew the gum. The world around him turned black and stayed that way until he awoke in a hospital to find a nurse with a strong Aberdonian accent cutting away his clotted hair with a knife. Gus Sivertz thought she was the most beautiful woman he had ever seen.

2

While Sivertz was lying unconscious in the mud, bleeding from his head wound, some of his comrades, unable to contain themselves, were still rushing forward against all orders, directly through their own barrage, to seize La Folie farm on the very crest of the ridge. They occupied it before seven o'clock – nothing more than a heap of ruins and fallen trees flattened by shellfire. An hour later the 3rd Division's final objective – the woods on the far side – was in Canadian hands.

On the crest of the ridge, over to the left, a dangerous gap had opened up between the two brigades of the 3rd Division: the RCRs hadn't kept up. The battalions on either side would have to send men over quickly to plug the hole in the line. Gregory Clark, the youngest and shortest officer in the 4th CMRs, got his orders at 8:30. He was to take an armed squad at once and meet a similar force from the Princess Pats at the centre of the gap and hold it until the RCRs arrived.

Off went Clark, a roly-poly figure loaded down with a Lewis gun and a sack of bombs, leading his men as they bobbed and wove from shell hole to shell hole, tripping over mine craters, ducking German grenades, spraying pockets of resistance with bombs and bullets, desperate to link up with the neighbouring battalion. At last he spotted a squad from the Pats stumbling toward him, led by a tall, gangling soldier, twice his height. As they flung themselves toward each other gratefully, the newcomer looked at Clark. "Don't I know you?" he said. Clark nodded slowly. It was the bully who had made his life a living hell back at school in Toronto. Clark was never so glad to see anybody in his life. Together the two former adversaries closed the gap.

Here too the Germans in the forward lines had been stunned by the speed of the attack. Otto Schroeder, a Berliner with the 262nd Reserve Regiment facing the 3rd Division front, had just got to sleep after a long, weary night of duty. Suddenly there came a heavy drumfire, and he awoke to the shouts of the dazed sentries, crying: "Outside! The British are coming!"

Schroeder was up in an instant, all tiredness gone, knowing his life was at stake. Even as he started to hand out grenades, the sound of rifle fire on his left told him the enemy had broken through and were rolling up the German positions. Schroeder's corporal ordered him into the dugout to bring up another box of hand-grenades. He was half-way back up the thirty-two steps when he heard the corporal shout: "Come up to the left! The British have already passed the trench." Schroeder dropped the grenades, climbed up into the trench, and found himself alone, except for a corpse draped over what was left of the parapet.

Very gingerly he made his way past the lip of the trench. All he could see in every direction were khaki-clad soldiers in the flat steel helmets the Germans dubbed "straw hats." To Schroeder they looked like men on a rabbit hunt; some, surprisingly, seemed drunk.

The situation called for ingenuity. Schroeder seized the nearest dead body, pulled it back into the trench, and lay down beside it like a corpse as the assault waves passed over. Suddenly, a strapping Canadian appeared and, more out of curiosity than anything else, stuck his bayonet into the corpse. That was the worst moment in Otto Schroeder's life. He couldn't stay still. The big Canadian saw him flinch and shouted: "Come on!" As Schroeder struggled to understand what he said, the Canadian shrugged his shoulders. As suddenly as he'd arrived, he disappeared, leaving the German alone once more.

Schroeder was off and running when another Canadian popped out of the ground, fired, and wounded him in the right forearm. As Schroeder stumbled on, bleeding from his wound, a familiar figure jumped out of some cover and greeted him. This was his friend Private Cordes, fortunately unhurt. Now the two men, grasping each other by the hand like two small, lost boys, began to wander aimlessly among the piles of Canadian and German dead mowed down by opposing machine guns.

At last they found a dugout. Their own heavy guns were now dropping shells directly on the ridge, and so the pair took cover on the dugout's top steps.

"Where are we?" Schroeder asked. Cordes thought they were still in enemy territory. Schroeder disagreed.

"We stay put until our division makes a counterattack," he declared.

As they were discussing this plan, a door in the dugout opened and a Canadian stepped out. Now an absolutely astonishing spectacle greeted them. Beyond the door, in the midst of the battle's fury, were six Canadians contentedly playing cards. They didn't even look up from their game or pay any attention to the two grey-clad Germans. It turned out they were medical orderlies. When the game ended, one sauntered over.

"Hello, Fritz," said he. "Are you wounded?"

Schroeder nodded. The medic looked at his arm and pronounced "Not good."

He bandaged him up and gave the pair something to eat and drink. When Schroeder had gained some strength, the orderly led him back to the dressing station, where he was treated by a Canadian doctor and sent farther back to Neuville St. Vaast. There he saw the reserve battalions and realized that the Canadians meant to hold Vimy Ridge at all costs. He was one of the lucky ones and knew it; hundreds of his comrades lay piled up in mounds on the bloody slopes they had vainly tried to defend.

3

Lieutenant-Colonel Chalmers "Whizbang" Johnston, the commanding officer of Gus Sivertz's battalion, pushed forward at nine o'clock that morning to set up his headquarters in the old German trench system. On the way he noticed the advancing troops trudging along like sightseers on a Sunday stroll, swapping cigarettes or stopping along the way to eat their iron rations. These were the members of the reserve battalion, 5th CMRs, whom Sivertz had encountered as he moved back.

One man had been left behind, a luckless private named Harold Carter, not much more than a child, really, who had lied about his age when enlisting and was only sixteen on the day of the attack. Carter had had the misfortune to slip and tumble back into the trench when the company went over the top at 6:50 that morning. Two members of the Lewis gun team had already been wounded and were lying at the bottom when Carter fell on top of them. Unable to proceed, they loaded the youth down with four bags of Lewis gun panniers and helped push him out of the trench.

By this time the three waves of his battalion had moved on, and young Carter, struggling with the sack around his neck as well as his rifle and other equipment, found it hard going over the pitted terrain trying to catch up. This enforced slowdown probably saved his life. It seemed to him that all the Germans in the Kaiser's army had opened up on him personally. He ducked into a shell hole, lay in the water, and tried to keep out of sight.

Three times he tried to climb out of the pit; three times enemy bullets splashed around him, throwing mud in his face. He tried putting his helmet on his rifle and raising it above the lip of the pit. More bullets splattered around him. He lay in the mud, silently noting an observation balloon, loose from its moorings, sailing back toward the enemy lines. Once again he raised his rifle. This time there was no reply. His battalion had finally managed to clear out the Germans who had hidden in the shell holes waiting for the first waves to pass over so that they could emerge to harass the troops from the rear. Carter cautiously gathered up his sacks of ammunition, slung them around his neck, climbed out of the muck, and toppled unscathed into the Zwischen Stellung trench to the cheers of the Lewis gunners who surrounded him.

Over on the left, the 7th Brigade had advanced with the same split-second timing as the 8th, moving in section rushes between the series of vast caverns that made up the Crater Line. The brigade reached its first objective right on the dot of 6:02 A.M.

But now there was trouble! The plans had gone awry. The brigade had come within range of the German machine guns on Hill 145. The guns had not been silenced and were wreaking terrible damage, especially on the Black Watch on the extreme left of the front.

Bill Breckenridge, manning the phones in the signals dugout well to the rear, got the first hint of trouble when his buzzer sounded and an officer's voice shouted indistinctly over the sound of the barrage: "What's the hold up on our left? The flank is open. Get it closed without delay; the Germans are sniping our men and I'm going to lose every man unless that flank comes up immediately."

But the flank did not close. No one seemed to be able to make contact with the neighbouring battalion. Shortly after that, the line went dead.

Nevertheless, the 7th Brigade continued to advance, following the barrage as it crept toward the final objective. Harold Barker, the RCR scout, let his eagerness get the best of him and was hit by his own curtain of shells. During training at Bruay among the tapes that represented trenches, Barker had felt a growing impatience waiting for the simulated barrage to creep forward. It took so long to get moving! The significance of those mounted officers carrying flags, cantering slowly across the counterfeit battlefield, had never quite sunk in. Now, after waiting so long in the cramped trenches, he was eager to push forward. He'd been told that he was the connecting file between "C" and "D" companies – that it was his job to make sure the men on both sides of him kept up. But Barker couldn't wait. There didn't seem to be much opposition from the Germans. He plunged ahead, felt something pound into his back, and fell to the ground, bleeding from wounds in the back, mouth, chest, and leg.

As he lay squirming in the mud a dozen of the enemy walked past him and offered to help. Dizzy from his injuries, Barker no longer knew where he was – just that he had been captured and was now a prisoner of the Germans, who were lugging him across the battlefield. Only when they reached the Grange Subway did it dawn upon the dazed and baffled scout that it was the Germans who were *his* prisoners.

The wounded were only too well aware that they would have to fend for themselves until the stretcher-bearers arrived. Their friends could not stop; the line had to be maintained. David Moir, the machine gunner with the RCRs who had slept with a corpse the previous night, saw one of his battalion sitting on what was left of his legs, calmly smoking a cigarette. Moir was impressed by the man's coolness, for he was bleeding to death and no one could stop to help him. Moir called for a stretcher-bearer to staunch the wounds, but by the time he arrived it was too late.

As Moir stumbled forward he came upon one of the enemy cowering in a shell hole. Moir was as scared as the German, but it was the German who surrendered, tearing off his wristwatch and belt as souvenirs. The man was so relieved to be captured that Moir thought he was going to kiss him.

But the going was hard. Hill 145 was still holding out, and the fire from this uncaptured fortress was withering. By the time Moir and his men reached the crest, only three members of the fourteen-man gun crew were left to set up their weapons. Moir himself came face to face with a wounded German who seemed to be reaching for his rifle just as Moir rounded a traverse in the enemy trench. One of the RCRs stabbed the German to death with his bayonet. To Moir, the look of hatred on the dying man's face seemed to say: *Okay, buddy, I'll remember you and be looking for you in the next world.* Moir would always remember that and wonder about it, sadly. Had the German been intending to kill him, or was he merely trying to surrender? He would never know.

The gun crew, what was left of it, was ordered to set up its weapons in a trench the battalion was digging a hundred yards in front of its main forward line – a precaution against a possible German counterattack. From this spot, Moir could look right down on the hamlet of Avion, nestled at the foot of the ridge. But he had little stomach for sightseeing. From Hill 145 directly above them to the left, machine guns and shells pounded the new emplacements. Moir and two others took shelter in one shell hole, while the fourth, a new man named Walker, sought refuge in another hole twenty-five feet away. Moir thought it safer to have two men to each shell hole and so crawled over to join Walker. The new man was sitting quietly reading his mail, which had arrived late the previous night. Moir spoke to him, but Walker didn't reply; and Moir now saw why. One of the bullets from Hill 145 had struck him in the neck, killing him instantly.

The stench in the RCRs' trench was dreadful. The decomposing body of a German, uncovered by the diggers, hung over the back wall. To Moir's astonishment and disgust a new machine gunner – a replacement for the dead Walker – began tearing the body out with his bare hands to see if there were any souvenirs in the corpse's pockets. The Canadians were known for this incorrigible habit. The Germans had a saying: ''The British fight for glory, the Canadians for souvenirs.'' How thin, Moir thought to himself, is the veneer of civilization.

4

Back at the signals dugout of the Black Watch, a linesman covered with mud staggered in, threw himself on a bunk, and began to give details of casualties. It was the first news of the battle that Bill Breckenridge had had since the line went dead. Now, he and another were detailed to go out and repair it. They followed the wire out into the tunnel and over into the Duffield Crater until they found the break. As he mended the wire and tested the line, Breckenridge could see the British planes flying above him, glittering in the brief noonday burst of sunlight. The Canadian guns were still roaring, but the German shelling was weak.

At that moment, a German rolled over the lip of the crater.

"What's the matter, Heinie?" asked Breckenridge's fellow linesman. "Are you hit?" The German only tossed his head in agony. He'd lived through the barrage but was bleeding from two wounds in his arm and two more in his chest. The two signallers could only feel compassion and guided him back to the regimental aid post. By now the enemy was so thoroughly cowed that the medical officer of Breckenridge's battalion, Captain Hale, actually captured five prisoners, his only weapons being a pair of scissors and a flashlight.

Some of the captives died from their own fire. George Kilpatrick, the battalion's padre, and a wounded officer were helping a German back to their lines. The prisoner was walking between them when suddenly he slumped. An enemy dumdum bullet had torn out his heart.

When the battalion moved its headquarters to the crest of the ridge, Breckenridge and the signallers moved as well. The Black Watch was consolidating its position four hundred yards ahead of the 4th Division troops on its left, who were still struggling to seize Hill 145. Thus the battalion was forced to curl its front around to close the gap and form a defensive flank to prevent a German breakthrough. In the first four hours of the battle the Black Watch lost two hundred men.

One of the wounded, Roy Henley, was surely the youngest Canadian in action that day. He too had lied about his age and somehow managed to get past the recruiting officers even though he was only thirteen when he enlisted. On the day of the battle he was fourteen. By nine that morning, Henley had a bullet hole through his water bottle and two through his kilt. Two more bullets had grazed his foot, actually tearing his sock; yet there wasn't a scratch on him. The sixth time he wasn't so lucky. A piece of shrapnel struck him in the back, and for him the battle was over. But he survived that and another wound at Passchendaele and lived to fight and survive again in the Second World War.

At battalion headquarters, the commanding officer of the Black Watch, Major S.C. Norsworthy, felt a growing sense of frustration. The 54th (Kootenay) Battalion of the 4th Division was supposed to be on his immediate left. Where were they? When Breckenridge handed him the field telephone he could hear the C.O. shouting over the line to the Brigade Major of the 7th, impressing upon him the seriousness of the position.

"Can you get the unit on the left to do something?" Norsworthy shouted. "If they can't clean out that machine-gun nest I'll take a dozen men and clean it out myself."

But it would take more than a dozen men. During the past hour the Black Watch had lost fifty dead and wounded from the sniping on Hill 145. Something would have to be done, Norsworthy kept saying, but nothing could be done until the hill was taken. The Kootenay battalion seemed to be in disarray. A few members of the unit had made contact with the Black Watch, but the main body was nowhere to be seen.

Meanwhile a ration party had arrived at headquarters, and Bill Breckenridge and a fellow signaller were ordered to take the rations to the battalion's advance headquarters beyond the crest of the ridge. It was not an enviable job. The gap between the two divisions was still open, and the German snipers were busy. The runner sent out to guide Breckenridge was suffering from shell shock, having just seen two of his

257

friends killed by his side; he had lost his bearings and was no longer sure of his direction.

The trio set off across the shell-torn slopes, tripping over wire, sinking in mudholes to the waist, crawling over corpses. Suddenly the guide turned to the others, white-faced, and announced that he was lost. They stumbled on in the general direction of the front line, their rifles further encumbering their progress, the shrapnel and stray bullets hissing above them.

A German 5.9 shell hit twenty yards ahead, sending up a geyser of mud that showered them as it fell. Breckenridge had jumped into a shell hole to escape the blast and was now stuck fast in three feet of muck. Another shell landed beside them with a crump, piling more earth on him.

"For God's sake," cried Breckenridge, "pull me out and let's beat it before we get hit!"

The other two hauled and grunted and the signaller emerged, leaving half his clothing on the barbed wire at the bottom of the hole. They ran two hundred yards to another shell hole, sat on its edge with their legs in the water, and began to laugh uncontrollably, partly out of nervousness, partly out of relief.

"She's a great old war," Breckenridge said. "That damn fool of a Fritz almost got us."

"It was close enough," his companion replied. "The mud saved our necks."

After two hours of stumbling about the lines they finally found their advance headquarters and tossed the rations off their shoulders.

"Here are your blinking rations," Breckenridge growled, and explained their close shave.

"That's too bad," said one of the headquarters men. "We've got all kinds of German rations here. If we'd have known we would have called and told you to remain at your H.Q."

He waved an arm around the dugout to indicate mountains of German rations stacked in every corner. Breckenridge nodded glumly, went into the dressing station, handed the medical officer a jar of rum – the one item the Germans hadn't left – and then headed back to his own lines.

Over on the right, Private George Johnston of the 1st CMRs was talking to a German prisoner, a former cook who'd worked in New York and spoke good English.

"I'm sorry for you," said the German.

"Why?" asked the astonished private. "You're going back to live in a prison camp."

"Yes," replied the prisoner, "but you don't know if you're going to get killed or not. I'm not."

And that was all too true, for the battle was not yet over. The 4th Division had not been able to achieve its objective.

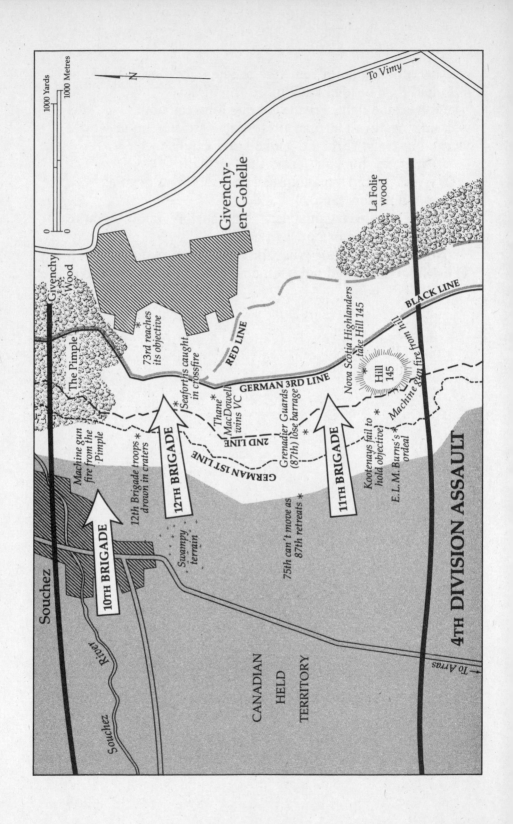

Souchez

To Vimy

Givenchy-en-Gohelle

La Folie wood

Givenchy Wood

The Pimple

*
73rd reaches its objective

RED LINE

GERMAN 3RD LINE

Nova Scotia Highlanders take Hill 145

*
Seaforths caught in crossfire

*
Thane MacDowell wins VC

*
Grenadier Guards (87th) lose barrage

Hill 145

BLACK LINE

Machine gun fire from hill

*
Machine gun fire from the Pimple

2ND LINE

GERMAN 1ST LINE

*
12th Brigade troops drown in craters

12TH BRIGADE

*
Swampy terrain

*
75th can't move as 87th retreats

11TH BRIGADE

*
Kootenays fail to hold objective

*
E.L.M. Burns's ordeal

10TH BRIGADE

Souchez River

Souchez

CANADIAN HELD TERRITORY

To Arras

4TH DIVISION ASSAULT

1000 Yards

1000 Metres

N

CHAPTER THIRTEEN

The 4th Division

1

What had happened to the 4th Division?

By mid-morning it had become terribly clear that the left flank of the Vimy assault was in chaos. Few of the attackers had been able to reach their objectives, and many who did had been hurled back; there were gaps all along the line. Worst of all, the fire from Hill 145, which was supposed to be seized by the battalions of Victor Odlum's 11th Brigade, was creating havoc among the neighbouring units of the 3rd Division digging in on the ridge to the immediate right.

The planners had badly underestimated the strength of this bastion, by far the toughest and best-defended section of the ridge. Although it lay only six hundred yards from the Canadian trenches, the slope was far steeper and higher than the gentler rises to the south. The Canadian guns had not been able to blast down to the honeycomb of concrete tunnels and dugouts – the deepest on the escarpment – that sheltered the German reserves. Nor did they realize that the Germans had carefully camouflaged a network of concrete machine-gun nests on their side of the crest. These hidden guns were purposely kept out of action until the moment of the attack. Thus, the division was lured into a hail of fire.

The 4th was also the weakest division in the Corps as a result of the abortive gas raid that had left it badly mauled on March 1. That débâcle had shaken the troops. Close to seven hundred men were casualties; a dilution of green troops had reduced the fighting capacity of the division. The worst blow was the loss of so many officers. Two of the battalions chosen to make the final assault on Hill 145 had lost their commanders. In addition, they had had to replace half their officers and NCOs just five weeks before the Vimy battle.

Victor Odlum's system of trench rotation, which made it

impossible for his battalions to train as a team, may also have contributed to the anarchy that reigned on his front that cold morning. The other divisions removed entire battalions from the line for rest and training. But Odlum's had to rehearse piecemeal because he maintained permanent battalion sectors in which smaller units were rotated. Because each battalion always had some men in the front line, its commander naturally kept his eyes focused on the front, where the danger lay, while lesser officers took over the training. Clearly, in the Canadian Corps senior officers were given a good deal of leeway, encouraged to act on their own initiative. Byng had let Currie have his way in the matter of trench raids. Watson of the 4th had let Odlum have his way in the matter of troop rotation. And Odlum let Major Harry Shaw, the acting C.O. of the Grenadier Guards (87th), have his way when he asked that the artillery leave one German trench undamaged. It was a major miscalculation.

This trench, in the very centre of the brigade front, formed part of the Germans' second line of defence. In hindsight it seems incredible that the commander of an attacking battalion would ask the artillery to hold off. At the time, however, Shaw's reasoning seemed to make sense. The trench was only a short distance from the Canadian line – not much more than the length of a football field; no doubt he felt his men could rush it before the Germans could recover from their surprise. The slopes facing him were steep; if the trench were destroyed by the Canadian barrage, the heaped-up rubble could form a barrier over which the men, sweating up the incline, would have to scramble. But if captured intact, it would provide instant protection from the guns on the heights above.

Whatever his reason, Shaw's request was granted, with devastating results. In the first six minutes, the Grenadier Guards lost half their number. Of eleven officers, ten were wounded – five mortally. The fire from the undamaged trench slowed the advance; the troops, unable to maintain the timetable, lost the protection of the barrage, which leaped over the German positions. Nor did they ever regain it. Some tried to escape over to the right, only to find themselves inextricably mixed up with two other battalions. Many of the Mississauga troops – the "Jolly 75th," who were supposed to back up the Guards – couldn't even get out of the assembly trenches because of the pile-up in front.

Jack Quinnell, the red-headed scout who had survived the March 1 gas raid, managed to force his way over the top directly behind the Guards. "My God," he said to himself, "there's no barrage at all." Ahead of him there was only mud, shell holes, and corpses. All Quinnell could see were hordes of the enemy in his path, pouring out of the galleries and passages unscathed, slaughtering the men in front of him. He jumped into a hole full of refuse and was pinned down by an explosion that half covered him with earth. He didn't dare move because he knew that if he popped into sight he'd be a dead man. He was certainly a sick one, suffering so badly from trench mouth he could scarcely speak and so seriously from trench foot he could hardly walk. But he didn't die. When he finally made his way to the rear he kept asking himself: *What went wrong?*

As a result of this stalemate, a dangerous enemy bulge appeared in the centre of the line – the kind that every commander fears – a salient bristling with machine-gun and mortar nests that the Guards had failed to destroy. From this vantage point the Germans could pound the flanks of Odlum's remaining troops on the Canadian right (already under fire from Hill 145) and those of the neighbouring 12th Brigade on the left, bogged down in the swamps in the teeth of a blinding snowstorm.

Now the 4th Division's attack was divided into two separate skirmishes with the salient separating them like a knife piercing the line.

The 12th ran into trouble early, for the terrain its troops had to cross was the soggiest in the entire Vimy sector. Scores of wounded men slid into the reeking shell holes and drowned. An eerie spectacle greeted the soldiers who finally relieved the 12th the next day – dozens of corpses sitting under the water at the bottom of the great slimy craters, as if pausing for a moment to rest.

The going was so hard that some battalions could not keep up with the barrage. This left them sitting ducks for the machine guns in the salient. The 38th from Ottawa, which was closest to the German bulge, had by-passed three large craters in the confusion, all swarming with the enemy. The battalion now found itself attacked from front, flank, and rear.

It was here that Major Thane MacDowell, a darkly handsome company commander from Lachute, won the Victoria Cross. With two battalion runners beside him, MacDowell leaped forward, bombed out two machine-gun nests, then acting entirely alone chased one of the survivors down the fifty-five steps of a long tunnel. Seventy-five feet underground, in the pitch blackness, he could hear human sounds. He shouted aloud, demanding surrender, his voice echoing in the confined space, but there was no answer. MacDowell kept going, turned a corner in the tunnel, and suddenly came face to face with two German officers and seventy-seven members of the Prussian Guard.

By rights MacDowell should either have become a prisoner or a corpse at that moment. Instead, with enormous aplomb, he called back to imaginary troops as if he were at the head of a small army. At that, all the Germans raised their hands. MacDowell was in a quandary. He knew that if he were to lead all seventy-nine of the enemy up the long stairway to the top the Germans would quickly overpower him and his two runners. He solved the problem by telling them off in small groups and sending these up in a series to the runners waiting up above. The first Germans to reach the top realized they'd been bluffed. One made so bold as to reach for his rifle. That was the end of him. MacDowell had already won the DSO for a similar capture of fifty Germans earlier in the war. Now he added the purple ribbon of the V.C. to his decorations.

The Winnipeg Grenadiers, following behind MacDowell's unit, were supposed to push on through to the next objective beyond the ridge. A few reached it but could not hold it; none returned alive. The rest of the battalion was unable to go further. By nightfall it had been reduced to two hundred disheartened men out of a total strength of seven hundred.

Stewart McPherson Scott, a subaltern with the Winnipeggers, was totally confused. He sat in a big shell hole all day long, gathering together the wounded as best he could. He had no idea where his battalion had got to. He was being harassed by his own artillery but had no way of letting the gunners know that their shells were falling short – the snow was too thick for his flares to be seen. And he had no way of getting word back to find out where the other companies and platoons might be.

Scott bound up the wounded who crouched with him in the shell hole; then, when dusk fell, he moved back a little where he found a confused mêlée of men from three battalions all mixed up together. Scott summoned the most reliable of the NCOs and did his best to straighten things out and hook up with the flanking units. For the next four days he stayed in the front line.

The other leading battalion of the 12th Brigade, the Seaforth Highlanders from Vancouver, was as badly off as its neighbours in the maze of shell holes and obliterated trenches. Under fire from the Pimple on their left and from the German salient on the right, they had lost all sense of direction. They too failed to reach their objective. By nightfall the battalion had only sixty men who were not killed or wounded. Of the thirteen officers, eleven were casualties. The Germans never let up. Harry Bond, a stretcher-bearer with the Seaforths, had the unnerving experience of trying to carry a wounded man back through the fire on a stretcher. Before he could reach his own lines a sniper had shot the wounded man through both hands.

Of the four battalions in the 12th Brigade, only the 73rd reached its objective that morning with minimal losses, thanks to the protective presence of the 10th Brigade, acting as an anchor between the Canadians and the British on their left. The 10th had orders not to move until the other two brigades seized their objectives. Its job was to take the Pimple on the following day. But the discouraging events of Easter Monday had postponed that plan.

2

In the other mini-battle on the right, the remaining two battalions of Odlum's brigade, faced by the unexpectedly strong opposition from Hill 145 and the flanking fire from the German salient, quickly lost their momentum. The 102nd Battalion from Northern British Columbia, dubbed "Warden's Warriors" after their popular C.O., managed to gain its objective half-way up the slope, but only at terrible cost. With every officer knocked out, a company sergeant-major took over until he, too, was put out of action by wounds in the hands and stomach.

The Kootenay battalion was supposed to leap-frog through and seize Hill 145, but that proved impossible. Caught in the crossfire between the German machine guns on their undefended left and the nests hidden on the hill above, the Kootenay troops were pinned down. A few struggled toward their objective; none returned. The rest were thrown back into the arms of Warden's Warriors, causing further confusion.

All that morning, while the other divisions triumphantly seized the ridge and drove the Germans back across the Douai Plain, the headquarters staffs in the subways along the 4th Division front received confusing and demoralizing reports. Runners sent out to get information were often killed before they could get back. Telephones were out of commission. At least one reporting aircraft was shot down before it could send a signal.

In the Cavalier Subway, at the battle headquarters of Warden's Warriors, reports were so confused that the acting C.O., Major A.B. Carey, decided to go forward himself. He took his own runner and a scout sergeant; the latter was killed almost immediately, but Carey wandered about the battlefield for three hours, vainly attempting to find his men, and then returned, in the guarded words of the battalion's war diary, "convinced that the battalion was securely dug in."

Eedson Burns, a twenty-year-old engineer with the brigade communications group – and a Second World War general – had reported initially by phone to Odlum that the attack was going well. Warden's Warriors had got past the German front line, and he himself had taken one prisoner, a diminutive Bavarian who hopped up and down in terror, in Burns's words "like a small boy who had wet his trousers," until he realized he wasn't going to be slaughtered. Burns sent him back on his own. Then, with his signals team, he began to work his way up the slope of the ridge. His plan was to get a telephone operating on top of Hill 145 as observation for the Canadian gunners, and so his group moved right behind the forward troops.

Suddenly he noticed a change. The troops hadn't been able to keep up with the barrage. As the shells passed them by, enemy machine gunners began to crawl out of their concrete shelters. Stragglers from several battalions began to join his party. Burns could see the German bullets smacking into the mud no more than a hundred yards ahead.

He leaped into a shell hole. As he did so a bullet creased his helmet. Burns looked up and saw one of the stragglers grinning at him in a peculiar apologetic way. "Get down, you damn fool!" Burns shouted. The grin faded, the man gently collapsed, his legs doubling under him, his eyes rolling upward until the whites showed. There was no blood, but he was stone dead.

Burns waited ten minutes, then headed back to round up the rest of the telephone section, crouching in a shell hole. Most were wounded; none could move; a German machine gun stuttered from a mine crater up ahead and to the left. Burns could see the machine gunners, exposed from the waist up, standing as if at target practice.

The effects of the March 1 gas raid were only too obvious. These were green replacements. Frustrated, Burns turned to a rifleman and told him to take a shot at the Germans. To his astonishment, the man gaped at him and confessed he'd never fired a rifle since arriving in France; that was the job of the snipers. Burns told him to loose off a few rounds anyway. None hit the target.

Burns now got on the phone to report the deteriorating

state of affairs to brigade headquarters, explaining that his signals party couldn't advance because the infantry had divided to the left and the right, leaving an enemy strong point directly in front. Odlum told him that was all poppycock. But nobody at brigade really knew what was going on. Up ahead, Burns spotted a scouting party, sent out by brigade to find out what was happening. It was blundering directly into the enemy. He couldn't warn them – the noise of the barrage made anything but close conversation impossible – so he leaped from shell hole to shell hole and headed them off. He suggested they might get forward by moving over to the right; he'd seen some 3rd Division troops there, but nothing of his own brigade. They took his advice.

Burns made his way back to the old German front line and there found a group of men lounging about with a Lewis gun so covered with mud that it wouldn't fire. He ordered them to clean it, gather up some Mills bombs, and wait for reinforcements. Fifteen minutes later, as he explored an old German dugout, a soldier ran down shouting: "Mr. Burns! Mr. Burns! Quick! Fritz is counterattacking!"

Up the stairs he went, doing his best to appear calm, only to find that the "counterattack" consisted of a dozen German prisoners being escorted back. At that very moment a German 5.9 shell landed in the midst of the group, blowing several into the air.

Burns could see the Germans still standing waist high in their trenches no more than fifty yards away. By now he was thoroughly frustrated and angry. He turned to one buck private and demanded to know what he thought his rifle was for. He seized it himself and got off several shots at the enemy gunners, who vanished below their parapet. Burns had no idea whether he'd scored a hit, but a moment later a bullet smashed into his own parapet, sending a shower of splinters into his face. At the same moment, a small, red-headed intelligence officer staggered into the trench, unable to speak, his throat emitting strangling, whistling sounds. He'd been shot through the jugular by the same bullet that had just missed Burns. As Burns tried to close the inch-long

268

split in the officer's neck, the man's face turned scarlet, then purple, and he died.

Burns now tried to work his way around to the right to see where his brigade had got to. A bullet struck his gas respirator. That was enough. He made his way back to brigade signal headquarters and gave his report.

Over in the Cavalier Subway, the commander of the Kootenay Battalion, Lieutenant-Colonel V.V. Harvey, was also totally confused by the scattered reports coming in. Clearly his men had been unable to take Hill 145. Even now, at the headquarters of the neighbouring Black Watch, Bill Breckenridge was listening to his people demanding to know what had happened. Harvey couldn't tell them.

He decided to send his newest subaltern, Alex Jack, forward to try to find out what was going on and to do his best to reorganize the battalion. Jack, a former company sergeant-major, had been commissioned the week before and was assigned as a reserve officer at headquarters. Now he set off with a Lewis gunner and half a dozen middle-aged batmen carrying ammunition. As the heaviest fire came from the German salient on the left, they hugged the right flank. Harassed by sniper fire, they got too far over and found themselves in the 3rd Division sector. Just as they jumped into a captured trench, a sniper hit the Lewis gunner.

Jack left him and, using the trench as cover, headed to the left where he eventually came upon remnants of his own battalion and some of Warden's Warriors. All the officers of both units were casualties and so Jack, the youngest and newest of all, aged twenty-five, found himself in command of two battalions.

But he knew what to do. He sorted out the men, placed three Lewis guns on the exposed left flank with the remaining ninety men of his own unit, then moved the men from the 102nd over to the right to link up with the Black Watch. That done he went forward to find out what was going on up front. He knew there must be scores of men pinned down in shell holes by snipers. One volunteer, Private Bob Hall from the Arrow Lakes district of British Columbia, came with him, and the two managed to crawl for six hundred yards to the far side of Vimy Ridge. There, looking down on the Douai Plain, they marvelled at the sight of peaceful farmers' fields, unmarked by war.

They were now in the main German trench system. Jack posted Hall at one end of the German communication trench and then began to explore the lateral trench, noting that the machine-gun posts on both sides were still manned. Somehow the two Canadians had got right into the enemy position without being observed. It was time to beat a retreat.

A sniper perched in what was left of a tree spotted them. Both men tried to duck the bullets, but Hall was hit in the back. Jack, crawling on his stomach along the bottom of an empty trench, tried to pull the wounded man to shelter. Two bullets in quick succession chipped the chalk above his head. Hall was dead; Jack got back alive to report that the Kootenays were so badly shattered they could not move past the position held by Warden's Warriors.

3

By early afternoon, Victor Odlum at 11th Brigade headquarters in the Tottenham Subway was haggard with worry. He had never felt so helpless. He had sent thirty scouts out to find out what was going on; only one had got back, and his report was confusing. But one thing was clear: Burns's account had not been poppycock after all. The set-piece attack had disintegrated. If Hill 145 was to be taken that day, fresh troops would be needed. But where were they to come from? His brigade and the 12th were fully committed and badly cut up. The 10th, holding the line at its junction with the British corps, was tapped to attack the Pimple, once the rest of the ridge was in Canadian hands. There was only one source of fresh troops: the 85th Battalion, better known as the Nova Scotia Highlanders.

At this point the tangled narrative of the 4th Division's assault on Vimy Ridge takes on a chimerical quality. The

Nova Scotia Highlanders were an ugly duckling battalion. They belonged to no brigade. They had never fought a battle. Two hundred were still in England, laid up with mumps. The others had only recently arrived in France, and on the channel crossing they had all been seasick. Most were big, strapping fellows, but their tasks were menial: building and filling dumps, digging deep dugouts and assembly trenches, carrying and stringing wire, lugging forward loads of ammunition, escorting and guarding prisoners of war. They were, in short, a work battalion, not a fighting unit. The others sneered at the Maritimers as "the Highlanders without kilts." Now these hewers of wood and drawers of water were assigned to do what the other battalions had been unable to do: attack and seize the stubborn defences in front of Hill 145.

The battalion's history was a curious one. It had been raised in 1916 as part of a Highland brigade to be attached to the Canadian 5th Division. But the idea of another division was soon abandoned. Casualties had been heavier than expected, and the Canadians preferred to have four divisions at full strength rather than five weak ones. All but two battalions—the 85th was one—were broken up to reinforce existing units.

On the day of the battle, the Nova Scotians had been given the lowly task of digging a new communication trench from the rear lines and across the ridge, directly over Hill 145. Now they would have to exchange picks and shovels for rifles, machine guns, and grenades.

Two companies were assigned to the task: Captain Harvey Crowell's "C" company from Halifax and Captain Percy Anderson's "D" company from Cape Breton. When the two officers met with Odlum, shortly before four that afternoon, Crowell thought he'd never seen a more worried officer. Odlum was determined that as soon as dusk fell, the hill would be stormed and the flanking fire harassing the 3rd Division stopped. Zero Hour was set for 6:45 that evening. There would be a twelve-minute barrage behind which the Nova Scotians would attack.

Anderson and Crowell got their groups out of the Tottenham Subway, wading all the way to the jumping-off trenches,

271

which, with the melting snow, were now more like brooks. The men were soaked to the skin before they reached them. Now, still standing waist deep in water, loaded down with bombs, ammunition, tools, reserve rations, and drinking water, they waited for the barrage to explode. The battalion's adjutant, Major J.L. Ralston (a future Canadian defence minister), stood by encouraging the men.

"Well, Anderson," he chaffed, "they had to send you to take Vimy Ridge."

"Well," said Anderson, "we'll take it or never come back."

Just as the last man waded out of the tunnel and into the soggy trench, a message arrived from Odlum cancelling the barrage on the recommendation of the commanding officer of the Nova Scotians, Lieutenant-Colonel A.H. Borden, who was afraid it might obliterate the scattered Ottawa troops crouching in the shell holes up ahead. The news came too late to reach the company commanders on the far flanks of their units at the end of the wriggling ditch of a trench. And there simply wasn't enough time to let every man know what was or what was not happening.

Would the two companies jump off without waiting for the non-existent barrage? Tensely, Borden waited to see.

The snow had ended. Now, as the men waited in the water, the sun came out. Harvey Crowell on the far left turned to see the setting rays aflame over the broken spires of the old church at Mont St. Eloi. The same sun, he realized, would be blazing in the eyes of the Germans. That could save a lot of lives.

Zero Hour came; no barrage! Bewildered, Crowell checked his watch. Thirty seconds ticked by. Forty-five. At one minute, Crowell decided he must move. Lieutenant Manning of No. 9 platoon stood up in the trench so Crowell could see him; he, too, was worrying about the absence of the barrage. Crowell decided to go, guns or no guns. He waved his hand forward and the company climbed out of the trench. The instant Crowell stood up, the German machine guns began to stammer. Crowell's runner went down immediately.

German signal flares shot into the sky to bring down shell-fire on the Nova Scotians. The first shell exploded in the line before it had moved twenty-five yards.

To Crowell's dismay, Anderson's company was not advancing. It flashed through Crowell's mind that he'd made a terrible mistake. But the truth was that Anderson, too, had been waiting for the barrage. Finally, when he saw Crowell's men crossing the old German line well ahead on the left, he started forward.

Crowell's company was already forcing its way over the wreckage of that line – barbed wire, sandbags, bits of board, human limbs, all churned up into a muddy soup. One hundred yards ahead, five German machine gunners emerged from an undemolished dugout and opened up. Lieutenant Manning had already fallen, mortally wounded.

As the Nova Scotians plunged on, the hail of bullets increased. This is the moment that every commander fears. There was no cover; the troops had been ordered not to stop and fire back but to keep moving; but that was almost more than the human psyche could bear. The instinct was to slow down, to stop, to grovel deep into the mud – anything to escape that deadly fusillade. It would take only one man to falter; the rest would seize the opportunity to follow. Once down, the company would never rise again, and the attack would fail.

On the other hand, it would take only one man's example to turn the tide. As so often happened that day, such a man emerged. Corporal M.H. Curll, a rifle bomber from Mahone Bay, was worried that he'd shortly be facing a court martial. The previous night, drunk on too much rum ration, he'd been insubordinate to Captain Crowell. Now he leaped out of a shell hole firing a borrowed grenade rifle from the hip. Thus heartened, the others in the company followed directly behind. The German machine gunners turned and tried to flee. Curll and two of his platoon shot them down. But Curll's main concern was not the Germans. To set off the grenades the rifle bombers were supposed to use blank ammunition. His grenadier had forgotten to bring any, so Curll was forced to use live bullets. Now his rifle was useless and he was afraid he'd be charged with destroying government property.

This bold action marked the turning point of the advance. The Germans were overcome by the same tendency to panic that had been about to engulf the Nova Scotians. When a few turned to flee, more and more followed, and the 85th, enflamed now by blood lust, firing rifles and Lewis guns from the hip, swarmed up the hill, killing seventy of the enemy as they advanced.

Harvey Crowell could see the German gunners trying to climb out of their slippery trench. Three started to slide back down the hill, all whacking into each other until they landed at his feet. Crowell began to laugh at the spectacle when he suddenly felt as if a mule had kicked him in the back. An explosive bullet had made mincemeat of his shoulder, and the shock knocked him speechless. He could see his men rushing on past their objective, but he couldn't yell at them to stop. He feared his own guns would cut them down if they went too far. In the heat of their enthusiasm, they seemed to be prepared to chase the Germans all the way to the Fatherland. Pain or no pain, Crowell went over the crest to bring them back; it wasn't an easy job.

Percy Anderson's company had also roared past its objective. Anderson himself rushed into an enemy stronghold, shot the first German he encountered, captured the next, and told him to remove his belt. When the man hesitated, Anderson ripped it off himself. His men killed or captured the rest. As they dug in, Anderson heard someone groaning out in No Man's Land. The field was raked with fire, but the company commander went out himself, threw the man over his shoulder, and brought him back to the trench.

Within one hour the Highlanders without kilts had captured Hill 145 and exceeded their orders by going beyond it, a breach of discipline that their commander, Borden, didn't mention in the war diary. Now all of the crest, save for the Pimple, was safely in Canadian hands. But there would be two more days of fighting before the eastern slope and the northern tip were wrested from the enemy.

CHAPTER FOURTEEN

Mopping Up

1

All along the crest of Vimy Ridge, as darkness fell, men stood and gaped at the scene to the east. Captain H.S. Cooper of the Princess Patricias looked back at the khaki world he and his battalion had just vacated and asked himself: "How did the Germans let us do it?" Until this moment, he had not realized what a complete field of fire the enemy had had.

For others, scrambling up the ridge like tourists to drink in the view, it was a bit like playing hookey. Here they were, perched on forbidden ground, walking over territory that not long ago had been raked with death, eating mulligan and watching the fleeing enemy. To Elmore Philpott, a gunner with the 25th Battery, it was an extraordinary experience. He had never actually *seen* a German. To him and his friends, working the big artillery pieces far behind the line, the enemy was a faceless stranger who killed his fellow Canadians in the night. Now it seemed as if the entire German army was in retreat. As Philpott stood with the others on the ridge, a Biblical phrase popped into his mind: "The children of Israel looking at the Promised Land."

Archie Brown of the Winnipeg Grenadiers, looking down and across the sodden Souchez Valley, had a different view. To that drab monochrome a bright new hue had been added. The potholes, the shell holes, the little stream itself seemed to be brimming with a scarlet dye. It looked to Brown as if somebody had soaked the entire valley with blood.

George Frederick Murray looked back over the battlefield they'd taken that day and inwardly remarked how deceptively gentle the slope up which they'd panted and struggled now appeared. Along the edge of the ridge he could see smoke rising from fires made by the troops cooking their supper. Below and beyond, the occasional Canadian shell still dropped, spurting mud into small volcanoes. Back on the old Canadian assembly line a few guns still flashed. But the general aspect was one of calm after a storm. There seemed to be no semblance of order around him as small groups of men wandered about, their heads bobbing up and down above the shell holes. On the German side the ground dropped off steeply, honeycombed by all manner of dugouts in some of which he would soon come upon hidden luxuries – baths, easy chairs, electric lights, even pianos. Beyond, in the distance, Murray could see the Canadian shells still exploding on the roads that led north to the German-held communities of Lens, Avion, and Méricourt.

But the artillery could reach no farther, and for that reason the troops were frozen on the ridge. That morning, the Canadian Corps had been on the verge of a breakthrough – the one glorious moment that Haig, Nivelle, Joffre, and Foch had longed for in all those weary months of battering against the enemy's diamond-hard defences. Driven from their front trenches early in the day, the Germans had been thrown off balance; the Allies had the momentum. If the guns could have been brought forward to continue the pounding barrage, who knows what might have been gained?

The irony was that the very arm of the service that had made the capture of Vimy Ridge possible – the artillery – had rendered itself impotent. The guns had given the battlefield such a harrowing that they could not be hauled forward to hammer the fleeing enemy. The melting snow completed the work of the barrage. The heavier guns were bogged down. It took as many as one hundred horses and eight men to haul a single 60-pounder a quarter of a mile, and the horses were dying under the strain. It was almost as difficult to move the lighter field guns. By four o'clock on the dark morning of April 10, one battery of field artillery – the 3rd – had somehow managed to manhandle its guns three thousand yards farther than any other, but this was still not far enough. It was four days before the 5th Brigade of the 2nd Division could get its field guns through Neuville St. Vaast and into the ruins of Thélus. Most guns had to be withdrawn until new roads were built, old craters, trenches, and shell holes filled with rubble, piles of cut brush laid under the new thoroughfares, and a narrow-gauge rail line extended to the ridge top. Five thousand men were set to work to repair the famous plank road; it was so slippery that no gun could negotiate it. The only hope the artillery had of keeping up the pressure on the fleeing Germans was to use their own captured guns. By then, the enemy was consolidating near Lens and any hope of a breakthrough was lost.

The critical moment in the battle had come about a little after 7 A.M. when the Germans' triple line of forward trenches was overrun. This would have been the time to bring in the cavalry on the right of the line to exploit the breakthrough. Some of Byng's staff had tried to plead with the commander to abandon the rigid artillery timetable and speed up the attack, once the Germans were on the run. Why give them time to breathe? But Byng had received explicit orders to capture Vimy Ridge and hold it as a bastion on the flank of the Arras offensive. He refused to throw off all restraint and interfere with the complex artillery plan that had to that point ensured the infantry's success. You did that at your peril, as the 4th Division discovered.

Masses of cavalry were stationed in the Arras area, and it's possible that Byng might have committed them to a flanking attack – but they weren't under his command or even under that of his superior, Henry Horne. Haig had taken them under his own wing, and Haig was difficult to reach. After the Brown Line was secured Byng sent two small troops of the Canadian Light Horse – ten mounted men each – to probe the German defences in Farbus Wood and Willerval on the Douai Plain. The move was disastrous. The troop that entered the wood, hampered by the trees, lost half its men, largely to German machine-gun fire from the unprotected flank of the 1st Division (for the British were still not in position). The other was cut to pieces; only two of its members got back safely.

Von Hindenburg himself remarked on the British inability to exploit the success gained at Vimy – "a piece of luck for us.'' The High Command and, indeed, the Canadians themselves had been so obsessed by the ridge that they had scarcely considered what lay beyond. All the ingenuity, all the planning, all the innovative training had zeroed in on one objective. No one had really set his mind to the possibility of a breakthrough or how to exploit one. Nivelle, the Allied generalissimo, had said flatly that the Canadians couldn't take Vimy Ridge. Had Haig also believed that? Certainly he had made no plans to commit his cavalry in the event of any quick success. It was as if the capture of the ridge was an end in itself.

2

In the dressing stations behind the old Canadian lines there was no sleep. Before the Battle of Vimy Ridge was over, the doctors, stretcher-bearers, and medical orderlies would treat 7,004 wounded men. Another 3,598 were past help. In short, one Canadian in ten was killed or wounded in the four-day battle for the ridge. That is not a high ratio by Great War standards, but to that number must be added another 9,553 casualties suffered at Vimy in the months before the battle. Sniper fire, artillery fire, and trench raids took their toll. Put bluntly, to take Vimy Ridge it cost Canada twenty thousand casualties, about a quarter of whom would never go home.

The stretcher-bearers trying to clear the battlefield also worked without sleep. Enemy sharpshooters picked off even the walking wounded. One medic tried to lead five bleeding men back to the dressing station only to have three killed en route; the other two crawled back on their hands and knees.

There were not enough bearers available to bring the wounded back immediately. Some were simply given hasty first aid in the field, then left in a shell hole for safety until stretchers were available. One man, Howard Leaming, woke up in the dark of the night in pain and, feeling totally abandoned, pulled out a gun, determined to shoot himself. At the last moment, he paused and thought, ''I didn't join the army to be a coward." He survived with a steel plate in his head for another fifty-two years.

The men holding the ridge could hear the wounded moaning around them. Lewis Buck spent a sleepless night with badly injured men in a cold German dugout, trying to kill rats with a captured pistol. Scores of other men lay out all that night on the battlefield, groaning in pain and facing the German sniper fire. When they were brought in twenty-four hours later, their clothing was so stiff with filth it broke the medics' scissors. For forty-eight hours the men of the medical corps worked continuously, dressing every kind of wound and setting every kind of fracture from skull to ankle. It was makeshift work. No doctor could follow his case through. In the forward stations each man got the same treatment whether his wound was slight or mortal: a bandage to hide the dirt, some bits of gauze to mask the protruding viscera.

The scenes in the dressing stations were heart-rending, even to senior officers who had seen a good deal of war. Brigadier-General Macdonell's voice broke when he saw the wounded from his brigade. "Poor boys," he said, "poor boys."

The dead were often buried where they lay, in communal graves in mine craters and shell holes – as many as one hundred to a single grave. It was heart-breaking work for many who recognized familiar faces among the corpses lying in the mud. One young stretcher-bearer, William Klyne of the 3rd Battalion, lost fourteen of his friends and buried three of them personally.

The sick and the wounded were sometimes mixed together with the dead. Cy Peck, the pugnacious C.O. of the Canadian Scottish, suffered so dreadfully from stomach cramps that he was finally ordered off the field by his medical officer, but only after the battalion had seized its objective. Jack Quinnell, who had survived his battalion's abortive attack, was taken back, unable to go on because of his trench mouth and trench feet – he hadn't had his shoes off for days – and thrown into an ambulance full of corpses. "They're all dead in here," he heard someone remark.

"No, they're not!" Quinnell managed to cry out through his bruised gums.

The corpse of David Moir's fellow machine gunner Private Walker still lay out in No Man's Land, to the sorrow and frustration of his best friend, another machine gunner named Pratt. Pratt couldn't bear the idea of his dead buddy lying out in the open, exposed to the elements, and suggested to Moir that the two go out and bury him. Moir hesitated. *That's like putting your head in the lion's mouth*, he thought nervously. On the other hand, he was the only man in the section who knew where Walker's body was. As Pratt kept urging him, a line from a Robert Service poem popped into Moir's head: "A friend's last need is a thing to heed." He agreed to risk it.

They waited for dark. But by then, after the continual shelling, the terrain had been transformed: every shell hole looked like every other shell hole. Every stump looked like a German; Moir could swear that some even moved. *Surely*, he thought, *Fritz will be sending out patrols to probe our defences*. In their haste the two gunners hadn't even brought sidearms or grenades: they'd be sitting ducks! At last they found the body, got out their entrenching tools, scraped out a shallow grave, and buried it. But they were now completely lost, blundering about, stumbling into the lines of a strange unit. A Canadian sentry almost shot them, but fortunately they had the right password. The sentry thought they were both crazy.

And the battle was not yet over. The north end of the ridge was still in German hands. The Nova Scotia Highlanders kept a precarious hold on the crest of Hill 145, but the enemy was still dug in directly beyond. That night ten volunteers crept out with rifle grenades to attack some of the concrete dugouts holding out on the steep slope. The work was dangerous: the first shots had to tell – there would be no second chance. The men got the job done, cleaned out all the dugouts, killed every German. The following morning, the C.O. sauntered over and spotted Lyle Pugsley, a twenty-two-year-old farmer from Beaconsfield, Nova Scotia. "Aren't you one of the ten who went out last night in the attack on the dugouts?'' he asked. Pugsley nodded. ''You may have won a medal,'' the C.O. told him. ''Draw a number from one of the slips in this helmet.'' Pugsley drew but didn't win. One of the others, a man from River Hebert, was awarded the M.M.

Meanwhile, on the same front, Brigadier-General Victor Odlum had gone forward after dark to try to sort out the remnants of his tattered brigade. They were all in a state of confusion. Odlum started on the left flank and worked his way along to the right, unit by unit, moving some men forward, straightening out the line, placing the troops in position just over the crest of Hill 145. Like the medics, he had no sleep; it was daylight before order was restored. Just as Odlum and two of his staff finished the job, a lone German rushed at them. To the Brigadier's vast relief, he didn't open fire. All he wanted to do was surrender.

In the smoking ruins of Thélus that same Tuesday morning, Private Lewis Robertson of the RCRs came upon a bizarre sight. He had been sent out to bury the dead but now spotted four Albertans seated in a shell hole about four feet deep, playing cards. Their heads protruded over the lip of the cavity, and they seemed to be waiting for something – a signal of some kind. It was then that Robertson noticed that each had a little blood coming from the ears. They were all dead of concussion, their bodies otherwise unmarked. Robertson had to tear the cards out of their hands before burying them in the crater.

3

There was no rest for the 4th Division. The eastern slope of Hill 145 and the woods at its base were still held by the enemy. Fresh troops would have to clear them out. That meant that the attack on the Pimple, scheduled for Tuesday, April 10, would have to be postponed. To this point, the men of the 10th Brigade had not been blooded. They were all Westerners from Vancouver, Calgary, Regina, Moose Jaw, and Winnipeg. The success or failure of these final phases of the Battle of Vimy Ridge would depend upon them.

Two battalions of the 10th – the 50th from Calgary and the 44th from Winnipeg – were hurriedly moved south into the sector precariously held by the battered remnants of Odlum's brigade. Their task was to pass through the captured trenches, vault over Hill 145, and reach the far edge of La Folie Wood at the bottom of the ridge. It was mid-afternoon before this transfer could be effected and a new barrage pattern drawn up to protect the attacking waves.

Now the same scenes that had illuminated the battlefield the previous day were repeated on the northern crest of the ridge. As they trudged forward under that floating canopy of hot steel, men began to topple into the mud. Victor Wheeler's temples throbbed as he staggered up the slope with the Calgarians, bowed beneath his crushing load of signal wire, Mark 3 telephones, Lucas lamp, binoculars, bombs, and equipment. He watched as the first man of his battalion, Sergeant Harry Diller, was struck by a cluster of shrapnel. "Lucky devil," somebody said. "He's got a blighty." Wheeler could see the gaps between the men around him widening as the German machine guns hammered away. He felt his insides writhe: would there be enough men left to take the objective? It seemed as if he might be the very last man to face the Germans, the carnage was so fearful: men on both sides were impaled on the broken wire like rag dolls or thrown face forward to splash and drown in the bloody water of the shell holes.

Over on Wheeler's right, Private John Pattison was about to win the Victoria Cross. Pattison was forty-two – old enough to have a son serving in the same unit. As the battalion plunged forward and the Germans raked the front line with machine-gun fire, Pattison spotted an enemy stronghold. Hunched over, jumping from shell hole to shell hole, dodging the traversing bullets, he got within grenade range of the enemy, stood erect, lobbed three bombs, and put the guns out of action. The attack had slowed some of the men crouching in shell holes to escape the fire, but now it picked up momentum as the men behind Pattison moved in with bayonets. Pattison survived the assault but not the war. Seven weeks later, he was killed in front of Lens. His son, following tradition, wore his decoration.

The Winnipeggers advanced on the right of the Calgarians. Sergeant Wesley Runions was cheered at the sight of his commanding officer, Lieutenant-Colonel Dick Davis, who had rebuilt the battalion following the Somme débâcle, nonchalantly swinging his cane – the only weapon he carried – as casually as if he were on a Sunday jaunt. His officers had followed his example; none carried rifles. But just as they leap-frogged through Victor Odlum's weary troops, a whiz-bang exploded on the crest, and a cloud of shrapnel tore into Runions's stomach and shoulder. As the medics bound up his wounds, pulled off his outer clothing and snipped off his undershirt, the nose of the German shell fell out. Runions recognized the legendary quality of his close call: he had been spared by a circumstance that had already become a wartime cliché. The shell had struck a New Testament in his tunic pocket. The little book had stopped it from tearing out his heart.

Sergeant Ed Russenholt with the Winnipeg battalion was also heartened by the sight of Davis swinging his cane. He was badly shaken by a grisly spectacle that had faced him when the battalion went over the top. As he watched, the lines of men ahead of him parted to right and left, leaving a gap as if to avoid some hidden obstacle. He couldn't understand what was happening until he reached the spot himself and saw what it was that had caused them to make the detours. In front of him lay a long triangle of khaki-clad bodies, about one hundred and fifty yards broad and narrowing to a ghastly apex. These were the corpses of the men who had jumped off the previous morning to walk directly into the traversing fire of the German machine guns in the undamaged trench. They lay face down, these dead men, with their rifles in their hands, the bayonets fixed, all pointing forward to their objective as if signalling a ghostly advance.

Now, as he passed over the crest of the ridge, Russenholt could see the devastation caused by the machine guns. On Hill 145 the fire had been so heavy that balls of barbed wire the size of kitchen chairs had been beaten as hard as iron.

In the plain below, the Germans were burning their papers. William Darknell spotted them from the ridge above – a long line of men throwing boxes of documents into an open fire. He trained his machine gun on them and mowed them down.

Within one hour the two battalions had secured their objective and were digging in. But the cost was fearful: the attacking companies of the Calgary battalion lost 228 men, more than a quarter of their total strength, killed, wounded, or missing. Bob Forrest, a runner with the unit, could not hold back his tears as he searched vainly for his buddies from Okotoks, Alberta. Eighteen had gone into battle; only one survived.

4

On the following day, Wednesday, April 11, the Canadians licked their wounds. A full twenty-four hours of rest and re-organization would be needed before the stubborn little Pimple could be attacked. As reserve battalions moved up to relieve the exhausted men in the front lines, the troops awoke to find that everything – horses, wagons, guns, and trenches – was covered in a thick blanket of snow. With the temperature still dropping, it was more like December than April. Andrew Macphail had already noted his first view of the rear areas: lorries mired, wagons in the ditches, a tram car overturned – its load of shells strewn like potatoes over the ground – a crumpled airplane poking its nose over a bank. With the field cleared of wounded and two thousand prisoners in the 2nd Division's cages, Macphail and his colonel headed out on a tour of inspection of the forward dressing areas. They had no idea what they were in for.

The terrain was worse than the Somme. They tripped over wire and old bones, pit props and iron stakes, praying they wouldn't set off an unexploded shell lurking beneath the surface. They skirted craters as wide as a small lake and others deep enough to hold a cathedral. The evidence of German defeat was everywhere – the old enemy line was all but indistinguishable from the ruin around them. The Canadians had ploughed and harrowed the enemy, "riddled him like a sieve" in Macphail's words. Looking down from the slopes of the ridge, he was reminded of a tumultuous sea suddenly frozen and turned to earth.

The engineers were laying a new tram line, so they followed the stakes to what had been the Lens-Arras road, now only a borderline of stumps. German shells began to fall amid the ruins of Thélus; they took refuge in a half-dug gun pit. A young soldier had clawed a coffin-sized hole out of the earth and was sound asleep in it. Macphail crawled in beside him.

The shelling stopped. The two doctors moved out, seeking a regimental aid post supposed to be hidden in a church cellar. Before they could find it the shells rained down again. They scrambled from crater to crater but even as they moved other craters formed. Ahead of them the earth exploded once . . . twice . . . three times. Just twelve feet away three new cavities appeared.

By noon the German guns had been temporarily silenced by the Canadian artillery. The church was rubble. The two officers helped set up a new medical post in a cave, then headed north to inspect a second post. They had only a vague idea where they were, for every landmark had been obliterated. When the shelling started again, Macphail was certain his end had come. Instinctively, he tried to protect his right hand from shrapnel wounds. Somehow they escaped, found the post, ordered it evacuated, and searched about to get their bearings. The only landmark on the horizon was the broken tower of the church at Mont St. Eloi, three miles to the west, stark against the glowering sky. With the shells still bursting around them, they hurried back through a field of corpses.

The dead lay everywhere that day: in the shell holes, the craters, the ditches, and by the roadsides. Indeed, they outnumbered the living. Two days before, this muddy plateau had teemed with men. Now only a few clusters could be seen: burial parties picking up the corpses, gunners hauling the artillery forward, a work party extending the tram line, a few others laying signal wires, digging gun pits, or putting up a wireless station. The Canadian Corps had gone to earth, hiding in holes and niches, catching its breath. Even the shellfire seemed to Macphail to have lost its power. Fragments splintered on his helmet, thudded into the mud, or splashed in the pools of bloody water without affecting him. Nonetheless, he didn't breathe freely until he reached the old Canadian front line. He and his companion had spent seven hours under fire, unable to relax for a single moment in all that long day.

5

The Pimple – a small wooded knoll at the northern end of the ridge – was another German stronghold. Strengthened with concrete pillboxes, bristling with machine guns, most of them still undamaged, it was a maze of tunnels, dugouts, holes, trenches, and entanglements, all carefully camouflaged and protected by mines, barbed wire, and booby traps. In the pits and craters on the slopes, the German snipers and gunners waited for the inevitable assault.

The original plan had called for a British brigade on the left to attack this objective. But four days before the battle the task had been assigned to the Canadian 10th.

Parts of the 10th had already been blooded two days before in the battle to secure the eastern slopes of the ridge below Hill 145. Now, on Thursday, April 12, other companies of the same two battalions – the 50th and 44th from Calgary and Winnipeg – together with the 46th from Regina and Moose Jaw were assigned to complete the job.

Once again at dawn the Westerners left their trenches to toil up the hill behind the furore of the creeping barrage and in the teeth of a raging snowstorm. It was still dark; the blizzard had wiped out the dawn's first light. But this time the snow was the soldier's friend. The men on both sides groped blindly in the blizzard, but it was the German machine gunners who suffered most, for they were unable to see the Canadians stumbling forward. The whirling snow was as much of a shield as the curtain of shells.

There was no respite for the signallers. For the second time in two days, Private Victor Wheeler, the twenty-one-year-old with the Calgary battalion, went over the top with his equipment. Until this moment, he had been numb to gruesome spectacles around him. Now, for the first time, the horror and tragedy of war struck home. A German 5.9 shell exploded in the midst of his section, blowing some men sky high, tearing others to pieces. One of his closest friends, Harry Waller, was blasted into the mouth of an old mine shaft, so badly ripped up it was difficult to pull him free. Waller had been Wheeler's intimate companion for two years, one of three brothers, all in the same battalion. As Wheeler cradled Harry's head in his arms, something inside him snapped, and he felt his throat choke with sobs. Waller's back was twisted out of shape, one arm and one leg were broken, a shin bone protruded through the flesh, and shell fragments stuck out of his head. His eyes were already filming over as his brother Art knelt above him, weeping. His wounds were mortal, but it took him five days to die. Wheeler couldn't linger. The Calgarians swept forward, leaving the two brothers alone on the battlefield.

The postponement of the battle had given the Germans time to bring up fresh troops, the élite Prussians of the 5th Guard – six footers all, who sneered at the Canadians as "untrained Colonial levies."

In spite of that, the despised colonials captured the Pimple in less than two hours. By then the Germans were pouring out of the shell holes begging for mercy. Not all got it. Some of the Calgarians remembered the gruff advice of the battalion's second-in-command, Major J.R.L. Perry, a tough Boer War veteran, who had told them: "I don't want any *angels* in my battalion, when you get to France. I don't want you to take any *prisoners*! I hope you understand."

The snow was so heavy that some men lost their sense of direction. When Allen Hart, a private with the Winnipeggers, reached the top of the ridge, he didn't know which way to go. To him the battle had taken on an unearthly aspect. Encased in a cocoon of sound and in the white mantle of the blizzard, he could see in the gun flashes the ghostly shapes of men falling around him. It did not occur to him that these men were hit. He simply thought they'd fallen into a shell hole or lost their bearings, as he had. Like so many others during these days of battle, he had no clear picture of what was going on. Later that same morning he found himself on the far side of the ridge, all alone, with no idea of how he'd got there. Over to his left he spotted some troops. These were Japanese Canadians from the reserve battalion – the 47th from British Columbia. It added to the weirdness of the occasion – the Orientals squatting on their haunches, grinning because the fight was over and they were still alive, and the soft snow still falling, mercifully concealing the ghastly carnage of war.

AFTERMATH

I suppose you're all feeling pretty fine about the war news these days. There's an absolutely different atmosphere about the war out here than there was a year ago. Everyone is in wonderful spirits. I can't see now what the Germans have to gain by holding out much longer. . . . A German officer, Prussian Guard, who was taken prisoner in the scrap said that the defeat at Vimy Ridge was one of the hardest blows that the Germans had received in the war. . . .

Lieutenant Irving Findley,
7th Brigade trench mortars,
to his father, April 21, 1917

AFTERMATH

1

Gad Terence Neale stood on the top of Vimy Ridge gazing down at the scene below and felt a surge of unexpected emotion. His overall feeling was one of exhilarating freedom. It was, he thought, rather like climbing over a neighbour's fence and looking into a yard that had been hidden from you all your life. Until a couple of days before, this had been forbidden territory; like the others in the corps, he had had no idea of what it was like on the far side of the ridge, only an overwhelming curiosity. Now he was able to look down on a rainbow world. In the woods below, the shattered trees were coming into leaf. Beneath them, daffodils, forget-me-nots, violets, primroses, and bluebells were bursting into flower. In the distance the fields were turning emerald green. This sudden relief from the monochrome of mud seemed unreal – almost as unreal as the suddenness of the victory the Canadians had achieved.

Neale was an Englishman, born in Watford, a market town in Hertfordshire. Bored by his work as a postal clerk, he had come to Canada in April of 1914. Having no skills or training he'd been advised to find work on a farm, and so had gone to northern Saskatchewan. There he got a job with his own kind, among the survivors of the Barr colony of English immigrants who'd arrived a decade before. A year later, at the age of seventeen, he'd gone to Lloydminster and enlisted. Now, at nineteen, he'd survived his first battle.

Young Private Neale could scarcely be called a Canadian. His five brothers were serving in British units. He himself had spent fewer than eighteen months in Canada, largely among recently arrived English. But now, standing on Vimy's crest, he could no longer think of himself as English. He was part of a corps of young Canadians who had accomplished

290

the impossible and done it with flair and dispatch. After the monotony of the trenches, Vimy had given Gad Neale new hope. For the first time he and his fellows had punched a hole in the four-hundred-mile line of German trenches. The British hadn't done it; the French hadn't done it; *they* had done it – the Canadians.

The world applauded. Robert Borden, who was in London at the time, was ecstatic: ''. . . all newspapers ringing with praise of Canadians,'' he scribbled in his diary. ''CANADIANS SWEEP VIMY RIDGE,'' cried the *Morning Post*. The rest of the press was just as enthusiastic. The *Nottingham Guardian*, in a long editorial entitled ''Canadian Valour,'' wrote that the battle ''will stand out as an imperishable addition to the glory of the gallant colonials.'' Philip Gibbs, the best-known correspondent of the war, hailed it as ''the Canadians' greatest day in the war since the capture of Courcelette.'' Only the good grey *Times* refused to devote a leader to the victory or mention the Dominion troops in its initial coverage of the Battle of Arras, an oversight that Borden thought disgraceful.

The American papers were, if anything, more generous. The New York *Tribune*, in an editorial entitled ''Well Done, Canada,'' wrote that ''every American will feel a thrill of admiration and a touch of honest envy at the achievement of the Canadian troops. . . . No praise of the Canadian achievement can be excessive. Canada has sent across the sea an army greater than Napoleon ever commanded in the field.'' The *New York Times* wrote that the battle would be ''in Canada's history, one of the great days, a day of glory to furnish inspiration to her sons for generations.''

In this there was truth. The war had been dragging on for more than two and a half years. In battle after battle hopes had been raised only to be dashed. Vimy was a limited victory, to be sure. But it was a decisive one, its topography easily understood by civilians. All through the war a ridge of land had barred the way; the Canadians had captured that ridge with blinding speed. The British to the south had done well too, on the first day, but they had not all reached their objectives, and as the days wore on, the Battle of Arras ground to another disappointing halt. The Nivelle offensive to the south failed, dooming its over-optimistic commander to obscurity. But Vimy Ridge remained in Allied hands; the Germans never regained it; indeed, they did not even try. So the ridge became a physical symbol, marking a turning point in the war for the troops in France and the people back home. It was "the grandest day the Corps ever had," in the words of Arthur Currie, who was almost immediately appointed to succeed Byng as Corps commander – to the fury of Garnet Hughes, who badly wanted the job.

For those who fought at Vimy, from Private Gad Neale to Fighting Frank Worthington, a future general, the brief, ·explosive battle was a turning point of a different kind. It turned both men, and thousands of others, into Canadians. Until this point the Old Country immigrants, new to Canada, had thought of themselves as British. Worthington, a Scottish-born soldier of fortune, had spent only nine days in Canada when he enlisted in 1917 in the 73rd Battalion. "I never felt like a Canadian until Vimy," he was to say. "After that I was a Canadian all the way."

In the days before Vimy, the Canadian Expeditionary Force had poked fun at themselves, in the Canadian fashion:

> *We are Sam Hughes's army*
> *Twenty thousand men are we.*
> *We cannot fight, we cannot march,*
> *What bloody use are we?*

Now that rueful attitude was replaced by something quite different.

"They said in Lethbridge . . . we were a bunch of booze fighters but we showed them today what we could do," one private soldier in the Canadian Scottish remarked to his platoon officer, Cyril Jones, after the battle.

Claude Williams wrote home that "the Canadian has lived down his reputation as a 'rag-tag' army and is now considered the best in the B.E.F. The Imperials think a great deal of the 'Byng Boys'. One feels proud to be a Canadian out here now."

292

Letters like that one plus the newspaper hyperbole conveyed a new spirit. A few days after the battle, Clifford Wells had time to post his mother "the most thrilling letter I have ever written you. . . . I hope you will find it the same. The greatest victory of the war has been gained, and I had a small part in it."

Byng wrote home to his wife that "the Canucks . . . are just bursting with bonhomie and grinning from ear to ear." The discipline and training had told and some went out of their way to thank the general for it. They had shown the sceptical French that the job could be done. Everybody liked the anecdote told by a young gunnery officer from the 25th Battery who, returning from England on Easter Monday, got the news in a café at Houdain that the ridge had been taken. A group of French officers at a nearby table who heard shook their heads. "C'est impossible," one declared. Then he was told that the Canadians had done the job. "Ah! Les Canadiens!" he responded. "C'est possible!" Or so the story went.

Vimy convinced the Canadians that they were the finest troops on the Western Front. By naming them assault troops in the battles that followed, the High Command confirmed that belief. (The honour was not always appreciated by the private soldiers who found themselves exposed in the vanguard.) Ed Russenholt, the Lewis gun sergeant who'd been with the 44th in the attack on April 10, recovering from wounds a year later in an English hospital found an enormous difference in the soldiers who came to visit him on leave. They had, he noted, a pride, a confidence, and a professionalism that hadn't existed in the early days. Russenholt came to believe, with thousands of others, that the Canadian nationality was born on that chill Monday in 1917.

This was no longer a corps of amateurs. Indeed, it was one of the most professional units on the Western Front, for the French and the British had already sacrificed the flower of their armies at Ypres, Verdun, and the Somme. As Byng wrote, "the good old Canucks behaved like real, disciplined soldiers" at Vimy.

In losing their amateur status, the Canadians also lost

their innocence. Gone was the naïve enthusiasm, the carefree indiscipline that had marked the earlier years. The war was no longer a lark, no longer an adventure, but something to be endured by men who knew their job.

That attitude comes out strongly in the letters that Claude Williams was writing home that spring. Williams, who had once been so eager to get into action as a machine gunner that he was prepared to stow away on a ship to France, now wrote to a friend in Hamilton a month after the battle:

". . . Although for me it is only about a year's service in France, it seems as if I had been born out here and have never known anything but everlasting mud and perpetual shellfire. Now all of us feel ready for peace at the right time; the fire-eaters who, before experiencing heavy action only wanted to 'get a poke' at Fritz, have already simmered down and cannot 'get their time' soon enough.

"I think it is only natural. None of us have lost our nerve but the novelty has worn off and we have seen too much of the shady side of fighting to love it for the mere sake of adventure. When called upon, we are cheerfully ready to do anything we are told but do not feel the same wild enthusiasm as formerly. We are all steadied and sobered up. . . ."

At that point one of Williams's closest friends was in hospital suffering from shell shock. A second was bedridden with shrapnel in his lung. A third had lost an eye. The remainder were suffering from hives, an allergy connected with imperfect diet but also with stress. The Claude Williams who wrote home from the blackened slopes of Vimy in the late spring of 1917 was a different man from the one who had arrived in France the previous October, eager to get in on what he called "the fun."

2

It has become commonplace to say that Canada came of age at Vimy Ridge. For seventy years it has been said so often – in Parliament, at hundreds of Vimy dinners and in thousands of Remembrance Day addresses, in newspaper editorials, school texts, magazine articles, and more than a score of books about Vimy and Canada's role in the Great War – that it is almost an article of faith. Thus it is difficult to untangle the reality from the rhetoric. Was Vimy the source of Canada's awareness of itself as an independent nation or the product of it?

It is a historical fact that Canada entered the war as a junior partner of Great Britain and emerged as an equal, her status confirmed when she, with the other Dominions, was given her own vote at the League of Nations. But did this really spring from the victory at Vimy? Or was Vimy simply used as a convenient symbol, a piece of shorthand to stand for a more complicated historical process that, in the end, was probably inevitable?

Does it matter? What counts is that in the minds of Canadians Vimy took on a mythic quality in the post-war years, and Canada was short of myths. There is something a little desperate – a little wistful – in the commentaries of the twenties and the thirties and even later, in which Canadians assured one another over and over again that at Vimy, Canada had at last found its maturity.

No overall hero emerged from the Canadian Corps – no Wellington, no Cromwell, no Washington. Byng, who could have been one, was British. Currie, who should have been, was undermined by rumours. The real heroes were the masses of ordinary soldiers who fought and died in the belief they were making the world a better place, and their inventive leaders who stubbornly refused to follow the old rules of war. The single word *Vimy* stood for them all and helped to soften in Canada the bitterness of the post-war years. Canadians could grumble that Ypres, the Somme, and Passchendaele were bungled by the British. But Vimy! That was Canada's, and nobody could take that victory away. In the years between the two World Wars, every schoolchild, every veteran's son, every immigrant was made aware of it.

It is difficult now to conjure up the intensity of the Vimy fever that swept across the country in those two decades.

After the first burst of publicity the impact of the battle was blunted everywhere but in Canada. It was, at best, a limited tactical victory. Canadians made much of the fact that the ridge remained as an anchor point to protect the British flanks for the rest of the war. But it's hard to believe it greatly affected the outcome. Only in Canada is it called the Battle of Vimy Ridge. Elsewhere it's part of the British Battles of Arras. Liddell Hart, in his definitive history of the Great War, gives it no more than a paragraph. The Americans quickly forgot it and today have never heard of it. But at home it became part of the cultural baggage that every loyal Canadian carried. The word popped out of innumerable broadcasts, interviews, and news stories. Anyone who had served at Vimy was described in the press not as a Great War veteran but as a Vimy veteran (and still is). The word, of course, was short enough to fit any headline, but there was more to it than that. Vimy dinners were held annually to mark the victory (and still are). Parks, schools, city streets bore the name. The sacred word was carved on a stone high up in the Ottawa Peace Tower. Some families even named a child Vimy. In the drumfire repetition of that word, that slogan, could be sensed the longing to tell the world and ourselves that we had passed through the fire and not been found wanting.

The Great War was much more a *Canadian* war than was the Second. The sacrifices were greater. More than sixty thousand Canadians were killed between 1914 and 1918. In the Second War, in spite of a huge increase in population, the number of dead was only forty-one thousand. And the chances of getting killed were much greater in that earlier war, where one man died for every eleven who enlisted. In the Second War the odds were only one in twenty-six. The symbols differed, too. If the symbol of the First War for Canadians was the Vimy victory, that of the Second, surely, was the Dieppe débâcle.

The Great War was a searing experience, one that all Canadians were determined to mark and remember. In every city, town, and hamlet monuments went up, flanked, usually by captured German guns, the evidence of victory. Even in

296

Dawson in the far-off Yukon, an Egyptian obelisk was raised to commemorate the war dead, and two German field pieces were trundled all the way from the battlefields of Flanders across an ocean and a continent to be set up in a little park in a ghost town not far from the Arctic Circle. The park is rank with weeds today, the field guns have been taken away, but the granite monument still stands, tilted slightly by the permafrost, to remind natives and tourists alike that Canada had fought as an equal partner with Great Britain.

These Great War monuments make a statement that the memorial stadiums and memorial hockey rinks of the later conflict do not. Carved in the granite or marble of the plinth are the familiar slogans: "Lest We Forget", "Is It Nothing to You?" "Their Names Will Live Forever", and the more plaintive "They Did Not Die in Vain," all suggestive of the gnawing suspicion that the Great War *had* been fought in vain and that the men who died would soon be forgotten. But there is a more subtle message: the very presence of the cenotaph with its bronze plaque and its flanking guns reminds the viewer that Canada finally played its part on the international scene, not as a vassal, but as a partner. *See these guns! We captured them. We helped win the war!* To thousands of Canadians, raised on the myths of 1917, that was what the word "Vimy" meant.

The outpouring of best-selling anti-war novels from Britain, the United States, France, and Germany had no real counterpart in Canada. There were a few such books, of course, but they had little impact. Our imperishable contribution to the international literature of war was neither cynical nor disillusioned: It was John McCrae's "In Flanders Fields," with its challenge to "take up the quarrel with the foe" that every schoolchild memorized.

Certainly there was a revulsion toward war and a naïve belief that it could (or should) never happen again; everyone raised in those days remembers it. Yet this was tempered in Canada by the elation that was always felt when the word "Vimy" came up. You might attack the war and all its horrors, but you would not attack Vimy. Vimy stood for more than a battle won; it also stood for Canadian ingenuity, Canadian dash and daring, Canadian enterprise – phrases that have long gone out of fashion in the endless discussions about the Canadian character and the Canadian stereotype.

The men who fought at Vimy weren't bland or boring. The techniques that won the battle were innovative. The Canadians who went over the top, knocking out machine-gun nests and sweeping the trenches of enemy gunners, had a certain *élan*. These were the same men who burned down the movie tent at Valcartier, rioted aboard the *Sardinia*, and when Sam Hughes kept them waiting at Salisbury Plain, responded with jeers and catcalls and then, to a man, walked off the parade-ground. The men of Vimy do not seem to fit in with Northrop Frye's description of the Canadian "instinct to seek a conventional or commonplace expression of an idea."

Have we lost some of this *élan*? Does it require a battlefield or a hockey rink to bring it to the surface? Something has happened to us in the decades since Vimy. The early years of the century leading up to the Great War were yeasty, adventurous times, in which more than a million newcomers performed the daring act of leaving their roots behind to find a place in a new world. The country in those years brimmed with the optimism implicit in its Prime Minister's remark about the century belonging to Canada. That enthusiasm spilled over into the trenches of Artois. A remarkable number of the men who brought new ideas to the Vimy battlefield and fought with such grace and aplomb were the same adventurers who had poured into the pioneer West in the first decade of the century, determined to be unfettered by Old Country traditions.

The loosening of Imperial ties, which began in Canada with immigrant influx into the West, was accelerated by the Great War in general and by the Vimy experience in particular. The Canadian soldiers could not help comparing their own officers with stiff-necked British counterparts and noticing how the family feeling in the Canadian Corps contrasted with the social divisions in the British.

George Hambley was one who took these attitudes back to Canada. On the Friday after the battle, when Hambley and his fellow gunners were on the crest of the ridge, an Imperial officer happened along with a group of British soldiers. He'd lost his way, but as Hambley put it, "he was a Lord or a Duke or something and when he found out we were only privates he wouldn't talk to us." He was a mile off his course and on the wrong road. It was too dark for him to read his map. But he refused any help from the Canadians who tried to steer him on his way. Hambley noted: "The way he snorted at us as 'Canaeyedians' showed extreme contempt for us as colonial troops." Off he went, disdaining Hambley's attempts to set him right, and promptly marched his men right into the German lines. Hambley heard the sound of machine-gun fire and later learned that the entire group was either killed or captured.

It was not just the private soldiers who brought these attitudes back to Canada. Canadian officers who were to become social and political leaders and opinion makers in the next generation had also noted the British and French military traditions that clung to rigid formulas and outworn concepts, placing seniority over merit, confusing merit with social class, discouraging innovation and thwarting criticism. Vimy was a classroom for future politicians (J.L. Ralston, Leslie Frost, Douglas Abbott), future jurists (James McRuer, J. Keiller MacKay), future opinion makers (Conn Smythe, Gregory Clark), and a host of future generals from Harry Crerar and E.L.M. Burns to Andy McNaughton himself. It was not that any of these men had ceased to venerate the British connection – most were staunchly pro-British – but they simply had no further reason to believe the British were their superiors. Canada no longer considered herself a colonial vassal of Great Britain. And, of course, she had never considered herself a colonial vassal of the United States.

3

The men of Vimy who survived the war returned to Canada to take up lives disrupted by the conflict. Some, such as Lewis Buck, whose brother Bill was killed two months before the

Armistice, suffered nightmares for months afterwards. Working in the field with a team of horses one day, Buck heard a loud noise he couldn't identify. He thought it was a shell and instinctively threw himself on the ground. *My God*! he thought, *I may never get over this*. But in the end he did. So did Bill Breckenridge, who spent three months in hospital back in Canada, suffering from shell shock. He too recovered, to become a sales manager for Pittsburgh Paints in Sherbrooke. But he could never talk about the war without emotion.

Others, like Gad Neale, felt lost in civilian life. The army had been mother and father to him. In the 46th Battalion he had found his niche. Among his comrades he was an identifiable person. There was always a friend to turn to, somebody to pick him up when he fell. Neale was still not old enough to vote when the war ended. He had faced the cold, the mud, the lice, the rats, and the Germans. Yet civilian life held more terror for him than any of these. His mother was dead, his comrades were scattered, the rest of his family was still in England. He was alone. But he didn't go back to England. He remained a Canadian and, in the end, made a life for himself, first as a farmer, later as a ship's master, and then as a real estate broker.

The veterans were dovetailed into every branch of Canadian society in the peacetime years, many of them in key positions in industry and politics. Claude Williams went back to medical school and became a successful doctor. Corporal Curll, the hero of the Nova Scotia Highlanders, became an executive of the Royal Bank. His captain, Harvey Crowell, founded his own accounting firm in Halifax. David Moir, the machine gunner, became an executive of Imperial Oil. Andrew McCrindle joined the actuarial department of Sun Life. William Pecover went back to teaching. George Hambley became a United Church minister in Manitoba. Gus Sivertz helped start a newspaper in Vancouver. Jack Quinnell went to college, worked for Ford, went into the construction business, and served as a staff sergeant in the Engineers in the Second World War.

Victor Odlum took up his newspaper publishing again and later became a distinguished member of Canadian legations. Cy Peck won the Victoria Cross in 1918, served in the B.C. Legislature and the Parliament of Canada, and became aide-de-camp to his old general, Julian Byng, at Rideau Hall. Andrew Macphail returned to McGill as Professor of Medical History and pursued a long career in both medicine and literature. Duncan Eberts Macintyre had several careers – from furniture manufacturer to real estate developer. Energetic to the end, he died of a heart attack at the age of eighty-nine after chopping a week's supply of firewood.

Few veterans would forget the comradeship of the trenches; when the harsh conditions and the stress of battle faded, memories of those intense friendships remained. Interviewed in the decades that followed – generally on the Vimy anniversary – they were wont to remark that in spite of everything, the war was an experience they wouldn't have wanted to miss because of the closeness, because of the comradeship. They tried to recapture some of that closeness and to keep the memory of Vimy green at Legion dinners, Armistice Day ceremonies, and in countless published memoirs. Gus Sivertz wrote a veterans' column for the Vancouver *Sun*. Ed Russenholt became his battalion's historian and wrote of its triumphs at Vimy for the Winnipeg press. Victor Wheeler spent fifteen years of his life assembling a mass of material about the 50th (Calgary) Battalion's role in the war. It was not published until after his death.

Others – Will Bird was one – retained their connection with those days by returning to the site of the battlefield. In 1922 the French government had turned 250 acres in the area of Hill 145 over to Canada in perpetuity as a memorial park. The government's response was remarkable in its spiritual and religious overtones. To Mackenzie King the site was "one of the world's great altars." To the Speaker of the House, Vimy was "hallowed ground." To the Deputy Prime Minister, Ernest Lapointe, it was "sacred." Vimy, in short, had become a Canadian shrine.

To mark this briefest of all battles, the Canadian government commissioned the most massive of all monuments. From a vast concrete plinth – forty thousand square feet in size – would rise twin spires of flawless Adriatic marble, each 226 feet high, symbols of Canada's two founding races. There was nothing modest about this memorial; perched at the very crest of the highest point on the ridge – Hill 145 – it would be seen for miles in every direction.

The stone for this sacred pile was identical with that which had withstood fifteen centuries of wear at Diocletian's palace on the Dalmatian coast. Canada was intent on erecting a shrine that would stand, not for a thousand years, but as its architect, Walter Allward, declared, *for all time*.

The memorial would be as much a statement as a monument, a boast as well as a symbol – "the most beautiful work in the world," in the words of the contractor. The hyperbole fitted. The Great Depression had begun. Money was tight. But nothing was going to halt the construction. *Look at us*, the monument would say. *We did what the British and the French couldn't do and we're proud of it*.

When Will Bird returned to the battlefield in 1930, the monument was under construction. Bird, who had missed the battle because of the mumps, was stunned to discover that the new park covered the very line he had occupied with the Black Watch. To him the effect was almost unbelievable. The trenches, saps, and posts that he knew so well had been preserved in concrete. Beyond them yawned the great craters. It was as if he had been transported back in time.

But it was the monument itself, rising just above the old lines, that caught Bird's imagination. It had been under construction for four years; it had six more to go. When he described it for the readers of *Maclean's* that year, he put his finger, perhaps unwittingly, on its subliminal purpose.

"Europe, when viewing the finished work," he wrote, *"will change her impressions of the Canadians as a people."**

*Author's italics.

4

Vimy fever reached its peak in 1936 in the most remarkable peacetime outpouring of national fervour the country had yet seen. At the height of the Depression more than 6,400 Canadians paid their way across the Atlantic to stand on Vimy Ridge to witness the unveiling of Walter Allward's memorial. The journey, which required five ocean liners for them all, was properly called a pilgrimage. It took two years to organize.

John Mould and his wife were two of those pilgrims who crossed the ocean in July 1936. Like so many others, Mould was English born. He'd come to Canada in 1910, settled in St. Catharines, and got work as a sign painter. The war cost him his teeth and part of his hearing. Now, at forty-five, he was back on familiar soil.

The Moulds travelled to Arras and, on Sunday, July 29, boarded one of the hundred buses that formed a long procession on the road that led to the ridge – a road lined with French peasants, the medals jingling and flashing on the men's black suits. There followed a three-hour wait in the section of the park designated "Canadian Pilgrims' Assembly Grounds." The Moulds sat on the edge of a large mine crater, furry now with grass, their legs dangling over the edge, and ate the box lunch they'd collected from the hotel at Arras. Then, with time to spare, they trudged up the slippery slope, still encumbered with wire and pocked by shell holes, toward Hill 145. Some of the women found it hard going. "No wonder they called it No Man's Land," Jack Mould heard one whisper.

"I wonder," he thought, "what she would have said about it twenty years ago?"

The memorial itself was fenced off by a barricade, but the Moulds could easily examine nineteen of the twenty carved figures that adorned the massive structure – none of them warlike effigies. One was swathed in a Union Jack and would shortly be unveiled by the King himself, the uncrowned Edward VIII, soon to be embroiled in a constitutional struggle over the problem of his mistress, Wallis Simpson.

By 1:15 that afternoon a contingent from England had swelled the gathering to eight thousand Canadians. Behind them, thousands more French citizens were waiting for the King. These included a scattering of young men and women seeking their Canadian fathers. A little apart from the Canadian veterans in their khaki berets was a sadder group – some twenty-five hundred war widows in blue berets. Eleven old soldiers blinded in the war occupied a special position.

At last the King arrived, flaxen-haired and boyish, medals glittering on his morning coat. Bands played. Officials bobbed and weaved. Crowds cheered as the King walked slowly through the lines, stopping to talk to a medal winner here, a one-armed man there. As he moved, the emotion grew, and Jack Mould noticed that the entire crowd began to vibrate, like grain caught in the wind. There were speeches and a flypast by the air force and the soft notes of "The Flowers of the Forest" echoing mournfully down the slopes. Then, just as the King stepped onto the rostrum, the sun came out as it had on that day so long ago when the victorious troops surged across the crest.

Jack Mould looked down on the throngs clustered on the grass of the ridge, with the yellow cornfields and the red-roofed villages shimmering in the sunlight. It seemed impossible that just nineteen years before this whole area had been a muddy, pitted desert. He looked about him – at the blind men and the armless men and the one-legged men, all listening to the soft English voice of their ruler, speaking of death and dedication, sacrifice and immortality, and "a feat of arms that history will long remember and Canadians can never forget." And he wondered what the blind men thought of it all.

Down came the flag, revealing a marble sculpture of a mourning mother. The barricade vanished and the crowd swarmed over the monument, searching for the names of friends and relatives carved on the wall of the plinth. The rows of names seemed endless – more than eleven thousand. This was all that was left of all those Canadian war dead whose bodies had not been recovered from the mud and who would never sleep beneath the crosses, row on row, in Flanders fields.

All that afternoon, the living milled about, making their communion with the dead. At six, the buses took them back to Arras. Like the battle itself, the pilgrimage had been a masterpiece of organization, due in good part to the abilities of the officer-in-charge, Lieutenant-Colonel D.E. Macintyre, D.S.O., M.C., the former Brigade Major of the 7th, who knew Vimy as well as he knew his own street.

The tour continued on through the battlefields of France and then across the Channel, where at the Royal garden party at Buckingham Palace some of the pilgrims – souvenir hunters to the last – pocketed the Royal spoons. Jack Mould, looking up at a fourth-storey window in the palace, saw Queen Mary gazing down on the crowd. He noted that she was not amused.

5

The Vimy Memorial would survive the Second War but not the weather. The biting wind still howls across the ridge, bringing with it gusts of rain and sleet. In April, when the flowers blossom in Paris, it is still chillingly cold on the steps that sweep up to Hill 145.

Like the memories of that other war, the memorial itself is fading a little. The weather has cracked the imperishable marble; this, after all, is not the sunny Adriatic. In 1984, with the quarries of Yugoslavia opened once again after a long hiatus, work of restoration began. It was needed. Some of the engraved names of the missing, whose only memorial was the vast wall of the plinth, were themselves missing – obliterated by the elements.

Each year half a million tourists visit the Vimy Memorial, although only a few are Canadians. The old crater line on the 3rd Division front still exists, after a fashion. A section of the trenches and a short length of the Grange Subway have been preserved and kept open for a generation with no real knowledge of static warfare. The visitors gasp at the closeness of the Canadian and German trenches. You could easily toss a football between them.

But this lovely little park, with its winding pathways, its greensward, its pines and maples, its asphalt roads, and its gleaming memorial, bears little resemblance to the dark slag heap of 1917. There is no feeling here of death or devastation, no sense of horror or of loss or of senseless human waste. The subway and the trenches are bone dry, and so are the great craters in which men once drowned – carpeted now with their blankets of grass. The trenches are as neat as the lawns, their sides plumb-bob vertical. The sandbags are as regular as bricks and on closer inspection turn out to be concrete counterfeits.

It is difficult for a student of the battle to orient himself here, for the slopes of the ridge are now clothed in forest, so that the crest is hard to find and the angle of ascent hard to assess. The Pimple, on private property, has vanished into the woods.

The archaeology of the battle remains hidden: two tons of ammonal lie beneath the lip of the Grange Crater and another seven and a half tons under the Broadmarsh. Human fragments, bones, bully beef tins, old bottles, wire, pit props, equipment, bombs, and shell fragments are all concealed by a soft covering of grass and foliage. A few artifacts have been gathered up and cemented into the walls of the subway for tourists to examine, but these scarcely convey the bewildering turbulence of Vimy.

One spectacle remains, however, and the effect is devastating. Beneath the pines and maples now rising from the slopes of the ridge and covering almost every square foot of the two hundred and fifty acres of the park lies one reminder of the battlefield that cannot be erased or glossed over. The slopes are green now with grass and not glistening with mud, but the panorama is still startling. Every bit of the terrain has been pounded out of shape into thousands upon thousands of pits and hummocks. Wherever one walks, wherever one looks, these myriad depressions, forming a kind of gigantic egg-carton effect, are there to remind the visitor that the flower of Canadian youth once passed this way to death and glory.

Was it worth it? Was it worth the cold and the lice, the rats and the mud? Was it worth the long hours standing stiffly in the trenches, praying that no sniper's bullet would find its mark? Was it worth it to crawl out into No Man's Land with a bag of bombs, seeking to mangle the men in the opposite trench before they mangled you? Was it worth that tense, chilly wait on the Easter Monday morning so long ago, when the world finally exploded and the enemy was driven from the heights at a cost in lives and limbs the High Command and the press described as "minimal?"

There was a time, less cynical, more ingenuous, when most Canadians were led to believe that the answer was *yes*. Nations must justify mass killings, if only to support the feelings of the bereaved and the sanity of the survivors. In Canada, long after the original excuses were found wanting –the Great War, after all, was clearly *not* a war to end wars– a second justification lingered on. Because of Vimy, we told ourselves, Canada came of age; because of Vimy, our country found its manhood.

But was *that* worth it? Was it worth the loss of thousands of limbs and eyes and the deaths of five thousand young Canadians at Vimy to provide a young and growing nation with a proud and enduring myth?

Now that the Vimy fever has cooled, a new generation sees the Great War for what it was. Many still visit the ridge to see where their fathers and grandfathers fought and died. Like Sergeant Gordon Rafuse of Berwick, Nova Scotia, they go back for sentimental reasons and without illusions. Rafuse's father was one of those who manned the big guns of the 7th Canadian Siege Battery on that April morning when the earth trembled and the wall of sound blotted out all human speech. Gordon Rafuse wanted his children to understand something about that particular moment in history and to see the spot where their grandfather had fought with the Canadian Corps.

They camped near Souchez, directly across the field from where his father's battery was dug in. The elder Rafuse had talked only rarely of the war, but his son remembered that he sometimes started up in the dark of the night, crying out aloud at the memory of past ordeals. It was ironic, as Rafuse later discovered, that he had had another relative at Vimy, a German lieutenant, Carl Rehfuss – his father's twelfth cousin – trying his best to return the Canadian fire from the opposite side of the ridge.

A few months later Gordon Rafuse, who was stationed at the time in Germany, sought out his distant cousin at Kiel-am-Rhine and the two men sat down to discuss the war – the forty-five-year-old Canadian and the eighty-two-year-old German who had been his father's enemy, both members of a clan that had sent out one of its branches to help found the town of Lunenburg, Nova Scotia, more than two centuries before. Neither had any stomach for the kind of war that had seen the Rehfuss descendants pitted against each other. It was, they agreed "a terrible waste of human life brought on by greedy people and tolerated for too long by silent majorities."

Was it worth it? The answer, of course, is *no*.

APPENDIX ONE

British Army Formations in the Great War

An *ARMY* was commanded by a full *General* or a *Lieutenant-General*.
It was made up of two or more *CORPS* commanded by a *Lieutenant-General*.
A *CORPS* contained several *DIVISIONS*, each commanded by a *Major-General*.
A *DIVISION* had three *BRIGADES*, each commanded by a *Brigadier-General*.
A *BRIGADE* comprised four *BATTALIONS*, each commanded by a *Lieutenant-Colonel*.
A *BATTALION* contained four *COMPANIES*, each commanded by a *Major* or a *Captain*.
A *COMPANY* was made up of four *PLATOONS*, each commanded by a *Lieutenant* (or *subaltern*).

APPENDIX TWO

The Canadian Battalions at Vimy

At the start of the Great War, Sam Hughes scrapped the traditional regimental designations and substituted numbers for almost all battalions except the Canadian Mounted Rifles. The existing militia battalions on active service continued to use both their original titles and their new numbers, for example, the 72nd Battalion (Seaforth Highlanders of Canada). Brand new battalions were formed on a regional basis. Thus recruits from the Kootenay district of British Columbia found themselves allocated to the 54th Battalion, while Calgarians were sent to the 50th, a circumstance that contributed to the *esprit* of the soldiers, who fought side by side with their friends and neighbours.

1st DIVISION (Right of the Line): Arthur Currie, C.O.
  2nd Brigade (Right)
    Right: 5th Battalion (Saskatchewan)
    Centre: 7th Battalion (British Columbia)
    Left: 10th Battalion (Calgary)
    In reserve: 8th Battalion ("The Little Black Devils,"
      Winnipeg)

  3rd Brigade (Left)
    Right: 15th Battalion (48th Highlanders)
    Centre: 14th Battalion (Royal Montreal Regiment)
    Left: 16th Battalion (Canadian Scottish,
      British Columbia)
    In reserve: 13th Battalion (5th Royal Highlanders)

1st Brigade (In Reserve)
    Right: 1st Battalion (Western Ontario)
    Centre: 3rd Battalion (Royal Regiment of Canada, Toronto)
    Left: 4th Battalion (Western Ontario)
    In reserve: 2nd Battalion (Eastern Ontario)

2ND DIVISION: Henry Burstall, C.O.
  4th Brigade (Right)
    Right: 18th Battalion (London, Ontario)
    Left: 19th Battalion (Central Ontario)
    In reserve:
      Right: 20th Battalion (Central Ontario)
      Left: 21st Battalion (Eastern Ontario)

  5th Brigade (Left)
    Right: 24th Battalion (Victoria Rifles, Montreal)
    Left: 26th Battalion (New Brunswick)
    In reserve:
      Right: 22nd Battalion (Canadien Français, "The Van Doos")
      Left: 25th Battalion (Nova Scotia Rifles)

  6th Brigade (In Reserve)
    Right: 31st Battalion (Alberta)
    Centre: 28th Battalion (North West)
    Left: 29th Battalion ("Tobin's Tigers," Vancouver)
    In reserve: 27th Battalion (City of Winnipeg)

3RD DIVISION: Louis Lipsett, C.O.
  8th Brigade (Right)
    Right: 1st Canadian Mounted Rifles
    Centre: 2nd Canadian Mounted Rifles
    Left: 4th Canadian Mounted Rifles
    In reserve: 5th Canadian Mounted Rifles

7th Brigade (Left)
Right: Royal Canadian Regiment (Toronto)
Centre: Princess Patricia's Canadian Light Infantry
Left: 42nd Battalion (Royal Highlanders,
  "The Black Watch," Montreal)
In reserve: 49th Battalion (Edmonton)

9th Brigade (In Reserve – not committed to the battle)
43rd Battalion (Winnipeg)
52nd Battalion (Port Arthur)
58th Battalion (Brantford)
116th Battalion (Nova Scotia)

4TH DIVISION: David Watson, C.O.
  11th Brigade (Right)
Right: 102nd Battalion ("Warden's Warrior's,"
  Northern B.C.)
Left: 87th Battalion (Grenadier Guards, Montreal)
In reserve:
  Right: 54th Battalion (Kootenays)
  Left: 75th Battalion ("The Jolly 75," Mississauga)
Attached and in reserve: 85th Battalion
  (Nova Scotia Highlanders)

12th Brigade (Centre)
Right: 38th Battalion (Ottawa)
Centre: 72nd Battalion (Seaforth Highlanders,
  Vancouver)
Left: 73rd Battalion (Royal Highlanders)
In reserve: 78th Battalion (Winnipeg Grenadiers)

10th Brigade (Left)
44th Battalion (Winnipeg)
50th Battalion (Calgary)
In reserve:
  47th Battalion (British Columbia)
  46th Battalion (Regina and Moose Jaw)

Author's Note

A great many books have been devoted to the Battle of Vimy Ridge, more perhaps than to any other battle involving Canadian troops in any war. It is not the purpose of this volume merely to repeat what has already been published (although the story is retold where it is necessary for background). Nor is *Vimy* intended to be definitive from a military or a tactical point of view. I have not thought it necessary to mention every battalion that took part in the action or every senior officer. There are several books, easily available, that do this.

My purpose, as in my two-volume work on the War of 1812, has been to tell not just what happened but also *what it was like*. I have tried to look at the Vimy experience from the point of view of the man in the mud as well as from that of the senior planners. The new material in this book comes from them – several dozen survivors of the battle, interviewed over the past two years – supplemented by the recollections in tape recordings of earlier interviews conducted two decades ago by the Canadian Broadcasting Corporation and, even more valuable, by unpublished letters, memoirs, and manuscripts acquired largely with the help of *The Legion*, the veterans' magazine. For these reasons I have not thought it necessary to append extensive source notes. The bibliography will make clear the personal papers and conversations from which this new material comes.

One thing that impressed me in the unpublished material is the eloquence of the writing. A good many Great War veterans obviously felt the need to record their experiences. Some did it to get it off their chests, others for the more important purpose of leaving a memoir for their sons and daughters. One of the latter was George Frederick Murray of the 5th CMRs, a man who never got past Grade 6 but who, at the request of his son Ernic, proceeded to fill in handwriting fifty quarter-inch-ruled loose-leaf sheets, every one of which is a pleasure to read.

This book also fulfils a second purpose. In these pages I have tried to continue my study of the Canadian character as it differs from the American and the British and also to chronicle the steps this country has taken toward nationhood. Vimy was clearly a milestone on that journey. In fact, the present book might be seen as a kind of sequel to *The Promised Land*, my account of the settlement of the North West in the years before the Great War. *Vimy* is peopled with many Westerners, some of them Old Country immigrants who had resolved to make Canada their home in the early years of the century. My own view is that the country has never overcome their loss in the First War; they were a different breed from the more cautious native-born. Who can say what these future entrepreneurs, lost in the appalling trench warfare of 1914-18, would have wrought if they had lived?

Acknowledgements

The names of the survivors of the Battle of Vimy Ridge interviewed for this book are listed in the Bibliography. Several, alas, have died in the interim. Almost all the others have entered their tenth decade. For their patience and their enthusiasm I am more than grateful. Without them, this book would not have been possible.

In addition I have drawn heavily on the oral history tapes in the Public Archives of Canada and on the published memoirs of three men – Will Bird, Duncan Eberts Macintyre, and Victor Wheeler. The memoirs of Lieutenant-General E.L.M. Burns, Dr. Robert Manion, and Ernest G. Black, and the letters of Donald Fraser were also useful. I have in addition drawn on several of the interviews appearing in Alexander McKee's *Vimy Ridge*, on the *Letters from the Front* of Bank of Commerce employees, as well as on personal material appearing in the various battalion histories.

The two biographies of Arthur Currie, that by Hugh M. Urquhart and the more recent work by Daniel G. Dancocks, provided useful background information on Currie, though the first makes no mention of his financial difficulties and the second glosses over them. These were first brought to light by R.C. Brown and Desmond Morton in an article in the *Canadian Historical Review* and are supported by letters and documents in the Borden Papers, Public Archives of Canada. Two other biographies, those of Julian Byng by Jeffery Williams and of Andrew McNaughton by John Swettenham, were very useful. Charles Winter's sycophantic treatment of his former employer, Sam Hughes, was not so valuable; most of my material on Hughes comes from other sources, notably the Borden and Foster papers in the Public Archives. Much of my background on Raymond Brutinel is drawn from Larry Worthington's *Amid the Guns Below*, and I want to thank her son, Peter, for drawing my attention to it.

My thanks, too, to Lieutenant-Colonel D.F. Spankie for his advice and counsel, to Bill Gray for allowing me to use material collected on the saps, subways, and craters in the Vimy sector, to Timothy Findley for lending me his uncle's letters from the Great War, to Dave Breckenridge for background on his uncle Bill, to Ben Sivertz for background on his brother Gus, to Frank E. Macintyre for background on his father, to Mrs. Audrey Ball for background on her uncle, John Mould, and to the Hon. J.V. Clyne for bringing to my attention his brother Harry's history of Tobin's Tigers.

My research assistant, Barbara Sears, who again devoted her unflagging energy and questioning mind to gathering much of this material, would like to thank the following for their assistance: Sylvie Robitaille and Jana Vosikowska of the National Film, Sound and Television Archives; Robert Grandmaitre, Map Division, Public Archives of Canada, Ottawa; Gordon Dodds, Bob Tapscott, and Michele Fitzgerald of the Provincial Archives of Manitoba; Eric Gormley, at the Glenbow Alberta Institute; the staffs at the British Columbia Archives, New Brunswick Museum, Provincial Archives of Nova Scotia, and the Historical Directorate, Department of National Defence, Ottawa; Don Wilson and Don Harrison, Department of Veterans Affairs, Ottawa; Reginald Roy, the University of Victoria; and from the Royal Canadian Legion: J.D. Bridges, Regina, Al Erikson, Prince Albert, William Jack, Saskatoon, Kenneth Rooke, Halifax, Alex Andrews, Kentville, James Sandford, Annapolis Royal, Lorraine Sherwood, Vancouver, Robert Horncastle, Saint John, and C.H. Graham, Ottawa.

Because of Jan Tyrwhitt Patton's extraordinary acumen I was persuaded to rewrite *Vimy*, and there's no doubt that without her counsel it would be a lesser work. Janet Craig, the best copy editor in Canada, saved me as usual from myself. Elsa Franklin's critique, which supplemented Ms. Patton's, convinced me that I was on the wrong track in an earlier draft. As always, the proofreading of my wife, Janet, has been impeccable. My research notes were organized by my former secretary, Caryle Jakobsen, and the various drafts of the manuscript were typed at blinding speed by my present secretary, Susan Blackwell. In a work of this complexity there are bound to be errors and omissions. These are mine.

Kleinburg, Ontario
April, 1986

Select Bibliography

Unpublished Manuscript Material

Public Archives of Canada:
MG27　　　　　Lord Beaverbrook Papers
MG26 H　　　Robert Borden Papers
MG26 J　　　　W.L. Mackenzie King Papers
MG26 II D7　George Foster Papers
MG27 III B7　R. J. Manion Papers
MG30 D150　Andrew Macphail Papers
MG30 E619　David Watson Papers
MG30 E100　A.W. Currie Papers
MG30 E15　　W.A. Griesbach Papers
MG30 E241　D.E. Macintyre Papers
MG30 E236　Villiers Papers
RG9 series 3, vols. 4912-4951, battalion war diaries

Department of National Defence:
Capt. Robert N. Clements, "Merry Hell the Way I Saw It"
Lieut. J.H. Fairweather diary
John Swettenham, "Two First World War Battles"
SGR II 202, Miscellaneous German Sources

British Columbia Archives:
Arthur Crease diary
Mrs. E.M. Garrard diary
Andrew S. Baird letters
Col. Cy Peck diary

Glenbow-Alberta Institute:
M742 Harold McGill Papers
F. Johnson, oral history interview

Manitoba Archives:
MG7 H11 George Hambley diaries

Ontario Archives:
MU4693 Lewis Duncan Papers
MU996 Matthew Ellis Papers

Provincial Archives, Nova Scotia:
MG100 Harvey Crowell Papers
MG23 A.M. Taylor war diary

Privately held papers:

Gordon Beatty, "Reminiscences of an Old Soldier"

William Breckenridge, "From Vimy to Mons"

Art Castle, "The Takeover of Vimy Ridge"

W.E. Darknell, "The Battle of Vimy Ridge"

Jules De Cruyenaere, "The Battle of Vimy Ridge and Hill 70"

Dr. E. Douglas Emery diary

T. Irving Findley letters

Eric Forbes diary

Bill Gray, Papers on subways, saps, and craters, Vimy Memorial Park

Bill Green, "Autobiography of World War One"

J.N. Gunn diary

R.A. Henderson letters and diaries

Arthur Jenkinson, "My War Experiences"

Harry Galt Lithgow letters

Harry Loosmore, "Recollections of Vimy"

H.W. Lovell manuscript

Andrew McCrindle, "From Private to Private in 36 Months or a Worm's Eye
    View of World War One"

John Mould diary

George Frederick Murray, "Account of Service in the Canadian Army During the
    Great War"

Percy Albert Murray manuscript

A.L.S. Nash, "The Story of the 40th Battery CFA, CEF 1915-1919"

William Pecover diary

_____ "A Memory of Vimy Ridge by One Who Was There"

Arthur C. Pollard, "Memoirs of a Soldier/Airman in World War I"

Ian Sinclair diaries

John Henry Stacey diaries

Frank Tamblyn diary

Alfred Thomson diary

George C. Walker, "Accounts of Events at Vimy Ridge"

Claude Williams letters

Len Youell letters

Newspapers

Toronto *Daily Star*, 1914,1917

Globe (Toronto), 1914,1917

Manitoba *Free Press*, 1914,1917

Edmonton *Bulletin*, 1914

Calgary *Herald*, 1914,1917

Mail and Empire (Toronto), 1914

Ottawa *Citizen*, 1914

Toronto *News*, 1914

Government Documents – Published

House of Commons, *Debates*, 1914-1918

Interviews

George Alliston; Harold Barker; J. Gordon Beatty; Roland Bird; Clifford Brown; D. Allan Brown; Lewis Buck; E.L.M. Burns; Benson Case; Art Castle; Robert Chambers; Jim Church; Dean Colpitts; Charles Dale; W.E. Darknell; George Drew; Dr. E.D. Emery; Robert England; Norman Evans; Len T. Fairey; Eric Forbes; Doug Forman; William Gale; Whitfield Ganong; Albert Gervais; Lester Giffin; Duncan Green; Eric Grisdale; William Hemming; Roy E. Henley; John Hill; Fred W. Hodges; Fred Holm; Leslie Hudd; George Johnston; James Johnston; Sam Kirk; William F. Klyne; James A. de Lalanne; William Lundal; Andrew McCrindle; D.I. McCullough; James McRuer; Bruce Menzies; David Moir; James Montgomerie; Gad Terence Neale; Harold Nixon; Frank Ormiston; Bob Owen; William Pecover; John Quinnell; Gordon Rafuse; George Raisbeck; A. Dodge Rankine; Fred Robertson; Lewis Robertson; Harold Rogers; Albert Rose; Wesley Runions; Gordon Shrum; Charles Sills; Cyril Smith; John Spears; Aubrey Staples; Fred Stapley; Alfred Thomson; James Todd; C.W. Topping; George Turner; James Wallis; Albert Welch; Harry Wilford; Claude Williams; Thomas Wood; Frank Yates; Len Youell

Public Archives of Canada:
Oral history tapes (interviews originally conducted for the CBC radio series "In Flanders Fields"): Percy Ackerley; T. Adams; V. Armstrong; F.C. Bagshaw; Stanley Baker; Capt. Royden Barbour; Robert George Barclay; Harry Bond; Arthur Bonner; Archie Brown; Bob Brown; Raymond Brutinel; Harold Campbell; Gregory Clark; H.R.N. Clyne; Henry Sloan Cooper; Richard Elmer Crowe; Harvey Crowell; N.G. Dean; G. Dorman; Cuthbert Joseph Dutton; James Ellis; Arthur Farmer; Leslie Fennel; Arthur Andrew Galbraith; T.C. Gaunt; T. Goodhall; Arthur Goodmurphy; George T. Hancox; Allen Hart; Thomas Hewitt; D'Arcy Higgins; P.J. Hopkins; W.J. Howe; Alex Jack; William Jenkins; Col. Kirkpatrick; Richard Leach; J.A. MacDonald; A. Manson; Douglas Marshall; H.C. McKendrick; W.S. McMactier; Andrew McNaughton; William Nickle; Victor Odlum; Daniel Ormond; M.E. Parsons; George Randolph Pearkes; Alfred Pearson; Elmore Philpott; Jack Pinson; R.S. Robertson; Clayton Ross; E.S. Russenholt; G. Scott; S. Scott; R.H. Sinclair; Gus Sivertz; John Stewart; Frank Thomson; Frank Vandenbosch; W.S. Wilson.

Published Sources

Allen, Ralph. *Ordeal by Fire*. Toronto: Doubleday, Canada. 1961.

Bank of Commerce. *Letters from the Front*, vols. 1 and 2. N.p., 1920.

Barnes, Leslie W.C.S. *Canada's Guns: An Illustrated History of Artillery*. Ottawa: National Museum of Man, 1975.

Beattie, Kim. *The 48th Highlanders of Canada*. Toronto: 48th Highlanders of Canada, 1932.

Bell, Douglas Herbert. *A Soldier's Diary of the Great War*. London: Faber and Gwyer, 1929.

Bennett, Capt. S.G. *The 4th Canadian Mounted Rifles 1914-1919*. Toronto: Murray Printing Company, 1926.

Berger, Carl. *The Sense of Power: Studies in the Ideas of Canadian Imperialism 1867-1914*. Toronto: University of Toronto Press, 1970.

Bird, Will. *And We Go On*. Toronto: Hunter-Rose Co. Ltd., 1930.

_____ *Ghosts Have Warm Hands*. Toronto: Clarke, Irwin and Co. Ltd., 1968.

_____ *Thirteen Years After: The Story of the Old Front Revisited*. Toronto: Maclean Publishing Company, 1932.

Bishop, William. *Winged Warfare*. New York: George Doran Company, 1918.

Bishop, William Arthur, *The Courage of the Early Morning*. Toronto: McClelland and Stewart, 1965.

Black, Ernest G. *I Want One Volunteer*. Toronto: Ryerson Press, 1965.

Blake, Robert (ed.) *The Private Papers of Douglas Haig 1914-1919*. London: Eyre and Spottiswoode, 1952.

Bliss, Michael. *A Canadian Millionaire, the Life and Business Times of Sir Joseph Flavelle, Bart. 1858-1939*. Toronto: Macmillan of Canada, 1978.

Borden, Robert Laird. *Robert Laird Borden: His Memoirs*, vol. 1. Toronto: McClelland and Stewart, 1969. (reprint).

Boudreau, Joseph A. "Western Canada's Enemy Aliens in World War One," *Alberta Historical Review*, vol. 12, no. 1, Winter, 1964.

Bray, R. Matthew. "Fighting as an Ally: The English-Canadian Patriotic Response to the Great War," *Canadian Historical Review*, vol. LXI, March 1980.

Brown, R.C. and Morton, Desmond. "The Embarassing Apotheosis of a 'Great Canadian': Sir Arthur Currie's Personal Crisis in 1917," *Canadian Historical Review*, vol. LX, March 1979.

Brown, Robert Craig. *Robert Laird Borden*. Toronto: Macmillan of Canada, 1975.

Burns, E.L.M. *General Mud: Memoirs of Two World Wars*. Toronto: Clarke, Irwin, 1970.

Byng, Viscountess. *Up the Stream of Time*, Toronto: Macmillan Co. of Canada, 1945.

Cameron, Kenneth. *History of No. 1 Canadian General Hospital CEF*. Sackville: Tribune Press, 1938.

Canada in the Great War, vol. 4, *The Turn of the Tide*. Toronto: United Publishers of Canada, n.d.

Carlyle, Randolph. "Our National Army," *Canadian Magazine*, vol. 31, no. 5 (1908).

Chaballe, Joseph. *Histoire du 22e Bataillon Canadien-Français*. Montreal: Les éditions Chantecler ltée., 1952.

Chapman, Guy. *A Passionate Prodigality*. New York: Holt Rinehart, 1933.

Cinquante Quatre: Being a Short History of the 54th Canadian Infantry Battalion by One of Them. N.p., n.d.

Clark, Gregory. *War Stories*. Toronto: Ryerson Press, 1964.

_____ "The Symbol" *Weekend Magazine*, April 4, 1967.

Clint, M.B. *Our Bit: Memories of War Service by a Canadian Nursing Sister*. Alumnae Association, Royal Victoria Hospital, 1934.

Clyne, H.R.N. *Vancouver's 29th*. Vancouver: Tobin's Tigers Association, 1964.

Corrigall, Major D.J. *The History of the 20th Canadian Battalion CEF*. Toronto: Stone and Cox, 1935.

Currie, J.A. *The Red Watch*. London: Constable and Co., 1916.

Dancocks, Daniel G. *Sir Arthur Currie*. Toronto: Methuen, 1985.

Dixon, Norman. *On the Psychology of Military Incompetence*. London: Cape, 1976.

Doyle, Arthur Conan. *The British Campaign in France and Flanders 1917*. Toronto: Hodder & Stoughton, 1929.

Drew, George A. *Canada's Fighting Airmen*. Toronto: Maclean Publishing Co. Ltd., 1930.

Duguid, A. Fortescue. "Canada on Vimy Ridge." Ottawa: Dominion Bureau of Statistics, 1936.

_____ "Canadians in Battle, 1915-1918," Canadian Historical Association *Annual Report*, 1935.

_____ *History of the Canadian Grenadier Guards, 1760-1964*. Montreal: Gazette Printing Co. 1965.

Durocher, Renée. "Henri Bourassa, les eveques et la guerre de 1914-1918," *Canadian Historical Association, Historical Papers*, 1971.

Ellis, W.D. (ed.) *Saga of the Cyclists in the Great War 1914-18*. Canadian Corps of Cyclists Battalion Assoc. 1965.

England, Robert. *Recollections of a Nonagenarian in the Service of the Royal Canadian Regiment*. Victoria: Robert England, 1983.

_____ "A Victoria Real Estate Man – the Enigma of Sir Arthur Currie," *Queen's Quarterly*, vol. 65, no.2.

English, John. *The Decline of Politics: The Conservatives and the Party System 1901-1920*. Toronto and Buffalo: University of Toronto Press, 1977.

Falls, Captain Cyril. *History of the Great War, Military Operations France and Belgium 1917*. London: Macmillan & Co., 1940.

Fetherstonhaugh, R.C. *The Royal Canadian Regiment*. Fredericton: Centennial Print and Litho Co., 1981 (reprint).

_____ *The Royal Montreal Regiment, 14th Battalion C.E.F. 1914-1925*. Montreal: Royal Montreal Regiment/Gazette Printing Co., 1927.

_____ *The 13th Battalion Royal Highlanders of Canada. 1914-1919*. Toronto: 13th Battalion Royal Highlanders of Canada, 1925.

_____ *The 24th Battalion CEF Victoria Rifles of Canada. 1914-1919*. Montreal: Gazette Printing Co., 1930.

"Fifth F.C.C. engineers at Valcartier," *Queen's Quarterly*, vol. 22, 1914–15.

Frost, Leslie. *Fighting Men*. Toronto: Clarke, Irwin, 1967.

Gibbs, Philip. *Realities of War*. London: Heinemann, 1920.

Gibson, Capt. W.L. *Records of the Fourth Canadian Infantry Battalion in the Great War 1914-18*. Toronto: Maclean Publishing Co., 1924.

Goodspeed, Major D.J. *Battle Royal, A History of the Royal Regiment of Canada 1862-1962*. Brampton: Royal Regiment of Canada, 1962.

_____ *The Road Past Vimy: The Canadian Corps 1914-1918*. Toronto: Macmillan of Canada, 1969.

Gould, L. McLeod. *From B.C. to Baisieux*. Victoria: Thos. R. Cusack Press, 1919.

Gould, R.W. and Smith, S.K. *The Glorious Story of the Fighting 26th*. Montreal: Montreal Standard, 1918.

Grafton, C.S. *The Canadian Emma Gees: A History of the Canadian Machine Gun Corps*. London: Canadian Machine Gun Corps Assoc. 1938.

Granatstein, J.L. and Cuff, R.D. *War and Society in North America*. Toronto: Thomas Nelson and Sons (Canada), 1971.

Grant, W.L. *In Memoriam: William George McIntyre*. N.p., n.d.

Grieve, Capt. W. Grant and Newman, Bernard. *The Tunnellers*. London: Herbert Jenkins, 1936.

Gunn, Lt.-Col. J.N. *Historical Records of No. 8 Canadian Field Ambulance*. Toronto: Ryerson Press, 1920.

Hayes, Lt.-Col. Joseph. *The 85th in France and Flanders*. Halifax: Royal Print and Litho, 1920.

Histories of the 251 Divisions of the German Army Which Participated in the War 1914-18. Washington: Government Printing Office, 1920.

Hodder-Williams, Ralph. *Princess Patricia's Canadian Light Infantry 1914-1919*. Toronto: Hodder & Stoughton, 1923.

Hogg, Ian V. *A History of Artillery*. Toronto: Hamlyn, 1974.

Horne, Alistair. *The Price of Glory: Verdun 1916*. New York: St. Martin's Press, 1968.

Ignatieff, George. "General A.G.L. McNaughton," *International Journal*, Summer, 1967.

Johnson, Melvin, and Haven, Charles. *Automatic Weapons of the World*. New York: William Morrow, 1945.

Johnson, A.E., and others. *Diary of the Eleventh, Being a Record of the 11th Field Ambulance*. N.p., n.d.

[Johnston, Lt.-Col. G. Chalmers] *The 2nd Canadian Mounted Rifles*. Vernon: Vernon News Printing and Publishing Co., n.d.

Jones, H.A. *The War in the Air*. Oxford: Clarendon Press, 1931.

Jünger, Ernst. *Storm of Steel*. New York: Doubleday, Doran, 1929.

Kay, Hugh R., Magee, George and MacLennan, F.A. *Battery Action!* Toronto: Warwick Brothers & Rutter, N.d.

Kay, Hugh R. *The History of the 43rd Battery C.F.A.* N.p., 43rd Battery Association, 1955.

Kerr, Wilfred Brenton. *Shrieks and Crashes*. Toronto: Hunter Rose Co., 1929.

Knightley, Philip. *The First Casualty*. New York: Harcourt, Brace Jovanovich, 1975.

Lewis, Lt. R. *Over the Top with the 25th*. Halifax: H.H. Marshall, 1918.

Liddell Hart, B. *History of the First World War*. London: Pan Books, 1972.

Lloyd George, David. *War Memoirs*. London: Ivor Nicholson and Watson, 1933-37.

Lower, A.R.M. *Canadians in the Making*. Toronto: Longmans Canada, 1958.

Ludendorff, General Erich. *My War Memories 1914-18*. London: Hutchinson, 1920.

MacBeth, Madge. "Life with Five Governors General," *Macleans*. 1 July 1953.

Macdermot, T.W.L. *The Seventh*. Montreal: Seventh Canadian Siege Battery Association, 1953.

MacDonald, F.B. and Gardiner, John J. *The 25th Battalion Canadian Expeditionary Force*. Sydney: Wayside Books, 1983.

MacDonald, J.A. *Gunfire, An Historical Narrative of the 4th Brigade CFA*. N.p., n.d.

MacDonald, Lyn. *Somme*. London: Macmillan, 1983.

Macintyre, D.E. *Canada at Vimy*. Toronto: Peter Martin Associates, 1967.

322

MacKenzie, C.J. "Andrew George Latta McNaughton," Royal Society of Canada *Proceedings*, 4th Series, 1967, vol. 5.

Macksey, Kenneth. *The Shadow of Vimy Ridge*. Toronto: Ryerson Press, 1965.

Macphail, Andrew. *Official History of the Canadian Forces During the Great War 1914-19. The Medical Services*. Ottawa: Department of National Defence, 1925.

_____ "Sir Arthur Currie," *Queen's Quarterly*. Spring 1934.

Manion, R.J. *Life Is an Adventure*. Toronto: Ryerson Press, 1936.

_____ *A Surgeon in Arms*. New York: D. Appleton & Company, 1918.

McDougall, Phyllis. "Henley of the Black Watch," *The Islander*, Victoria: November 1984.

McEvoy, Bernard, and Finlay, Capt. A.H. *History of the 72nd Canadian Infantry Battalion Seaforth Highlanders of Canada*. Vancouver: Cowan & Brookhouse, 1920.

McKee, Alexander. *The Friendless Sky*. London: Souvenir Press, 1962.

_____ *Vimy Ridge*. London: Souvenir Press, 1966.

McKenzie, F.A. *Through the Hindenburg Line*. Toronto: Hodder & Stoughton, 1918.

McMurray, Dorothy. *Four Principals of McGill University*. Montreal: Graduates Society of McGill University, 1974.

McWilliams, James L., and Steel, R. James. *The Suicide Battalion*. Edmonton: Hurtig, 1978.

Middlebrook, Martin. *The First Day on the Somme*. London: Allen Lane, 1971.

Moir, David Alexander. "At What Price?" *Legion Magazine*, April 1977.

Morton, Desmond. *A Peculiar Kind of Politics*. Toronto: University of Toronto Press, 1982.

Murray, Col. W.W. *The History of the 2nd Canadian Battalion (Eastern Ontario Regiment) Canadian Expeditionary Force in the Great War*. Ottawa: 2nd Battalion CEF, 1947.

Murray, W.W. "The Vimy Pilgrimage," *Canadian Geographical Journal*. vol. 13, no. 8, 1939.

_____ "Vimy VCs," *Macleans*, 15 February 1929.

Newman, James R. *The Tools of War*. New York: Doubleday, Doran, 1942.

Nicholson, Col. G.W.L. *Canadian Expeditionary Force 1914-1919*. Ottawa: Department of National Defence, 1962.

_____ *The Gunners of Canada*. Toronto: McClelland and Stewart, 1967.

Noyes, Frederick. *Stretcher-Bearers at the Double*. Toronto: Hunter Rose Co., 1936.

Ray, Anna Chapin (ed.) *Letters of a Canadian Stretcher Bearer*. Boston: Little, Brown, 1918.

Reeder, Col. Red. *Bold Leaders of World War One*. Toronto: Little, Brown, 1974.

Reid, Gordon. *Poor Bloody Murder*. Oakville: Mosaic Press, 1980.

Robertson, Bruce (ed.) *Von Richthofen and the Flying Circus*. Fallbrook: Aero Publishers Inc., 1964.

Robertson, Heather. *A Terrible Beauty – the Art of Canada at War*. Ottawa: James Lorimer & Co. in association with the Robert McLaughlin Gallery, Oshawa, and National Museums of Canada, 1977.

Roy, Reginald H. *For Most Conspicuous Bravery*. Vancouver: University of British Columbia Press, 1977.

_____ (ed.) *The Journal of Private Fraser*. Victoria: Sono Nis Press, 1985.

Russell, Arthur. *The Machine Gunner*. Kineton: Roundwood Press, 1977.

Russenholt, E.S. *Six Thousand Canadian Men, Being the History of the 44th Battalion Canadian Infantry 1914-1919*. Winnipeg: 44th Battalion Association, 1932.

Savage, Candace. *Our Nell*. Saskatoon: Western Producer Prairie Books, 1979.

Scott, Frederick George. *The Great War As I Saw It*. Toronto: F.D. Goodchild, 1922.

Seely, J.E.B. *Adventure*. London: William Heinemann, 1930.

Simson, Colonel D.C. Unwin. "The Vimy Memorial," *Canadian Geographical Journal*, January, 1943.

Singer, H.C. *History of the 31st Canadian Infantry Battalion CEF*. N.p., n.d.

Smythe, Conn, with Young, Scott. *If You Can't Beat 'Em in the Alley*. Toronto: McClelland and Stewart, 1981.

Stanley, George F.G. *Canada's Soldiers: A Military History of an Unmilitary People*. Toronto: Macmillan Co. of Canada, 1960.

Steele, Harwood. *The Canadians in France 1915-1918*. London: T. Fisher Unwin, 1920.

Swanston, Victor. *Who Said War is Hell?* Saskatoon: Modern Press, 1983.

Swettenham, John. *McNaughton*. Toronto: Ryerson Press, 1968.

_____ *To Seize the Victory*. Toronto: Ryerson Press, 1965.

Taylor, A.J.P. *The First World War: An Illustrated History*. London: Hamish Hamilton, 1963.

Thirty Canadian VCs. London: Canadian War Records Office, n.d.

Topp, Lt.-Col. C. Beresford. *The 42nd Battalion CEF, Royal Highlanders of Canada*. Montreal: Gazette Printing Co., 1931.

Trounce, H.D. *Fighting the Boche Underground*. New York: Charles Scribner's & Sons, 1918.

Unknown Soldiers by One of Them. New York: Vantage Press, 1959.

Urquhart, H.M. *The History of the 16th Battalion (Canadian Scottish), Canadian Expeditionary Force in the Great War 1914-1919*. Toronto: Macmillan Co. of Canada, 1932.

_____ *Arthur Currie, The Biography of a Great Canadian*. Toronto: J.M. Dent & Sons (Canada), 1950.

The Vimy Memorial. Veterans Affairs Canada, 1982.

Vince, Donald. "The Acting Overseas Sub-Militia Council and the Resignation of Sir Sam Hughes," *Canadian Historical Review*, vol. XXXI, March 1950.

Wallace, O.C.S. (ed.) *From Montreal to Vimy Ridge and Beyond*. Toronto: McClelland, Goodchild and Stewart, 1917.

Weatherbe, H. *From the Rideau to the Rhine and Back*. Toronto: Hunter-Rose Co., 1928.

Wheeler, Victor W. *The 50th Battalion in No Man's Land*. Calgary: Alberta Historical Resources Foundation, 1980.

Williams, Frank. "Vimy Ridge," *Montrealer*, April 1967.

Williams, Jeffery. *Byng of Vimy, General & Governor-General*. London: Leo Cooper in association with Secker and Warberg, 1983.

Wilson, Barbara. *Ontario and the First World War 1914-1918*. Toronto: Champlain Society, 1977.

Winter, Charles F. *Lieutenant General the Hon. Sir Sam Hughes K.C.B., M.P., Canada's War Minister 1911-1916.* Toronto: Macmillan Company of Canada, 1931.

Winter, Denis. *Death's Men*. London: Penguin Books, 1985.

Wood, Henry Fairlie. *Vimy!* Toronto: Macmillan of Canada, 1967.

Worthington, Larry. *Amid the Guns Below*. Toronto: McClelland and Stewart, 1965.

_____ *Worthy*. Toronto: Macmillan Company of Canada, 1961.

Index